Future of Business and Finance

The Future of Business and Finance book series features professional works aimed at defining, analyzing, and charting the future trends in these fields. The focus is mainly on strategic directions, technological advances, challenges and solutions which may affect the way we do business tomorrow, including the future of sustainability and governance practices. Mainly written by practitioners, consultants and academic thinkers, the books are intended to spark and inform further discussions and developments.

Reinhold Exner • Alexander Zunic

The Path to an Intelligent Enterprise

The Art and Practice of Business Intelligence Strategy

Springer

Reinhold Exner
Bruchsal, Germany

Alexander Zunic
Heidelberg, Germany

ISSN 2662-2467 ISSN 2662-2475 (electronic)
Future of Business and Finance
ISBN 978-3-031-69913-9 ISBN 978-3-031-69914-6 (eBook)
https://doi.org/10.1007/978-3-031-69914-6

This Springer imprint is published by the registered company Springer Nature Switzerland AG
The registered company address is: Gewerbestrasse 11, 6330 Cham, Switzerland

Preface

Business intelligence has been a key management and business priority for at least the last two decades. The ultimate vision of being able to make contextual business decisions in real time, anywhere, at any time, across all levels of the organization based on facts remains extremely compelling. However, even though we now have more technological means and computing power available than ever before, this vision of an “Intelligent Enterprise“ still seems somewhat unattainable for many organizations.

At the same time, new technological advancements such as artificial intelligence, big data, and cloud entirely change the game. The opportunities and risks associated with these ground-breaking technologies are huge and raise both managerial and ethical questions. However, answers to these questions are often discussed from a technology-centric viewpoint only. We strongly believe that business intelligence is essentially not a technology problem. Instead, it requires a strategic and business-centric approach to address questions, for example, regarding organizational competencies and skills, data literacy, attitude toward data and knowledge sharing while at the same time being aware of the risks and ethical implications.

A BI strategy aims to address these multi-facetted questions on a strategic level and with the entire organization in mind. It helps to provide clarity on the role of business intelligence in the organization and how it is connected with other business domains and strategies. A BI strategy is the prerequisite for managing business intelligence as a strategic business domain of its own right.

The need for a BI strategy is by no means new. From the beginning, BI strategies were driven by the recognition that strategic alignment is needed to achieve true enterprise-wide business intelligence and decision-making. However, in practice, BI strategies often fall short of achieving the intended goals.

When developing or further enhancing a BI strategy, it is common in practice to look for proven methods and approaches. Surprisingly however, our research shows that proven end-to-end methodologies and frameworks on how to build and implement a coherent BI strategy from scratch are scarce.

The objective of this book is to provide guidance and practical advice on how to develop corporate BI strategies, building on our own experience as consultants and BI practitioners. We support the reader by introducing practices and methods which have proven effective in practice.

Our book is structured in the following chapters:

In this Preface, we shortly describe the book's structure and content.

Chapter 1 deals with definitions and established terminologies of "Business Intelligence." The chapter illustrates typical situations and challenges within enterprises and the resulting areas for action. Moreover, emerging trends in the area of BI are described.

It is worth noting that a BI strategy can never be free of context. Its value strongly depends on the level of integration with other organizational strategies. For this reason, **Chap. 2** provides an overview of different strategies within an enterprise like overall corporate strategy, strategy for enabling the digital enterprise, finance strategy, sustainability strategy, and IT strategy. Of course, these strategies are by no means complete but they will serve as an anchor for strategic alignment with business intelligence.

It is crucial to understand these strategies in sufficient depth. This will allow deriving the strategic requirements toward BI as the key foundation for developing or revising a BI strategy. The details of how this can be achieved will be described in **Chap. 3**. In addition, Chap. 3 introduces a methodological process framework which enables the systematic creation of individual BI strategies. Last but not least, we will explore different maturity levels and bridge these levels to BI.

Based on a transparent view of the strategic requirements and expectations toward Business Intelligence, **Chap. 4** will first introduce approaches for creating a BI vision. Furthermore, the process model for developing a BI strategy and its individual components as well as the BI strategy process will be introduced. The reader will learn how to develop an initial BI strategy but will also experience how this BI strategy can continuously be adapted to new circumstances.

As we all know, strategies which are not translated into operations are usually ineffective and remain a theoretical construct. For this reason, Chap. 3 provides guidance on implementing BI strategies as well and contains four examples.

This leads us to the question of how BI is actually delivered to the end-consumer from an organizational point of view. Across and within organizations, we find different flavors and forms of dedicated BI organizations. No organizational structure addresses all requirements equally well—therefore, we will introduce in **Chap. 5** the reader to a variety of organizational design options and ways of evaluating the best-fit for a specific environment. First and foremost, this chapter focuses on the structure of a BI organization and how this structure can be embedded in a corporate context. In addition, we will explore the relevant processes which need to be designed to run within the BI organization. Finally, we will examine ways on how the value contribution of BI products and services can be measured and managed across the entire lifecycle.

In **Chap. 6**, we will discuss questions around BI architecture. First, we will describe the relevance of architecture in the context of BI strategy and which expectations and goals a BI architecture needs to balance. We then further explore design practices, models, and learnings from enterprise architecture and introduce the reader to an enterprise BI architecture framework to enable enterprise-wide business intelligence and decision-making. In the context of this framework, we will describe individual architecture layers and illustrate the strategic aspects and considerations involved in designing the enterprise BI architecture.

Finally in **Chap. 7**, we will summarize "The Path to an Intelligent Enterprise—The Art and Practice of Business Intelligence Strategy" and leave you, our readers, to take your next steps.

Bruchsal/Heidelberg, Germany

Reinhold Exner
Alexander Zunic

Acknowledgements

Reinhold Exner:

Looking back, writing a book is like running a marathon. You are embarking on a publishing adventure, and you don't know all the challenges that await you. You have to keep going for a long time, despite all the unanswered questions, to finally reach your goal.

I would like to thank my dear wife Jutta from the bottom of my heart for giving me the freedom to write this book and for supporting me throughout my book marathon. I know it wasn't always easy. I would also like to thank my three sons Jan Hendrik, Frederik, and Patrick, who have supported and encouraged me in this project. I am proud to have been able to experience such strong family support from all of you.

Special thanks go to my co-author Alexander, whom I would like to thank deeply for our collaboration and friendship. I will never forget how it felt to feel recharged after our intense professional discussions, and I would not want to miss the exchange of ideas, the many intense discussions, and our work together.

Alexander Zunic:

This book project was an intense and ambitious endeavor from the start involving many long nights and week-ends next to my day job as consultant. But in retrospect, this project turned out to be an exciting and rewarding experience, especially thanks to all the support I received both privately and professionally.

I want to particularly thank Xenia and also my brother Rocco for their patience with me and encouragement to write a book like this over such a long stretch of time. It was not always easy, but I am extremely grateful for all the support.

Finally, I want to thank my co-author Reinhold for the long-lasting collaboration on this project and our deep friendship. The fruitful exchange of ideas, constructive debates, and joint sessions after work will always be remembered.

Both of us:

A big thank you goes to our partner Springer, Heidelberg/New York and especially to Mr. Dr. Prashanth Mahagaonkar, Executive Editor—Books, Business, Management & Finance. Thank you for your patience, your professional support, and your helpful assistance with questions that kept coming up when we thought we were so close to our goal.

Additionally, we want to thank you Ms. Barbara Bethke, Associate Editor—Books, Information Systems/Business & Management and Mr. Christian Rauscher, Editorial Director—Books, Head of Business, Economics, Finance, Politics, Applied Statistics, who encouraged us to start this journey together.

We sincerely hope that our readers will enjoy this book with us and that they will be inspired to use it in their own work. Then we will have accomplished our goal.

Thank you very much to all!

Bruchsal, Heidelberg, January 2024
Reinhold Exner and Alexander Zunic

Contents

1 Case for Change 1
- 1.1 Introduction and History of the Term "Business Intelligence" 2
- 1.2 Key Characteristics of an Intelligent Enterprise 9
- 1.3 BI Strategy in a Nutshell 10
- 1.4 Typical Situation and Need for Change 11
- 1.5 Business Intelligence Trends 17
  - 1.5.1 Macro Trends 18
  - 1.5.2 BI Usage Trends 20
  - 1.5.3 Data Monetization Trend 22
  - 1.5.4 BI Technology Trends 22
- 1.6 BI Strategy and the Path to an Intelligent Enterprise 25

2 Strategic Anchors for BI Strategy 29
- 2.1 What Is "Strategy?" 30
- 2.2 Gearing BI Strategy with Other Strategies 40
- 2.3 Corporate Strategy 44
- 2.4 Strategy for "Going Digital" 50
- 2.5 Finance Strategy 59
- 2.6 Sustainability Strategy 69
- 2.7 IT Strategy 74

3 Tool Kit for Strategy-Aligned BI 87
- 3.1 The Strategy House Concept 88
- 3.2 How to Decompose a Given Strategy 94
- 3.3 How to Consolidate BI Requirements in a Meaningful Way 103
- 3.4 How to Improve Captured Input 105
- 3.5 How to Improve Strategic Alignment Maturity 115

4 From Vision to BI Strategy 125
- 4.1 BI Vision and Characteristics of a Good Vision Statement 125
- 4.2 Process Model for Developing a BI Strategy 132
- 4.3 Implementing a BI Strategy 140

5 Organizing BI Strategy . . . 151
5.1 Governance: Key Enabler for BI Strategy . . . 152
5.2 Dimensions of BI Governance . . . 155
5.3 Working Principles for BI Governance Design . . . 174
5.4 BI Organization Design Options . . . 177
5.4.1 Option 1: Virtual BI-CC . . . 182
5.4.2 Option 2: Virtual BI-CC with BI Management and Central Build Teams . . . 182
5.4.3 Option 3: BI-CC Without Operations (BI-DC) . . . 183
5.4.4 Option 4: Full BI-CC for Ramp-up Innovations . . . 184
5.4.5 Option 5: Full BI-CC (Line of Business) . . . 184
5.5 BI Organization Examples . . . 185
5.5.1 Virtual BI-CC . . . 185
5.5.2 Virtual BI-CC with Management . . . 186
5.5.3 Full BI-CC . . . 187

6 Architecture Foundation of BI Strategy . . . 189
6.1 Why Is BI Architecture Important? . . . 190
6.2 Relevance of BI Architecture in a BI Strategy . . . 193
6.3 BI Architecture Goals . . . 196
6.4 BI Architecture Expectations . . . 202
6.5 What Can We Learn from Enterprise Architecture? . . . 203
6.6 Enterprise BI Architecture Framework . . . 209
6.6.1 Business Architecture . . . 211
6.6.2 Information Architecture . . . 215
6.6.3 Data Architecture . . . 222
6.6.4 Application Architecture . . . 231
6.6.5 Technology Architecture . . . 234

7 Now Take Your Next Steps . . . 239

References . . . 245

Index . . . 247

About the Authors

Reinhold Exner is an Principal Business Transformation Consultant. Based on 14 years of leadership experience in various functions, including Head of Strategic Controlling and Head of BI at an industry world market leader, he is advising companies of various industries on their transformation journey to an Intelligent Enterprise based on latest ERP technology for additional 16 years now. He holds an MSc in Economics and Engineering (Wirtschaftsingenieurwesen) from Technical University Karlsruhe.

Alexander Zunic is an Principal Business Transformation Consultant. Based on 20 years of experience as project manager, product manager, management consultant, and BI architect, he is advising international clients of various industries on their data-driven transformation initiatives. Coming from a finance background, his current focus areas are corporate sustainability and business transformation towards the intelligent enterprise. Prior to his current position, he worked as a strategic purchaser at a large OEM in the consumer electronics industry. He holds an MBA from Aston Business School.

List of Figures

Fig. 1.1 Evolutionary path of reporting and analytical capabilities (© Exner/Zunic 2024. All Rights Reserved). 5
Fig. 1.2 Business Intelligence—Data to Impact (based on (Hackathorn, 2003), adapted by authors) 7
Fig. 1.3 Pragmatic framework to capture most burning BI issues (© Exner/Zunic 2024. All Rights Reserved). 12
Fig. 1.4 Example of capturing the most burning issues (© Exner/Zunic 2024. All Rights Reserved). 14
Fig. 1.5 The Gartner Hype Cycle (Gartner et al., 2023) 23
Fig. 2.1 Gearing of corporate and BI strategy—foundation of value-adding BI initiatives (© Exner/Zunic 2024. All Rights Reserved) 41
Fig. 2.2 Corporate BI in a wider context (© Exner/Zunic 2024. All Rights Reserved). 42
Fig. 2.3 BI strategy in different organizational contexts (© Exner/Zunic 2024. All Rights Reserved). 43
Fig. 2.4 Customer Journey (© Exner/Zunic 2024. All Rights Reserved). . . . 47
Fig. 2.5 Exemplary design options for a business intelligence setup in a multi-business model enterprise (© Exner/Zunic 2024. All Rights Reserved). 49
Fig. 2.6 Value add of business intelligence growths with each stage of the digital journey (© Exner/Zunic 2024. All Rights Reserved) . . . 51
Fig. 2.7 Relationships between the corporate digital stage and BI domain (© Exner/Zunic 2024. All Rights Reserved) 55
Fig. 2.8 Views on efficiencies (© Exner/Zunic 2024. All Rights Reserved) 67
Fig. 2.9 The everlasting challenge of any CFO—"do more with less" in business intelligence context (© Exner/Zunic 2024. All Rights Reserved) 68
Fig. 2.10 Interrelations of sustainability strategy with other strategies (© Exner/Zunic 2024. All Rights Reserved). 73

Fig. 2.11 Gravitation pattern of customer expectations, based on Kano, adapted from Yadav (2015) (Visualization adapted from: Yadav, S. (2015, December 18). The Kano Model—A tool to prioritize the users' wants and desires. Interaction Design Foundation—IxDF. https://www.interaction-design.org/literature/article/the-kano-model-a-tool-to-prioritize-the-users-wants-and-desires, last checked 16.10.2023) . . . 77
Fig. 2.12 The "Tornado of Exponential Growth"—infinitely fueled (© Exner/Zunic 2024. All Rights Reserved). . . . 79
Fig. 3.1 Key components of a house—very simplified . . . 89
Fig. 3.2 House of Strategy, adapted from Friedag and Schmidt (2016). . . . 90
Fig. 3.3 Roof of the House of Strategy, adapted from Friedag and Schmidt (2016) . . . 92
Fig. 3.4 O-A-R—Objective–Action–Ratio, adapted from Friedag and Schmidt (2016) . . . 93
Fig. 3.5 Adjusted guiding structure for strategy decomposition (© Exner/Zunic 2024. All Rights Reserved). . . . 95
Fig. 3.6 Collection of information—strategy-driven approach at a glance (© Exner/Zunic 2024. All Rights Reserved). . . . 100
Fig. 3.7 Different paths from strategy ideation to strategic monitoring (based on Müller-Stewens & Lechner, 2005) . . . 101
Fig. 3.8 Structuring results of analysis (© Exner/Zunic 2024. All Rights Reserved) . . . 106
Fig. 3.9 Looking into the details—example of improvement potential (1/3) (© Exner/Zunic 2024. All Rights Reserved) . . . 107
Fig. 3.10 Looking into the details—example of improvement potential (2/3) (© Exner/Zunic 2024. All Rights Reserved) . . . 109
Fig. 3.11 Looking into the details—example of improvement potential (3/3) (© Exner/Zunic 2024. All Rights Reserved) . . . 110
Fig. 3.12 Interconnectivity of BI Content, BI processes, BI structures, BI tools and the BI customer . . . 111
Fig. 3.13 Area of conflict between different governance views or philosophies (© Exner/Zunic 2024. All Rights Reserved) . . . 113
Fig. 3.14 BI strategy development—embedding results into overall BI strategy document (© Exner/Zunic 2024. All Rights Reserved) . . 114
Fig. 3.15 BI Maturity model—path to the Intelligent Enterprise (© Exner/Zunic 2024. All Rights Reserved). . . . 119
Fig. 3.16 Simplified process model illustrating different assessment types (© Exner/Zunic 2024. All Rights Reserved). . . . 119
Fig. 3.17 BI Maturity model—Exemplary BI maturity assessment result (as-is). . . . 122
Fig. 4.1 BI vision in a time horizon context—The big picture . . . 126
Fig. 4.2 How to develop a BI vision (© Exner/Zunic 2024. All Rights Reserved). . . . 128

Fig. 4.3 Relationship between BI vision and BI strategy (© Exner/Zunic 2024. All Rights Reserved). 133
Fig. 4.4 BI strategy development lifecycle (© Exner/Zunic 2024) 135
Fig. 4.5 BI strategy lifecycle embedded in wider corporate environment (© Exner/Zunic 2024. All Rights Reserved). 137
Fig. 4.6 Strategic impulse—trigger for change (© Exner/Zunic 2024. All Rights Reserved). 141
Fig. 4.7 Strategic impulse—working approach based on BI framework (© Exner/Zunic 2024. All Rights Reserved). 142
Fig. 4.8 Implementing a BI strategy—basic example (© Exner/Zunic 2024. All Rights Reserved). 143
Fig. 4.9 Key elements of BI strategy development at a glance (© Exner/Zunic 2024. All Rights Reserved). 148
Fig. 5.1 Positioning of BI in the organization (© Exner/Zunic 2024. All Rights Reserved). 154
Fig. 5.2 Governance framework—key dimensions (© Exner/Zunic 2024. All Rights Reserved). 156
Fig. 5.3 The BI product lifecycle (© Exner/Zunic 2024. All Rights Reserved) 159
Fig. 5.4 BI portfolio management along life-cycle (© Exner/Zunic 2024. All Rights Reserved). 163
Fig. 5.5 BI governance framework—across product stages (© Exner/Zunic 2024. All Rights Reserved). 165
Fig. 5.6 BI governance framework—governance elements (© Exner/Zunic 2024. All Rights Reserved). 169
Fig. 5.7 BI governance provides a clear set of rules (© Exner/Zunic 2024. All Rights Reserved). 173
Fig. 5.8 Exemplary elements of a "Stable Core" (© Exner/Zunic 2024. All Rights Reserved). 178
Fig. 5.9 Approach for evaluation of best organizational BI-CC option (© Exner/Zunic 2024. All Rights Reserved). 179
Fig. 5.10 Virtual BI-CC (© Exner/Zunic 2024. All Rights Reserved). 186
Fig. 5.11 BI-CC with management (© Exner/Zunic 2024. All Rights Reserved) 187
Fig. 5.12 Full BI-CC (© Exner/Zunic 2024. All Rights Reserved) 188
Fig. 6.1 BI architecture—balancing areas of conflict (Westenberger, 2018) 197
Fig. 6.2 BI architecture—the three modes of agile (© Exner/Zunic 2024. All Rights Reserved). 199
Fig. 6.3 BI architecture—moving the boundaries of information capture & insight (© Exner/Zunic 2024. All Rights Reserved). 202
Fig. 6.4 Zachman framework™ (Zachman, 2008) 204
Fig. 6.5 Federal Enterprise Architecture (FEA) Framework (Zachman, 2008). 206

Fig. 6.6 High-level comparison of Enterprise Architecture Frameworks (© Exner/Zunic 2024. All Rights Reserved) . . . 207
Fig. 6.7 Enterprise BI architecture framework (adapted from TOGAF® Content Metamodel) (The Open Group®, 2018) . . . 210
Fig. 6.8 Business architecture–key artifacts (adapted from Osterwalder & Pigneur, 2010) . . . 213
Fig. 6.9 Information architecture—semantic modeling (© Exner/Zunic 2024. All Rights Reserved) . . . 217
Fig. 6.10 The three pillars of information architecture (adapted from Rosenfeld & Morville, 2002) . . . 217
Fig. 6.11 Unified reference data architecture (© Exner/Zunic 2024. All Rights Reserved) . . . 227
Fig. 6.12 Alternative views on BI application architectures (© Exner/Zunic 2024. All Rights Reserved) . . . 233

List of Tables

Table 1.1 Quick-Scan—Hotspot-Definitions 15
Table 1.2 2022 Gartner Hype Cycle predictions for business intelligence, data management, and artificial intelligence 24
Table 2.1 Different KPI categories in the "going digital space" 57
Table 2.2 Illustrative "make" or "buy" example with BI implications for finance functions 65
Table 2.3 Layered architecture of business intelligence-as-a-service 83
Table 3.1 How to decompose a given strategy—sequence of activities 97
Table 3.2 How to decompose a given strategy—sequence of activities and example 98
Table 3.3 Structure for decomposing a strategy—example. 104
Table 3.4 Exemplary guiding questions for determining BI process maturity 120
Table 4.1 Implementing a BI strategy—basic example and working sequence 143
Table 4.2 Implementing a BI strategy—example on BI information delivery 144
Table 4.3 Implementing a BI strategy—example on BI organization. 145
Table 4.4 Implementing a BI strategy–example on BI business operations . . 146
Table 4.5 Implementing a BI strategy—example on BI information technology enablement 147
Table 5.1 Relevant governance aspects in various BI lifecycle phases. 161
Table 5.2 Illustrative example on how the BI product portfolio could be governed 162
Table 6.1 Comparison of different modes of agile 200
Table 6.2 Suitable aspects of available Enterprise Architecture frameworks for BI architectures 208
Table 6.3 Inventory of information assets (© Exner/Zunic 2024. All Rights Reserved) 220
Table 6.4 Characteristics of a data strategy 224

Case for Change 1

In the past decade, a wide range of predictions emerged regarding the future of enterprise business intelligence. They range from the notion of "BI is dead," or "AI is the next BI" to "BI is the path to the Intelligent Enterprise." If we are honest, none of these prophecies have materialized so far. We believe that business intelligence will be around for a long time and in fact continue to evolve and take different forms providing new levels of actionable insight. At the same time however, many companies have gone through a painful learning curve when it comes to BI, and some have in fact concluded that enterprise business intelligence is too complex, too costly, too little value adding, and not worth the effort. In this book, we want to make a case "pro" enterprise BI and outline a strategic approach.

However, to convince stakeholders of a strategic approach to enterprise BI, we need good answers to the following questions: What is a BI strategy good for? Why is BI strategy development important? What are the key drivers and expected benefits of a BI strategy? What do I need to change to be successful and what does success look like?

These fundamental questions will guide us in this chapter.

Since there is no unique definition of business intelligence, we will first begin with a brief overview of the history of BI, including how the meaning of the term "business intelligence" originated and evolved over time.

For quick readers, we recommend our one-pager with a very brief description of what a BI strategy is not, and of course what a BI strategy is (in a nutshell).

A good starting point for a BI strategy is to know your baseline/as-is situation. Companies mostly know their pain-points and are not interested or willing to spend too much time and effort on in-depth analyses of their current situation and opportunities for improvement. For this reason, we will describe a proven, concise, and practical guide for the practitioner how to quickly identify and make explicit the burning issues in the BI space.

R. Exner, A. Zunic, *The Path to an Intelligent Enterprise*, Future of Business and Finance, https://doi.org/10.1007/978-3-031-69914-6_1

Knowing your challenges is one thing, but knowing where the markets and competition are heading is much more helpful in developing a forward-looking BI strategy. Therefore, in the following chapter, we explore and contextualize some of the dominant BI trends, including the underlying drivers of change.

In the final section, we summarize our initial findings and recommendations to provide some initial guidance for BI strategy development. At the heart of this is the development of a transparent way of aligning business value expectations with the value contribution of BI. The documentation of this ambition and commitment to the organization is what we call the "BI strategy."

1.1 Introduction and History of the Term "Business Intelligence"

Before talking about BI strategy, it is essential to first define the term business intelligence (BI) itself. This book aims to provide hands-on guidance for practitioners; thus, our readers should not expect an exhaustive treatment of the many definitions of business intelligence. Instead, the main objective is to provide a solid understanding of what BI is all about. Based on this, we will then jointly take further steps towards BI strategy development. This will be the focus of the subsequent chapters.

The term "business intelligence" has been in use for many decades in both the business and IT communities. It is notable that the term has survived for so long and remains a top priority for many organisations. However, there is no consistent definition of the term, and it can mean different things to different stakeholders. This lack of clarity must be addressed before we continue with further details.

It's important to realize that there is no "ONE" universally accepted definition of "business intelligence" that holds true for every viewpoint. Thus, it makes sense to look into some origins, to extract key elements of business intelligence and potentially to even build a first basis to challenge our own point of view. And finally, to get the understanding of business intelligence aligned right from the beginning.

One of the earliest authors, who used the term "business intelligence" is said to be Hans Peter Luhn in the IBM-Journal 1958 "A business intelligence System". Referring to Webster's New Collegiate Dictionary, G. & C. Merriam Co., Springfield, Massachusetts, he defined business intelligence as: "[…] a collection of activities carried on for whatever purpose, be it science, technology, commerce, industry, law, government, defense, et cetera. The communication facility serving the conduct of a business (in the broad sense) may be referred to as an intelligence system. The notion of intelligence is also defined here, in a more general sense, as "the ability to apprehend the interrelationships of presented facts in such a way as to guide action towards a desired goal.""[1] (Luhn, 1958) Reprint Courtesy of IBM Corporation ©

In 1989 or 1993, depending on source, Howard Dresner from Gartner proposed "business intelligence" as an umbrella term to describe "concepts and methods to improve business decision making by using fact-based support systems." Based on (Cebotarean, 2011)

Peter Chamoni/Peter Gluchowski contributed to the definition by describing business intelligence systems "[...] which, on the basis of internal performance and accounting data as well as external market data, are able to support management in its planning, controlling and coordinating activities." (Chamoni & Gluchowski, 2016)

In 2009, Gartner defined BI as "an umbrella term that spans the people, processes and applications/tools to organize information, enable access to it and analyze it to improve decisions and manage performance." (Gartner et al., 2009)

The term "decision support" should not be confined only to managerial decisions but can include operational and shop floor decisions as well.

When we dive deeper into the history of business intelligence, the term "data warehouse" inevitably comes up. But what is a data warehouse and how does it help us understand business intelligence? A data warehouse is the technical solution for storing data relevant to decision-making. Decades ago, companies used to run their business on the so-called mainframes, which were large, monolithic, and very expensive computers. In those years, there was no thought of separate reporting systems as we know them today. Furthermore, it was not advisable to run reports on these computers as this would have reduced the runtime performance for transactional processing, i.e. it was a question of prioritizing between transactional processing, i.e. the core business and decision support. During this time, many companies began to reduce the burden of decision support by exporting data from the mainframes to spreadsheets for reporting purposes.

But this approach led to a rapidly growing number of spreadsheets serving multiple functions and stakeholders across the organization. As a result, when someone tried to create a consistent, overarching view, it proved very cumbersome, error-prone, and often confusing to decision-makers as multiple versions of the truth became visible.

During this time, the data warehouse concept was born. A few essential characteristics are worth to mention even today. Therefore, we will quickly summarize them.

- The first characteristic is about *organizing and structuring the data*. This means that the data is organized based on multiple, but specific subject areas such as business functions like pre-sales, sales and marketing, supply-chain, etc., or business objects like customer, product or services, sales orders, or production orders, returns, and many more. By structuring a data warehouse

[1] H. P. Luhn, "A Business Intelligence System," in IBM Journal of Research and Development, vol. 2, no. 4, pp. 314–319, Oct. 1958, doi: 10.1147/rd.24.0314.

in such a way, it becomes easier to provide information on such pre-defined topics.

- Data in a data warehouse is typically historical or close to real time to support reporting and analysis. Most of reporting queries consider a timeframe which can range from minutes to days, months or even multiple years. For example: "Show me the revenue for product x during the last months." To make this data retrievable in a very short time, it needs to be *organized "by time."* This contrasts with transactional systems, where mainly the current transactional data is relevant.
- In transactional systems, the purpose is to complete a business process. Once the process is complete, the primary objective, such as fulfillment and invoicing of a customer order, is achieved. Typically, after a period of time, this transactional data is archived and no longer available in the transactional systems. If executives want to know about past business process performance, this approach would limit the analysis to only the accessible data that is currently in use but not completed at that point in time. For this reason, it is important for later analysis that the data is *stored persistently*, regardless of how old it is. It is also important to *keep the historical data unchanged*, regardless of who analyzes it, when, from what perspective, and for what purpose.
- A data warehouse typically *combines data from various sources* such as different lines of business like finance, sales, supply chain, and many more. In addition, various sources can include, but are not limited to relational or object-oriented databases, flat files, structured and semi-structured data, metadata, and master data from within the organization or even outside the company. The more different sources are to be integrated, the more the complexity increases to combine the data. Key is to achieve a level of quality that users can trust the data and make reliable decisions based on the data, regardless of how many sources are combined.

From historical point of view, the business intelligence success book started with what we call nowadays "reporting." Reporting was and still is mainly perceived as a static presentation of one or few performance indicators in combination with a certain pre-defined number of perspectives like time, geography, products, responsibility centers, and others. Today we call these "dimensions." This pre-definition was given by a limited number of knowledgeable experts or managers who requested certain views to explain what has happened. If a new requirement emerged to have another view available for decision-making, a new report was generated to meet the requirements. Furthermore, during early times of business intelligence, the technology was able to print spreadsheet like reports, so once a performance indicator combined with a set of analytical dimensions was printed, it was "frozen." No chance to "play with the dimensions" by user interaction or having user interaction at all.

With growing demand for more dimensions and more details, the number of reports in different departments was significantly increasing and at the same time it

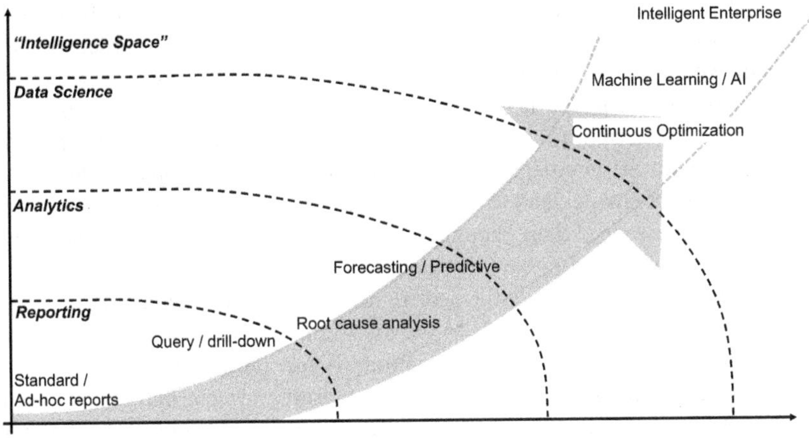

Fig. 1.1 Evolutionary path of reporting and analytical capabilities (© Exner/Zunic 2024. All Rights Reserved)

became clear that an increasing number of reports with little to no use were produced without any value add.

The next step was the technology-enabled flexibility which allowed the user to interact with the computer system to add or change dimensions or to replace one dimension by another. In addition, the feature of "drill-down" from higher aggregated figures down to more granular figures within the same set of dimensions was providing valuable insights. These features provided much more flexibility to the experts; however, once printed the selected set of performance indicators and dimensions was still frozen. Like the previous example on reporting showed, the underlying question that was answered was still the same: "what has happened?" The high-level evolutionary path of reporting and analytical capabilities is shown in Fig. 1.1 above.

One of the fundamental differences between reporting and analytics is the ability to interactively explore the data, to perform multi-dimensional analysis along various dimensions that provides meaningful business insights ("business intelligence" in a narrow sense) that ultimately supports decision-making.

One of the emerging requirements was and still is the translation of "what happened" in the past to the future "what is going to happen?" This can be seen as the birth of "analytics" and is visualized as the second evolutionary layer in Fig. 1.1. In the illustration above, the different layers are intentionally separated by dotted lines, as the separation is more of a blurring than a fixed boundary.

Gartner defines the term "analytics" in its IT Glossary as: "Increasingly, analytics is used to describe statistical and mathematical data analysis that clusters, segments, scores, and predicts what scenarios are most likely to happen." (Gartner, Gartner Glossary: Analytics, n.d.). In other words, analytics can be seen as a systematic and logical approach to examining given, typically complex data sets in order to better understand them, determine their structure, and derive their essential characteristics. Analytics also aims to gain additional insights in order to actively shape the situation that caused the existing data sets in the future.

These requirements led in the past years to new terms like "prediction," "forecasting," or "prescription." The underlying principle is the same: understand the past, learn about the interdependencies and root causes, develop a model based on the before, run the model, and validate the results based on facts once they materialize. The more advanced these methodologies and models become, the more are we moving to the third evolutionary layer in Fig. 1.1, called "Data Science."

Once we are able to predict the near future this certainly again will not be sufficient. It quite automatically leads to the question "how can we avoid any risks or damages or, for example, stock-out-situations, before they materialize?" Or in other words, we are aiming for not only an early warning system but system-provided recommendations for concrete corrective action/countermeasure to avoid emerging negative results before they hit us in reality.

Prescriptive analytics extends the analytical approach beyond data analysis by evaluating the underlying business facts, and in particular the dependencies, to identify inherent and typically hidden rules. Based on these identified data-embedded rules, prescriptive analytics aims to reuse and derive these rules to provide targeted instructions to the user to identify an actionable set of the best possible actions. These activities can result in improved real-world business activities ("impact") as well as identified needs for further exploration of the data. In other words, prescriptive analytics aims to generate data-driven recommendations to achieve defined outcomes.

When we think about the next level of support, beyond providing targeted instructions on what to do and what not to do, we need to consequently close the loop. So far, we have only learned what happened and why it happened. We know the underlying dependencies and have fact-based arguments about what is most likely to happen next. We also have recommendations and instructions about what to do. However, and this is the crux of the matter, we have not necessarily put those instructions into practice. One possible reason for this is that, based on our human intuition or gut feeling or other individual reasons, we have come to the conclusion that despite all the data, findings, and instructions, we as individuals still feel that we "know better." In other words, the loop is not necessarily closed. Consequently, if we insist on closing the loop, we need to question the "know better" attitude and discuss ways to remove the remaining barrier. In this sense, we can oversimplify this barrier as "human constraints."

In this sense, we can expect to enter another, the fourth evolutionary layer in Fig. 1.1, called the "intelligence space." Data-driven continuous optimization, based on identified rule sets, requires the idea of removing human constraints, thus further increasing the level of automation toward machine learning/artificial intelligence (AI) and ultimately the "Intelligent Enterprise."

Whatever technology is provided to the decision-makers, if the decision is not made in time or the execution is weak the overall result will be poor as well.

Key Considerations for Developing a BI Strategy

- Decision support is not a decision made. Moreover, even a decision made does not necessarily change anything by itself. It is only when the decision is translated into actions and consequently put into practice that the decision will materialize into a concrete and intended impact. This intended impact will result in revised data as a basis for performance evaluation. In this way, it is possible to prove whether the previous facts have been transformed into new facts as a result of the impact.
- In other words, the main goal of Business Intelligence is not just to improve insight to action.
- The main goal of Business Intelligence is the acceleration of *SPEED TO IMPACT*. Figure 1.2 below illustrates the closed loop of decision-making.

Another key factor we need to consider as well is the individual decision-making style of any decider, the "human factor." For instance, one decision-maker may rely fully on facts aiming for a solid grounded data-driven decision-making, while others may tend to rely on their experience-based gut feeling or intuition. None of these approaches does necessarily result in inferior decisions. In addition, it must be considered that adding more data does not always lead to faster or better decision-making. In fact, having too much data and facts can have the opposite effect and cause decision-making to come to a standstill.

Defining individual strategies to come to best possible fact-based decisions, while recognizing personal biases or inclinations is and will be an important factor regardless of the technology used. Personal biases or preferences include, for example, the separation of the relevant from the irrelevant, focus on selected assumed

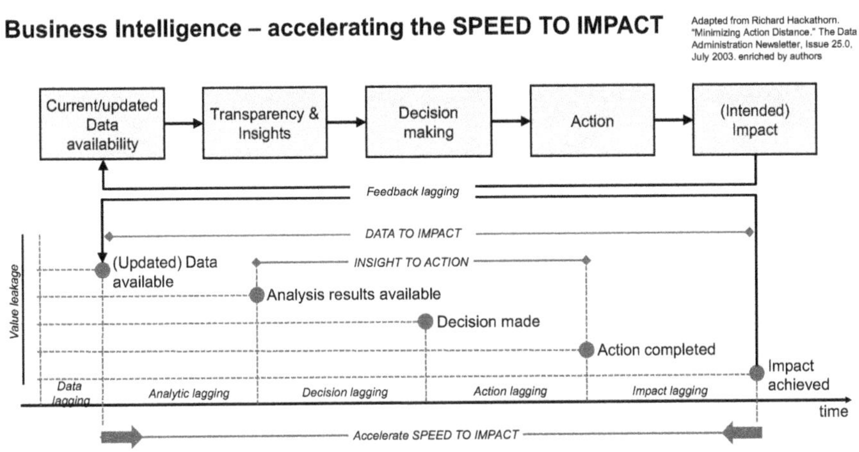

Fig. 1.2 Business Intelligence—Data to Impact (based on (Hackathorn, 2003), adapted by authors)

relevant data sets and personal preferred approaches to balance multiple and partly inconsistent information.

Based on this brief journey through history, we can now describe some key characteristics of Business Intelligence. In doing so, we were able to distinguish between "intelligence," which summarizes the core purpose of SPEED TO IMPACT, and its primary target audience of decision-makers, the "business."

Please note that the above descriptions are not intended to provide an exhaustive history and definition of "Business Intelligence." Rather, they are intended to provide suggestions for dealing with the fundamental objectives and principles of business intelligence.

Based on this view, we now can summarize as follows:

The *Purpose* of "Business Intelligence" Is To

- Interact with data to perform multi-dimensional analysis providing meaningful insights.
- Identify or even better anticipate relationships between facts which should guide necessary actions for achieving targets.
- Support decision-making with its planning, steering, and coordinating activities.
- Integrate strategies, processes, and technology based on distributed and non-harmonized corporate, market, and competitive data.
- Analyze information by using defined processes of mathematical and statistical data analysis that cluster, score, and predict what scenarios are most likely to happen.
- Know about underlying concepts, methods, and constraints on how to make and improve business decision-making itself.
- Optimize processes and enable a company to react quickly.
- Speed-up strategic and operational actions based on timely decisions made grounded on business intelligence capabilities (SPEED TO IMPACT) (see Fig. 1.2)

The *required capabilities* of "business intelligence" are to be provided by

- Systems that are based on internal performance and accounting data as well as external market data capable to support decision-makers.
- Applications, infrastructure and tools and good or even better, best practices.
- Skilled people who are willing, capable, and mandated to use data to improve business performance.
- A defined set of rules which transparently defines how the processes, methodologies, organizational units should work together ("way of working").

1.2 Key Characteristics of an Intelligent Enterprise

Although we have more technology and computing power than ever before, the vision of the Intelligent Enterprise still seems somewhat unattainable for many organizations. Today, the Intelligent Enterprise is more likely to be seen as a catchy vision than a reality or a well-defined roadmap. However, some guardrails have emerged in recent years.

The scope and variety of data and data management technologies has increased significantly over the past decade. The accelerated progression of data-driven optimization, based on data patterns and inferred rule sets previously identified by advanced algorithms, consequently, requires in future the removal of human constraints. These human constraints are, among others, the increasing human inability to keep pace with the highest complexity of machine-developed (self-learning) algorithms and program coding, 24/7 availability, limitations on physical location with time zones, and others.

Devices are becoming increasingly "smart" and connected. Digital twins, or digital representations of physical assets, provide new insights into complex, interconnected supply chains and production processes at the level of products, processes, and entire plants or factories. In other words, physical assets are becoming increasingly blurred with their digital representations.

One of the key characteristics of the "Intelligent Enterprise" is that the entire organization is built on continuous and reinforcing agility and innovation. This also includes the systematic root-cause analysis of identified variances between actual and target performance levels throughout the entire value chain. Not only the options for decision-making and the best option selected as the final decision are recorded, but also the resulting realized actions to overcome the deviations. The success rate of achieving the intended impact is determined, continuously monitored, and recorded to serve as a basis for similar decision scenarios. In addition, this way of working and thinking is no longer limited by organizational boundaries, but is extended to an even broader, cross-company business network. In this way, the organization can be described as an "Intelligent Enterprise."

The vision of the "Intelligent Enterprise" requires a further significant increase of the level of automation in all business domains toward machine learning, artificial intelligence (AI), and other emerging innovations. These developments are impacting transactional processing, digital assets, and automation of the decision-making and execution process. They are multi-dimensional, connected, reinforcing themselves and due to their endlessness cannot be reasonably contained. In this sense, we can expect to enter a new universe, we call "intelligence space" (please refer also to Fig. 1.1).

Key Characteristics of a Visionary "Intelligent Enterprise"

- Ultimate level of automation in all business domains including transactional processing, integration of physical and digital assets.
- Highly automated decision-making and execution process.
- Extensive usage of machine learning, artificial intelligence (AI), and other latest innovations.
- The accelerated continuation of data-driven optimization.
- Way of working and thinking is no longer limited by organizational boundaries, but is extended to an even broader, cross-company business network.
- The acknowledgment of human value contribution, but ongoing removal of human constraints such as manual, repetitive, cumbersome, and error-prone activities.

1.3 BI Strategy in a Nutshell

We recommend this chapter for readers aiming to capture the essentials of this book quickly. But sometimes a phrase is catchy, and we change our minds during reading. To continue reading in more detail, we briefly reference the relevant chapters.

A BI strategy is not a destination, it is a journey. With this in mind, we encourage our readers to take the first step on this journey. Each BI strategy journey is unique, and not all aspects need to be considered in every case, depending on individual situations and preferences. The following chapters should be seen as an invitation to explore the various aspects that contribute to a BI strategy.

Let us start with "*What a BI Strategy is NOT?*"

- Just an IT guideline for BI
- Just a high-level statement of direction
- Just a collection of BI requirements
- Just a blueprint or framework for a BI implementation project
- Just a product-centric innovation roadmap
- Just a BI project portfolio
- Just a document owned by IT

By stating what a BI Strategy is not, we still miss "*What is a BI Strategy?*" and what the BI strategy journey looks like.

• A company-specific definition of BI, BI strategy, its purpose, and value contribution to the overall strategy	Please refer to Chap. 1
• A clear statement of BI goals and objectives derived from strategic business initiatives and/or corporate strategy	Please refer to Chap. 2
• A framework to align BI initiatives and requirements across the company	Please refer to Chap. 3
• A structured process of incrementally improving the maturity of BI via a roadmap with clear evolution stages and targets—including a regular assessment of BI maturity	Please refer to Chap. 3
• A set of corporate BI standards that should be followed by BI projects and initiatives	Please refer to Chap. 4
• A description of the individual building blocks to achieve the objectives—including clear ownership and funding – Data Governance standards – Corporate BI alignment processes/roles/BI-CC – Architecture standards – Technology standards	Please refer to Chaps. 5 and 6

1.4 Typical Situation and Need for Change

"'Time is money,' thus let's get to the essentials quickly." This or similar mindset is quite common. In other words, in most cases, executives are not interested in spending too much time and effort in deeply exploring as-is situation and opportunities to improve. Instead, they quickly want to learn about the key opportunities for improvements and successful ways to tackle the prioritized issues.

For this reason, we describe a proven hands-on approach for the practitioner on how to quickly identify burning topics in the BI space.

Quite often companies are struggling with developing a common and mutually agreed understanding on pain-points, challenges, and opportunities within the business intelligence domain. One reason of this might be that different viewpoints on BI exist within the organization and additionally different wordings are used to describe similar aspects.

While businesses typically view BI as a key enabler for decision support, IT views BI predominantly as a technology- and data-driven enabler for the business. Thus, wordings include different terminologies used by businesses and IT for describing the same or similar phenomena, which can result in difficulties to understand each other (communication barriers). Furthermore, the perception of criticality and urgency differs between businesses and IT as well. For this reason, it makes sense in a first step to develop a common basis for assessing if and in which key areas issues exist and which of them should be addressed with priority.

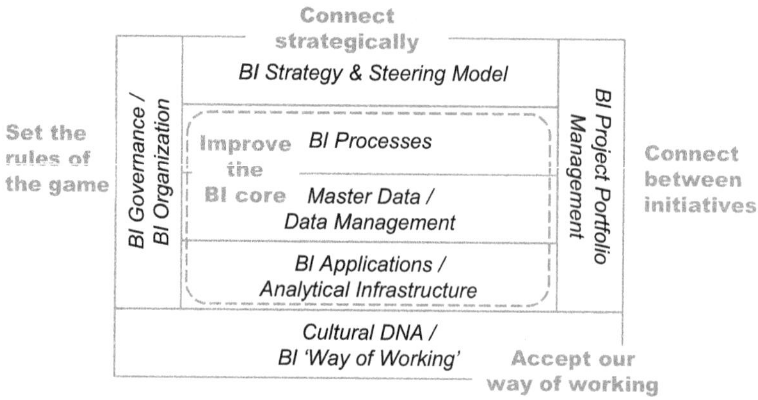

Fig. 1.3 Pragmatic framework to capture most burning BI issues (© Exner/Zunic 2024. All Rights Reserved)

Executives are typically not interested in spending too much time and effort in deeply exploring as-is situation and potential issues. They rather are forced to improve the situation quickly.

How could such an approach look like?

The following approach provides proven hands-on guidance. It might not be exhaustive in every single detail and certainly we could spend quite a lot of time finding the best possible framework. However, the framework should be used just as a starting point. Once we gain momentum and basically agree on a "need for change" we have accomplished our target. Further tailoring can be done later, if needed.

1. The basic idea is first to agree on a conceptual framework or canvas, which can guide us to group pain-points, challenges, and opportunities in a well-arranged and easy to digest way. This canvas could look like illustrated in Fig. 1.3.
2. Next, we collect challenges, pain-points, opportunities in context with business intelligence. This can be done based on own experiences, meetings with colleagues, participation on BI conferences, Internet sources, and others.
3. Based on the beforementioned findings, we note each of these in a separate text box. It is important that we keep the description crisp, lean, and easy to understand. The appearance of the text boxes should be neutral, hence not unintentionally highlighting any of the content compared to any other.
4. Next, we position the text boxes in the different sections of the canvas where they fit best.
5. Once we have finally arranged the text boxes within our canvas, we are ready to go for conducting an assessment in practice.

To capture the most pressing BI issues, we suggest using a canvas. In practice, it is advantageous to use a canvas that is easy to explain and introduce, as this allows participants to contribute even if they are not familiar with BI in all its details. The canvas aims to address the following areas of investigation:

1. How well is BI strategically connected?
2. How well are initiatives connected to achieve synergies between them?
3. Are the rules in place adequate to serve the BI organization?
4. How does the overall way of working in the company affect BI? And finally
5. How do the core BI components meet the requirements?

The basic reason for choosing the above five areas is that they are broad enough to easily capture burning issues, but still engaging enough to motivate the majority of BI and non-BI experts to be able to share their views.

Based on the above, we now concretize these in a canvas as illustrated in Fig. 1.3. Our final canvas consists of seven building blocks, which are:

1. BI Strategy & Steering Model
2. BI Processes
3. Master Data/Data Management
4. BI Applications/Analytical Infrastructure
5. Grounded by Cultural DNA/BI "Way of Working"

Framed by

6. BI Governance/BI Organization
7. BI Project Portfolio Management

First step is to develop a common and holistic view of the BI status quo. Based on the beforementioned step 4, we arrange the "problem statements" (text boxes), depending on which section of the canvas they fit best. It is not a black or white decision where to assign a "problem statement." A brief discussion within a small group of participants will guide you to the suitable answer. It is key to avoid enforcing consensus on individual problem statements right at the beginning. Instead, it is advisable to complete this later. Key reason and benefit for this approach is to actively engage stakeholders or workshop participants to voice their gut feeling and individual impressions without risking them to get talked down.

Neither it is recommended to jump direct into the details of the problem statements or start discussing various possible definitions of any of the pain-points. Jumping right into premature conclusions should also be avoided. Instead, it is valuable to initially listen to a spontaneous "gut" feeling for deciding whether a specific pain-point is valid for the own perception or not. In case the pain-point is predominantly perceived as "valid" it will be marked with red color, in case "not valid," i.e., the pain-point (hot-spot) is not existing or is not perceived as relevant, it will be marked with green color. A binary decision should be moderated as mandatory to encourage clarity of opinion. A blurring color or usage of "orange" should be avoided. Running such session in a time-boxed manner is advisable.

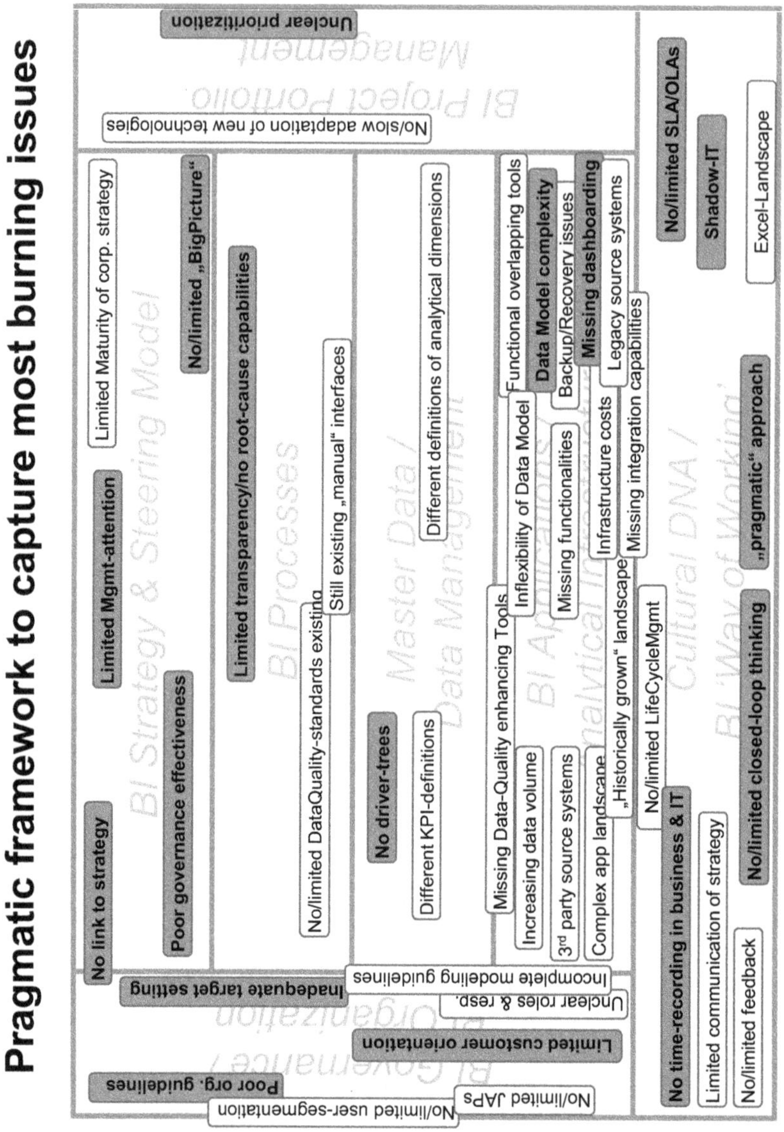

Fig. 1.4 Example of capturing the most burning issues (© Exner/Zunic 2024. All Rights Reserved)

Table 1.1 Quick-Scan—Hotspot-Definitions

Hot spots	R/G*	Descriptions	Evaluation/feedbacks
1. No/limited "big picture"	R	Ability to holistically understand the vision and objectives of BI	No concrete vision and BI strategy of future state BI landscape; what depth of description is appropriate?
2. No link to corporate/ divisional strategy	R	Degree of alignment/cascading between strategic business objectives/plans and BI	Business strategy "x y z" and other strategic pillars like M&A (clear financial strategic objectives defined) are not yet aligned with BI strategy
3. "Pragmatic approach"	R	Approach often used to prioritize speed of delivery higher than quality and sustainability of results	Many ad-hoc requests; no integrated holistic concept; side-reporting
4. No/limited closed-loop thinking	R	Degree to which the performance management system integrates all processes and tools needed to iteratively (closed loop) identify, analyze, and act on performance deviations/issues	No/limited systematic approach; action plans partly existing; many side-tools which are not integrated and different ownership of these tools; action plans partly existing; targeted granularity of data undefined
5. Shadow IT	R	Bypass to "official" IT without central governance/ownership	Siloed BI solution landscape; side-reporting with usage of spreadsheets; no overarching ownership established
6. No driver trees	R	Ability to analyze value drivers influencing financial performance alongside a pre-defined logical structure (hierarchy)	Structural relationships between data entities (hierarchies) not consistent or undefined limiting drill-down-capabilities
7. Limited transparency/no root-cause capabilities	R	Ability to analyze and understand details of identified performance issues using analytical capabilities	Limited capability to connect performance data long the value chain (revenue–order entry–quotations–leads/opportunities–customer visits)
8. No time recording in business and IT	R	Ability to trace and plan fact-based efforts spent on reporting and planning (both business and IT)	No time recording, thus no baseline to measure efficiency gains in BI delivery
9. Inadequate target setting	R	Effective and efficient target setting, deriving operational plans and monitoring these plans	Limited planning of quantities; no integrated planning across supply chain; missing connect between demand and supply
10. Limited customer orientation	R	Degree to which reporting delivers the right content to the right people at the right time	Limited knowledge and adoption of existing tools and capabilities (silo); deeper understanding of internal BI customer segmentation and specific requirements required
11. Limited management attention	R	Degree to which management acknowledges and strategically values the importance of BI	No regular meeting cadence for BI established; No ownership "Mr./Mrs. BI" (SPOC) existing
12. No/limited SLA/OLAs[a]	R	Degree to which reporting performance metrics have been defined and agreed with the business via SLAs and delivery units via OLAs	SLAs not established in a harmonized/ standardized way. Not existing at all in BI/reporting environment

(continued)

Table 1.1 (continued)

Hot spots	R/G*	Descriptions	Evaluation/feedbacks
13. Poor governance effectiveness	R	Degree to which governance procedures and ownership have been established for reporting content and data	"Historical grown"; no/limited responsibilities; one of the core topics within BI
14. Poor organziational guidelines	R	Existence and adherence to corporate reporting guidelines, incl. standards on design, definitions, notations	"Historical grown"; no/limited responsibilities; one of the core topics within BI
15. Unclear prioritization	R	Degree to which issues and needs have been captured, documented, and classified/prioritized	Ad hoc prioritization existing but dedicated structure existing on how BI-related issues will be captured and prioritized
16. Missing dashboarding	R	Ability to provide easy to read, often single page, self-service user interfaces (usability, commenting)	Inadequate dashboarding capabilities; no self-service established, predominantly IT-driven BI delivery
17. Data model complexity	R	Scope and complexity of reported information, data relationships, and data quality	Single reporting hierarchy existing but parallel hierarchies are requested; profit-center structures integrated with product structures, harming flexibility Reconciliation issues across data silos and data models

SLA Service Level Agreement, *OLA* Operational Level Agreement
R Red, *G* Green

This approach is particularly valuable when different stakeholder groups are involved to contribute with individual and potentially divergent viewpoints.

The resulting picture could finally look like illustrated in Fig. 1.4.

The benefit of this approach is that we can discover a first pattern indicating the focus areas (where we find multiple "red" elements). This immediately can help to provide an initial "big picture" view of the hot spots which should be followed-up in subsequent steps.

As already introduced, we now can go into the details by clarifying and aligning the interpretation of the hot spots. This again is most likely a mutual (follow-up) exercise. It is recommended to conduct this with the same participants. Table 1.1 shows exemplary hot spots with their definition and reasoning. Column "R/G" indicates "Red / Green" statements. In Fig. 1.4, the gray boxes are the red ones.

This approach provides a good and meaningful source for further evaluation and steps developing a new or refining an existing BI strategy. Table 1.1 shows an exemplary overview and description of the identified "hot spots."

Above problem statements show an initial pattern with hot spots predominantly in:

- Cultural DNA/BI "Way of Working" (5 "red" topics)
- BI Strategy & Steering Model (4 "red" topics)
- BI Governance/BI Organization (3 "red" topics)

- Some in BI Applications/Analytical Infrastructure (2 "red" topics) with less hot spots in BI Processes (1 "red" topic), Master Data/Data Management (1 "red" topic), and BI Project Portfolio Management (1 "red" topic)

Do you recognize yours? In this case you would like to adapt the approach to your needs.

1.5 Business Intelligence Trends

In this chapter, we will analyze key business intelligence trends both in terms of technological innovations and changing business expectations. Both dimensions are important, because they significantly influence the BI value contribution. At the same time without an adequate management approach and strategic assessment of these trends, the value contribution will likely not be optimal. Hence, we will also provide some advice on how trend analysis and assessment can be integrated into the BI strategy development process.

Many organizations struggle to keep pace with the rapid evolution of technology and related business expectations in the business intelligence and data management domains. The interconnected nature of business intelligence requires responsiveness to change in many different areas.

Moreover, the BI domain itself is fuzzy because it is not an established business function like finance, for example. BI is not only relevant across all lines of business, it also spans across many different IT domains, such as software applications, data management, integration, security, technology platforms, and many more.

To be able to control and manage this complexity, a good practice in a BI strategy is to clearly describe and evaluate the main BI trends and drivers in the context of the organization's business intelligence goals and needs (as an organizational "point of view"). A key aspect of this is to understand the basic underlying macro trends, technology trends and their relevance to the organization. This is important because such trends can significantly disrupt existing approaches and practices and influence IT architecture and technology decisions. A BI strategy should ideally describe an approach how technology trends will be reviewed, evaluated, and phased into the organization.

To illustrate how this can be done, we introduce a model that takes a look at four main trend categories and describes the underlying trends from a business intelligence perspective.

- Macro trends
- Usage trends
- Data monetarization trend
- BI Technology trends

Let us first begin on a macro-level and take a look at which general trends will fundamentally impact the BI domain. Please note, the following trend descriptions are to some extent subjective and should be reviewed and described from an organization-specific point of view.

1.5.1 Macro Trends

Trend 1: New Generation of Users

Digital natives who are familiar with compelling digital consumer experiences are entering the business world. This generates new business user expectations. Business users increasingly expect information at their fingertips everywhere, on any sort of output device, tailored exactly to their information needs. They do not only want to search for and consume pre-defined reports, they want to explore and share insight within their communities and peers. In addition, this group of users is more inclined to analyze data interactively, experiment with data, and create their own analyses.

Trend 2: New User Experiences

Information consumers are increasingly demanding business intelligence applications that provide engaging user experiences, are flexible and lightweight, and deliver information as customized and personalized content that is easy to consume and digest. Formerly dedicated, and thus recognizable, BI applications are increasingly blending and seamlessly integrating with business processes and transactions ("embedded BI").

BI consumers are increasingly able and empowered to develop and deploy their own analytical applications and reports based on low-code/no-code platforms (citizen developers), increasing the agility of BI delivery.

Trend 3: New Technologies

The scope and variety of data and data management technologies has increased significantly over the last decade. Devices are increasingly becoming "smart" and connected. Digital twins, meaning digital representations of physical assets, enable entirely new insights into complex, interconnected supply chains and production processes on the level of products, processes, and entire plants or factories. New technologies such as blockchain enable the secure exchange of transactions between trading partners without the need for an intermediary acting as a trusted third party.

And we have seen many more exciting trends achieving increasing adoption in the business community on the path to becoming "Intelligent Enterprises."

From a business intelligence perspective, all of these trends essentially create a new playing field. Unstructured and semi-structured data are now an essential part of the game, and new data management approaches and integration technologies challenge traditional business intelligence best practices and architectures.

Although history shows that the majority of new "hyped" technology innovations do not survive in the long term, those that do tend to have a significant disruptive impact and cannot be ignored.

Some of the most prolific technology trends expected to have a significant impact on enterprise business intelligence are the following:

- Artificial Intelligence (AI)
  Artificial Intelligence is the simulation of human intelligence in machines programmed to think and learn like humans. It involves the development of algorithms and computational models that enable machines to perform tasks that typically require human intelligence. These tasks include problem-solving, learning, understanding natural language, speech recognition, visual perception, and decision-making.
  AI can be applied to different business use cases as illustrated below.

  – *Generative AI*—Unlike traditional AI systems that focus on solving specific problems or making predictions based on existing data, generative AI is designed to produce novel and creative outputs. It utilizes artificial neural networks that undergo initial training with a substantial amount of data and are then fine-tuned for specific tasks. Generative AI models can generate new content based on the information gathered during training for a new question or task.
  – *Natural Language Processing (NLP)* enables the recognition, translation, and generation of text or other content via large language models (LLMs) using massive sets of training data and model parameters. Such models can be used for text classification, document structuring or translation and can help make large semi-structured data sets accessible for analysis and decision-making.
  – *AI-Based Data Science algorithms* refers to the more traditional application of artificial intelligence. It is used primarily to classify or group data sets like, for example, identifying customer segments with similar buying behavior, detecting patterns and anomalies (for example, fraud detection), or proposing actions based on decision trees.
  – *Conversational, Dialog-Oriented AI* can engage in natural language conversations with users. These systems are designed to understand human language, generate appropriate responses, and simulate natural conversation. They typically assist users in complex workflow processing and task automation by guiding them via a dialogue-oriented conversational interface. Conversational AI is used in various applications, including chatbots and virtual assistants.

- Embedded Analytics
  Embedded analytics refers to the integration of business intelligence and analytics capabilities directly into operational applications, workflows, or processes. By enabling real-time analytics in the operational processes, the goal is to overcome the traditional separation between *O*n*L*line *T*ransactional data *P*rocessing (OLTP) and business intelligence on aggregated, non-real-time data (*O*n*L*ine *A*nalytical *P*rocessing) (Merge of OLTP and OLAP).
- In-Memory Analytics
  In-memory analytics revolutionizes the speed and efficiency of data analysis by processing and storing data in RAM, enabling organizations to perform complex analytics in real time. This approach also helps eliminate the need to store multiple redundant copies of data and create physical data aggregates for analysis and reporting purposes.

- Cloud BI
  Cloud Business Intelligence (Cloud BI) refers to the delivery of business intelligence applications, services, and tools via cloud computing technologies. It leverages the power of the cloud to deliver scalable, flexible, and accessible business intelligence services with shorter innovation cycles. We are already seeing widespread adoption of cloud-based analytics services, particularly as an entry point to a broader cloud strategy.
  In addition, cloud data integration platforms in a platform-as-a-service model (see Chap. 6) are becoming increasingly popular. These platforms provide the infrastructure and tools needed to integrate and manage data from disparate sources using open APIs and offering pro-code/low-code/no-code integration options. Especially in hybrid (cloud, on premise) landscapes, a cloud-based integration layer can be attractive.

Trend 4: New Governance

The increasing diversity of user groups, data-driven use cases, technology platforms, new ways of working, and other trends outlined above are challenging established control mechanisms and governance structures. There is a noticeable push toward more flexible and agile BI solutions with localized control and ownership, avoiding the constraints of a centralized control and change management approach. This includes potentially rethinking or (re)defining business intelligence ownership, data ownership, the scope of enterprise business intelligence, and change control management.

Managing this growing complexity while meeting higher user expectations is not trivial. In practice, many organizations are trying to strike a balance between centralized and decentralized control and are attempting to establish at least a minimum level of BI governance, while others have resigned entirely to impose any centralized governance on their BI environment (see Chap. 5).

1.5.2 BI Usage Trends

Changed business intelligence usage trends can be observed in three main areas.

- Broadening the use of BI beyond traditional reporting use cases
- Significant increase of data volumes accessible for analytics
- New ways of consumption through flexible self-service BI

Broadened Use Beyond Traditional BI

In addition to traditional business intelligence, which was primarily designed to meet the needs of corporate functions such as accounting, controlling, sales, and covered use cases like reporting, planning, forecasting, new forms of business intelligence like predictive modeling and big data analysis have emerged. These new use cases are fueled by the growing data demands and analytical capabilities of business communities as well as the increasing availability of data.

However, these new use cases do not render traditional business intelligence irrelevant or obsolete. On the contrary, business intelligence architectures built for the needs of management decision-making around a strong governance and steering model will continue to be a key cornerstone of the BI landscape.

Higher Data Volumes Accessible for Analytics

With the introduction of big data analytics into enterprise business intelligence, entirely new analytical use cases became possible. The ingestion and querying of mass data (both structured and unstructured) in real time enables the analysis of previously inaccessible data sources. Data essentially does not need to be prepared for a pre-defined analytical use but can be queried in its original format. Combined with trained AI-based analytical models, very powerful analyses and even simulations are within reach that were not imaginable only a few years ago.

The applications of such analytical scenarios are endless. They include, for example, sentiment analyses of customers retrieved from social media posts as an early indicator of perceived product quality and potentially future buying behavior, predictive maintenance of machinery based on real-time sensor data, smart-grids, and many more. The basic idea is to evaluate mass data from new data sources with high-performance technology and statistical methods for a variety of purposes. The analysis scope thus extends far beyond classical accounting tasks and also the analysis horizon expands from rear-view performance reporting to the prediction of future outcomes. The goal is to forecast developments on a very granular and individual level, as for example individual products, batches, specific target groups, or the end customer. We expect to see major innovation in this area and increasing experimentation/adoption within organizations, as this domain has the potential to be a competitive differentiator.

New Ways of Consumption

Another key trend, which has become an established practice in leading companies already, is a flexible self-service provisioning of BI. This enables business departments to consume and adopt BI capabilities and data without having to involve IT. Increasingly self-service BI allows end-users to not only consume but also to create and deploy new BI content on their own, which can be shared with other business communities. While self-service is important, information workers also need access to reliable, well-governed information sources. Self-service and own content delivery hence do not replace a central governance structure.

A BI strategy needs to acknowledge different forms of business intelligence use cases and changing usage behaviors. A useful starting point would be to interview a representative sample of BI users and non-BI users across the organization, varying by age, gender, hierarchy level, and department, to determine usage patterns and future requirements prior to reaching any conclusions. An important factor in achieving success will be the ability to integrate the diverse strategic demands without creating isolated organizational or technological silos. Chapter 6 (Data architecture) provides a few examples in this regard.

1.5.3 Data Monetization Trend

Another fascinating development is the monetization of data and BI services within existing or entirely new business models. Data that is collected along the duration of the customer relationship can enable entirely new product and service offerings, based, for example, on data-as-a-service or content-as-a-service models.

There are essentially three main approaches to data monetization.

- Commercializing value-adding data or data services as a new business model or revenue stream
  In this approach, companies create new value-added services by collecting and sharing data with customers and partners who pay for the data and/or service provided.
  Examples: The vendor monitors the customer's product usage to proactively identify maintenance and repair cycles helping customers avoid cost of failure/the vendor provides a benchmarking service to his customers who in turn agree to share their data/an insurance company uses telematics devices to collect a customer's driving data and can provide personalized discounts for safe driving behavior.
- Identifying up-sell and cross-sell opportunities to improve the top-line
  This is particularly common in a sales and marketing context. Customer data can be used to identify up-sell and cross-sell opportunities based on customer segmentation or buying behaviors and product selection patterns. It can also be used for an intelligent bundling of products to provide more attractive product offerings.
- Identifying waste and cost reduction potential to improve the bottom line
  The main focus here is to improve operational efficiency, mainly by automating manual tasks and achieving real-time insights into operational performance. Eliminating manual recurring tasks like manually recording data, performing side-reporting in spreadsheets, checking invoices, manually correcting errors, and performing reconciliations or running manual approval workflows can all help reducing operational cost and hence improving the bottom line—especially when they can be scaled across the organization.

A BI strategy should connect with other business strategies and identify drivers for data monetization and areas of BI value contribution. The more tangible the BI value contribution and business case are articulated, the greater the probability of obtaining necessary management commitment and funding.

1.5.4 BI Technology Trends

Although this book is not primarily about technology, technological developments cannot be ignored when developing a BI strategy. As we have already seen at the beginning of this chapter, a BI strategy should be able to clearly describe and

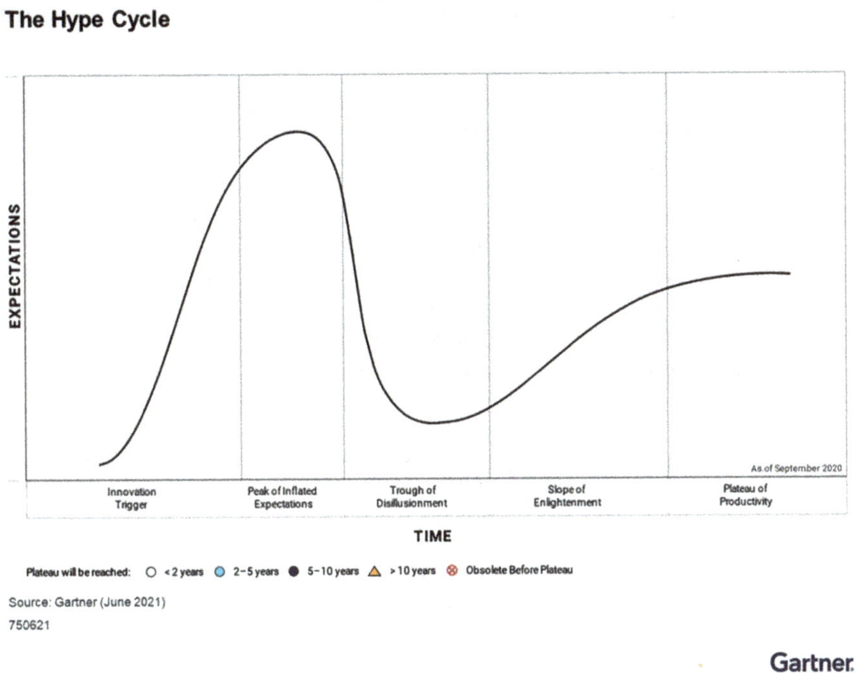

Fig. 1.5 The Gartner Hype Cycle (Gartner et al., 2023)

categorize the technology trends that affect the organization and provide a framework to continuously monitor and evaluate them in an organization-specific context.

An established source for tracing IT and technology trends is Gartner. Gartner regularly publishes market research and trend predictions on a wide range of IT topics and technologies, among them BI and analytics.

The Gartner Hype Cycle (Fig. 1.5) illustrates the product life cycle curve of various individual technologies and innovations, from initial emergence in the market to stabilized adoption.

Gartner's experience shows that the adoption of new technologies and innovations typically follows a common pattern. After the initial launch, technologies are often hyped, which can result in exaggerated expectations. If the expectations are not met, the innovation life cycle enters a so-called trough of disillusionment, which can lead either to a further life cycle stage of stabilized productive adoption, or to the withdrawal of the innovation from the market.

Individual technologies and innovations are regularly plotted on this life cycle curve. This makes it possible to track the evolving maturity of these technologies over time.

The Gartner Hype Cycle, or more generally, a framework for tracing the life cycle of technology, can aid in assessing the maturity of technology innovations.

A straightforward way to evaluate BI and analytics trends is to link the organization's designated BI innovation areas or strategic BI capabilities to the macro trends

Table 1.2 2022 Gartner Hype Cycle predictions for business intelligence, data management, and artificial intelligence

Macro trends	BI innovation area, capability	BI and analytics trends from Gartner Hype Cycles (2022)	Hype cycle phase[a]	Trend duration[b]
New generation of users	Data-driven decision-making and self-service analytics	Analytics and business intelligence hype cycle[c]:		
		• Embedded analytics	Phase 4/5	Long
		• Self-service data and analytics	Phase 4/5	Long
		• Data storytelling	Phase 2/5	Medium
		• Analytics catalog	Phase 1/5	Short
	Advanced analytics (Data Science)	Analytics and business intelligence hype cycle[c]		
		• Text analytics	Phase 4/5	Long
		• Prescriptive analytics	Phase 3/5	Medium
		• Edge analytics	Phase 3/5	Medium
New user experiences	Data discovery	Analytics and business intelligence hype cycle[c]		
		• Explainable AI	Phase 3/5	Short
		• Natural language query	Phase 3/5	Medium
		• Natural language generation (NLG)	Phase 3/5	Medium
New technology	Big data processing	Data management hype cycle[d]:		
		• Event stream processing	Phase 4/5	Long
		• Data lakes	Phase 4/5	Medium
		• Data fabric	Phase 3/5	Short
	Artificial intelligence	Artificial intelligence hype cycle[e]:		
		• Smart robots	Phase 2/5	Short
		• Generative AI	Phase 2/5	Short
		• Decision intelligence	Phase 1/5	Short
New governance	New forms of BI delivery and governance	Analytics and business intelligence hype cycle[f]		
		• Cloud analytics	Phase 4/5	Medium
		• Citizen data science	Phase 3/5	Medium
		• ModelOps	Phase 1/5	Medium

[a]Phase 1 = Innovation trigger, Phase 2 = Peak of inflated expectations, Phase 3 = Trough of disillusionment, Phase 4 = Slope of enlightenment, Phase 5 = Plateau of productivity
[b]Trend durations: short < 2 years, medium 2–5 years, long > 5 years
[c]Hype Cycle for Analytics and Business Intelligence (Gartner & Krensky, 2022)
[d]Hype Cycle for Artificial Intelligence (Gartner et al., 2022)
[e]Hype Cycle for Data Management (Gartner et al., 2022)

that affect the company as well as the corresponding BI technology trends identified by market analysts such as Gartner.

Table 1.2 illustrates this approach. The table maps major BI and analytics trends (shown in column 3) to the macro trends and required BI capabilities identified by the organization (columns 1 and 2). Moreover, it presents the maturity position of the BI trend as per the 2022 Gartner Hype Cycles for Analytics and Business

Intelligence, Artificial Intelligence and Data Management and indicates how long-lasting the trend has been (by comparing the Hype Cycles from previous periods).

Please consider the above approach as an indicative example only.

The trend analysis shows that in certain capability and innovation areas, BI trends have largely matured and been adopted on a wide scale, whereas in other areas like artificial intelligence trends are still in early innovation stages.

From a strategic viewpoint, it is advisable to treat these trends differently in terms of adoption. New trend areas will require room for experimentation and early failure whereas more mature areas have the potential to be put to productive use immediately.

1.6 BI Strategy and the Path to an Intelligent Enterprise

In this last sub-chapter, we will summarize our first learnings and recommendations to provide initial guidance on BI strategy development.

The very core is to develop a transparent way how to gear and match value expectation of the businesses with value contribution of BI. The documentation of this ambition and commitment to the organization we call "BI strategy."

In the subsequent Chap. 1, we will discuss how to gear BI strategy with other strategies.

The beforementioned BI pain-points, needs, and trends analysis are by no means intended to be exhaustive. However, they provide a solid foundation to understand starting point and help identifying first opportunities on a way forward.

Before we will equip our readers with in-depth inputs to develop a BI strategy in later chapters, we will summarize first learnings and additional recommendations to provide initial guidance:

- *Understand strategic value expectation and BI value contribution*
  Key anchor of BI value contribution is a close alignment between corporate and functional strategies with business intelligence. This alignment has multiple factettes. This can range from envisioning new strategic opportunities based on data-driven business models and data monetarization to BI technology enabling new decision support and latest innovations leading to new ways of working. However, this new way of working should not be limited to the transactional processes of day-to-day operations but should also consider the process of decision-making itself and the process of execution once a decision has been made.
- *Ensure business participation*
  One of the main challenges in BI adoption is that in many cases investment decisions are driven by IT departments ("we know technology") who have little insight into how the business operates and interacts with data and technology. This can easily lead to a situation in which the business does not feel sufficiently understood by IT. Potential consequences can be a bypassing of IT owned

solutions by business owned investments in BI tools. If this is done excessively, redundant and siloed solutions are being created.

- *Gearing value contribution with BI technology*
  Before making important BI technology investment decisions, think about value contribution and specific application areas carefully. This may sound obvious, but often technology decisions and investments are made without understanding the inherent demands they are supposed to serve. This includes, for example, a thorough analysis of your already available business intelligence capabilities, the degree of adoption of these capabilities, needs for replacement (for example of outdated technology), and an understanding of functional white spots in new BI domains.
- *Proactively incorporate organizational and governance drivers*
  Investments in innovations can sometimes be mis-used to fix problems which are not technology related. For example, data-driven decision support relies obviously on proper quality of operational data. Typically, the responsibility of operational data quality resides in multiple businesses with not necessarily identical way of working, and perception of data quality can differ. This is often caused by narrowed thinking of own data usage (silos), ignoring or underestimating the relevancy of data quality in a larger context. Hence, data quality issues, for example, will not alone be fixed by pure technology solutions or BI tools unless they are supported by an underlying process and governance environment. In addition, even when data quality is sufficient and all the facts are on the table, decisions are sometimes delayed. As a result, not trying to explore the underlying reasons can limit opportunities for improvement.
- *Don't let the hype take control—don't follow every trend!*
  Technology trends are by nature changing all the time and are typically overemphasized in the early stages of maturity. It is neither possible nor advisable to follow every trend as this will lead to confusion and potentially wasted resources. Therefore, it is important to define a methodology and ownership—make this part of your BI organization. Trends in technology innovation should not be the only main driver of your BI strategy—but you should take mature trends into consideration when building or revising your future BI vision and strategic BI capabilities.
- *Create environments for experimentation*
  Allow failure to happen (early). Establish innovation lab environments to test and explore new innovations in a risk-free environment. Manage and measure the results and experiences to judge solution readiness prior to further rollout and broad adoption. As a result of early technology adoption, new triggers for potential revision or enhancement of BI strategy can arise. Such a safe environment is in particular also relevant if you are adopting the ideas of the "Intelligent Enterprise" to decision-makers in senior and middle management.

Coming back to our core topic about BI strategy. *What should a BI Strategy describe?*

It is highly recommendable to use a concise, yet comprehensive style to provide answers to the below mentioned aspects. A pure listing of bullets could leave room for interpretation or misunderstanding and should be avoided.

Key Considerations for Developing a BI Strategy

- Describe your organizational specific definition and scope of Business Intelligence.
- Describe the fit-gap of current capability portfolio and ambition level as a result of an initial pain-point analysis.
- Describe how your company views the major macro trends applicable and how they will likely change user behaviors and requirements.
- Describe the full inventory of BI technologies you are using today including an overview of the number of applications and users (baseline).
- Cluster these technologies by purpose (what are they used for?), maturity (how mature is the technology?), and usage duration.
- Document the adoption of the available technologies (for example, by user satisfaction feedback or usage statistics) to rate existing pervasiveness.
- Continuously validate your BI strategy development and BI value contribution against the key characteristics of a visionary Intelligent Enterprise.

Strategic Anchors for BI Strategy

2

This chapter shall familiarize you with the notion of "strategy" as such. It will provide insights into selected corporate and business strategies, starting with a crisp illustrative definition. Based on this understanding, we can strategically anchor the BI strategy with the business.

The relevancy of corporate and business strategies for BI strategy must not be underestimated. If we do not sufficiently understand corporate and business strategies, including their objectives, level of ambitions, constraints, underlying assumptions, ways of working, terminologies, etc., we will hardly be able to discuss on a strategic level with our BI stakeholders and customers. And even more important, if we are not sufficiently equipped to participate in strategy discussions, how shall we convince our BI customers of our strategic BI value contribution?

In the subsequent sub-chapters, we will discuss strategies, starting with the overarching corporate strategy. Due to the utmost importance of digital data for BI, we will detail "digital" strategy in a dedicated sub-chapter. Despite the relevance of digital data, it is by no means self-evident that companies are entirely mature across all domains. Within the sub-chapter finance strategy, we will broaden our view to understand possible changes within finance that might become opportunities or challenges for BI. During the last years, the relevancy and urgency to make significant improvements in sustainability and de-carbonization globally led to new needs of information provisioning and decision-making beyond corporate boundaries. This will be discussed in Sect. 2.6. Finally, we will provide insights into IT strategy and its cross-dependencies with BI.

The tool kit itself for conducting the alignment will be described in Chap. 3.

R. Exner, A. Zunic, *The Path to an Intelligent Enterprise*, Future of Business and Finance, https://doi.org/10.1007/978-3-031-69914-6_2

What is strategy, and why is it important to start this chapter with a definition of strategy?

The notion of "strategy" is a frequently used term, but it is an often misunderstood concept applied in many different contexts. For example, the term "strategy" is sometimes used interchangeably with "planning" or "target setting." Furthermore, it can be used to describe a long-term or even visionary approach or plan. In a more informal setting, the term 'strategy' is often used to describe a high-level approach that does not delve into specifics or details. While these aspects of strategy may all be relevant to a certain extent, they remain abstract and do not provide sufficient guidance as to why strategy is important and how it is applied. It is important to recognise that, despite the established corporate disciplines of business strategy and strategic thinking, there is no universally accepted approach or even definition of 'strategy'. It is nevertheless beneficial to examine different definitions and techniques in order to challenge our own perceptions and gain insights into its purpose and applicability, particularly in the context of business intelligence.

The ambiguity of the term provides opportunities for discussing different perceptions and practices before drawing conclusions in a specific direction.

It is interesting to note that neither "business intelligence" nor "strategy" are clearly defined terms. It is therefore particularly important to be clear about what is and is not meant by the combined term "business intelligence strategy".

This book aims to provide guidance in developing a BI strategy. For this reason, it is essential to get the basics right from the beginning.

2.1 What Is "Strategy?"

Although the term "strategy" is used almost inflationary, it is by no means self-explanatory, and many academics have contributed to the question of "what is strategy" in the past. This book is intended to assist practitioners in the context of a Business Intelligence strategy, so we will present only a few thoughts. Of course, there are additional and different views that we will not cover. Our focus on some aspects should not be confused with an implicit evaluation. The purpose of this book is not to dive deep into the strategy discourse and its definitions.

Rather, this chapter can be seen as an invitation to explore strategies within one's own organization and to look for common definitions and understandings of what a strategy is and what it is not. Consistency with corporate strategy should be seen as key to avoiding a Business Intelligence strategy being perceived as a "foreign body" or, even worse, being ignored entirely. In other words, understanding strategy helps identify commonalities and discrepancies in strategy definitions to anchor a BI strategy.

One of the essential starting points of exploring strategies is to achieve a common understanding of how value is created for a customer in a sustainable way. This implicitly assumes common understanding on what "value" is and who the customer is. Reality shows that even those fundamental questions are sometimes easier to ask than to answer.

The idea of value creation contains various aspects. One of the well-known ones is the business process. The idea is that without a process, which is understood as a sequence of activities to achieve a specific outcome, no result can be achieved, or no product or service can be developed.

This idea of value creation can also be applied to business intelligence, as it encourages reflection on the business intelligence processes and their value creation sequence. This approach also inspires a rethinking of how the sequence of BI value creation is organized from an end-to-end perspective and, consequently, how essential activities can be separated from less important ones.

If you broaden this view to the entire organization, this approach supports clarifying how BI might be embedded in the overall process landscape of a company. In most organizations, Business Intelligence is not a core activity from a business perspective such as sales or production. However, in many cases, there is consensus that business intelligence supports the monitoring of business processes and decision-making on various levels. In recent years, however, it has become increasingly apparent that business models are evolving which are purely data-based, i.e. do not generate physical products. In such cases, the level of business intelligence contribution is typically higher. Even further, when the provision of business intelligence services is fully outsourced, business intelligence becomes the primary activity of the service provider.

However, what other aspects exist that support value creation? One of the critical connectors between all the different business processes and their activities is data. Data are bits and bytes in computers that represent physical reality. Data are the content that flows through the various processes with their underlying activities. Data become enriched along the activities and processes, so the data at the start of a process look different than at the completion of a process. Without data, the processes would be similar to empty shells. Imagine a well-designed business process without any data flow. The process is useless, as it does not change anything. Of course, we can, for example, imagine a craftsman shaping a workpiece with his hands or performing an activity that does not require data. However, such kinds of examples are increasingly the exception rather than the rule.

Business intelligence capabilities necessarily rely on high-quality data. These data are created within all activities within a company as well as by external sources such as business partners, customers, vendors, authorities, etc. The implicit assumption is that these data are consistently defined, created, shared, and used across the entire enterprise. Practitioners know that, more often than not, this assumption is not valid. Consequently, we typically see the emergence of multiple "versions of the truth" in organizations.

Let us further utilize the idea of value creation and rethink it within an international operating company with, say, three business units running different businesses in their regions but serving partly the same global customers. Due to the history of the exemplary company, which grew through mergers, each business unit has established its own business intelligence landscape with separated technology, systems, processes, end-user support, and many more.

In today's environment of striving for sustainable profitability, continuous cost reduction is a crucial lever. It is evident that there is little room for redundancies in such scenarios. The question is valid from a global perspective: "Which of the BI functions can be shared or centralized globally, which should remain regional, and what is the rationale for each of these decisions?" The idea of challenging the historically grown pattern of BI processes can also be used as a means to review and redesign the current setup of BI processes on a global scale. This common view can accelerate discussions on further optimizing the BI setup for this exemplary global enterprise.

The above-used scenario is very simplistic, and every practitioner knows about existing complexities due to multiple circular activities, loops, and cause-and-effect relationships that any high-level sequence of activities cannot adequately describe. Furthermore, the very idea of value creation along a process chain is still ambiguous, because in practice we find many variations of such terms, such as end-to-end processes like "order to cash," "procure to pay," or "record to report." Yet, there is no commonly agreed scheme of end-to-end process definition applicable to all organizations, which just needs to be put into practice. However, the idea of discussing such end-to-end processes from the very beginning to the very end in an organization or even beyond organizational boundaries adds value because these discussions help to challenge the way of thinking. Ideally, they encourage us to think in a strong, process-oriented way, without organizational boundaries such as departmental or functional boundaries. In doing so, this new way of thinking encourages us to break down silos of thinking and consequently acting.

In recent years, we have seen significant progress in discussing business processes. Interestingly, if we assess how data are discussed along these end-to-end business processes, more often than not, these discussions are still conducted quite siloed. In other words, what currently sounds obvious from a process point of view is not yet common practice regarding data flows in companies. Any practitioner knows the partly significant differences in data definitions and data qualities between corporate business functions such as finance, sales, production, and others and their respective data domains. Let us take an example: Sales drive revenue growth and, thus, are regularly part of a company's core processes, which underpins its strong internal position. This strong position again led to situations where lots of room was and still is given to sales to create their own data structures primarily to support sales activities. But on the other hand, they often sacrifice compatibility and consistency with other data structures, such as in finance. Again, finance is requested to serve multiple objectives, such as adherence to global and local financial reporting accounting principles such as IFRS or US-GAAP, adhering to further compliance standards, and supporting management accounting goals in a standardized way.

In recent years, the concept of the "customer journey," which looks from a typically external customer point of view on a company's business processes, has become increasingly valuable and important. The main idea of this concept is to change the focal point from what a company does in terms of business processes, typically viewed as end-to-end processes, to how these processes attract external customers. The basic idea is to identify and visualize the steps a customer takes when engaging with a company. Doing so makes it possible to gain greater visibility into the interactions and touchpoints between the organization and the customers. Each of these touchpoints can lead to positive, neutral, or even negative experiences, and the experiences can vary throughout the different activities within this process. As a result, a customer journey shows how real-life experiences meet individual customer expectations and, therefore, a company's ability to delight its customers. Of course, the more touchpoints exist between the customer and the company, the more sophisticated it becomes.

In today's highly computerized world, with instant access to online stores from anywhere, it is increasingly important to know customers and to predict and influence their buying behavior. Customers interact with the features offered, using multiple online channels simultaneously to select an item on Channel A while comparing prices on Channel B and chatting/asking a friend for their opinion on Channel C. This scenario can take place at home, in a store, while traveling, or in any combination. All of these interactions and touchpoints create data and contribute to an enormous data point puzzle. Business intelligence aims to manage the resulting massive amounts of data and find the value-adding "nuggets" in it. The ultimate goal of a customer journey approach is to improve the customer experience and eliminate any unpleasantness along the journey. However, business intelligence must not be seen as a spectator in this game. As we have discussed earlier, business intelligence is about "data to impact."

However, business intelligence must not finger-point to other functions; the same applies to business intelligence customers as well. Have you ever thought why a BI customer should think and act differently in a professional business context, while in a private context, all options for product and service selection and, in case of dissatisfaction, a change of service provider is used?

Added value needs to be measured from the customer perspective, not from the delivery perspective. For example, asking what key decisions with substantial financial impact have been made properly grounded by validated data will lead to much more valuable insights into BI customer satisfaction than simply counting several dashboards deployed. Furthermore, it is advantageous to continuously validate trends and monitor "early warning indicators." For example, you may learn that in addition to your internal data, decision-makers are increasingly asking for external data provided by executive assistants. Unfortunately, executive assistants have not been asked for BI requirements at all, as this group was not perceived as a relevant user group or BI customer.

Knowing your internal customers and customer groups is key. Internal customers must not be treated differently from external customers. If a customer is not happy, he looks for alternatives, bypasses officially released BI tools, uses corporate processes not as intended, undermines official rules and governance, tends to implement side reporting, and others. If you treat these "out of the rule" phenomena as an opportunity to detect the hidden reasons for their existence, you may uncover a significant potential for improvement.

Let us consider another example. Typically, no executive is willing to accept delays in getting decision-relevant material to the table as quickly as possible. On the other hand, subordinates usually do not want to be perceived as inadequately serving senior executives by referring to standard procedures, as this could potentially damage support and recommendations in the event of an application for another position. As a result, subordinates simply do "whatever it takes" to make the boss happy. Consequently, there is no perceived need for change from a senior executive's perspective because they are getting the material on time and in quality. When senior management, which is regularly seen as a key user group, is asked about their requirements, the answer is typically vague or ambiguous. Unfortunately, such scenarios tend to become self-perpetuating if not identified and resolved.

The existence of such scenarios should be seen as a call to regularly evaluate the existing business intelligence in detail to uncover structural inconsistencies or hidden rules caused by bypassing established standard procedures. Furthermore, happy customers today do not guarantee satisfied customers tomorrow. We will detail the changing customer perception of feature attractiveness in Sect. 2.7 of this book.

Business intelligence is much more than technology or processes, and so is the BI strategy. BI strategy development should include systematic and holistic identification of opportunities and key constraints and bottlenecks that impact the ability to deliver even better BI products and services along the customer journey. This should include processes and technology but must not be reduced to just the two. Based on the above example, it should be clear that even the simple question of "Who is the BI customer?" should be answered with care.

Any BI customer journey within a business intelligence organization must not conflict with the BI and overall corporate strategies. It is more convincing to be consistent between BI strategy and BI operations and is often called to "walk the talk." This should be valid within the BI context but also include the dependencies between BI strategy and corporate or functional strategies. If, for example, the overall corporate strategy of an exemplary manufacturer is to provide low-cost/low-price services to the end customers, a BI strategy of that particular company, prioritizing tailormade high-price BI tools and providing high-price services to internal customers would likely be questionable. However, if in the same company, the corporate strategy aims to simplify the usability of any used IT tools with a streamlined solution portfolio, low process complexities, and costs, this would support the workforce to move between departments to gain cross-departmental expertise more easily. A BI strategy consistent with this corporate strategy could, for example, support this strategy by implementing easy-to-use and training-free analytical tools, offering highly standardized and easy-to-digest BI self-services with very efficient deployment in the entire company. Such BI offerings contribute to overall corporate strategic goals and mutually reinforce value added. The corporate workforce will be able to easily switch between operational and analytical jobs. In addition, any of the activities would be consistent with the overall corporate strategy.

In practice, we can assume that any company that performs business intelligence in one way or another also has an IT organization. From an overall business perspective, which strives for continuous efficiency improvement, redundancies should be avoided. Instead, it is beneficial to exploit potential synergies by actively aligning who does what and provides internal services to whom. Translated to the BI context, this could result in opportunities for streamlining activities such as the unification of

- User-frontend design
- Roles and authorizations design
- Deployment approaches
- IT-helpdesk-support functions
- Global communications and marketing

"Make or buy" or "develop on your own or utilize already existing" either in your own company or externally allows you to rethink your entire way of working with business intelligence.

Before we detail aspects of how a strategy should be understood, let us first introduce some key aspects of a strategy within a business intelligence context.

- As we intend to develop a forward-looking and aligned set of activities, we need to understand our BI strategy as a plan. The plan includes all the activities needed to make the strategy a reality. The existence of this plan makes our forward-looking ideas explicit, as we describe these in writing. This will allow us to communicate to a broader audience in the organization and thus share our ideas and how we intend to translate these ideas into real activities.
- Next, we want to establish and grow the relevancy of business intelligence in our organization. Based on this ambition, we need to describe a future state/target position and consequently shape the position of business intelligence as part of organizational design. We will detail this later in Chap. 5.
- Furthermore, we also want to attract others by sharing our ambitions and ideas about value contribution. We want to provide a clear, concise, and digestible perspective that is attractive enough for BI customers and our business intelligence employees to join the journey.

Let us now detail the aforementioned key aspects and discuss more contextual information and details.

Business Intelligence Strategy as a Forward-Looking and Aligned Set of Activities

Our idea of understanding BI strategy development as a plan is driven by the need to establish a reliable, repeatable, predictable, and scalable method of BI strategy development. Based on these requirements, we need a structured approach to identify possible future state scenarios and translate these first theoretical options into a set of real-world actions to make the most attractive option a reality. It is worth mentioning that in this context, we also aim for impact. Conducting just some activities but ending up again in the very same situation is a waste of effort. Hence, with our set of activities, we aim to create a new reality. This requires, among other things, documenting, sharing, and delegating the intended direction of action, in other words, a strategic plan.

Interpreting a strategy as a plan allows us to put our point of view on the table and align with others. With the idea of alignment with others in mind, we must not confuse a business intelligence strategy with a fixed framework with explicit constraints. Alignment also means being open to new emerging ideas and experiments, not restricted to a pre-defined and fixed way of how it should be.

Considering today's business reality, which often involves global operations, multiple organizational bodies, and different languages in different time zones, it is almost obvious that such a strategy should exist in writing. In this sense, a plan can also serve as a seed or friction for controversial discussions to develop a mutually agreed upon, aligned strategy.

In the corporate context, strategies are usually managed by management representatives. However, this should not be confused with the initiation of strategies or strategy updates, which can take place throughout the company and are typically not restricted to management.

Business Intelligence Strategy as Part of the Organizational Design

We want to establish and grow the relevance of business intelligence in our organization. Ideally, business intelligence will become a valued and regular contributor to other fact-based strategy developments. Consequently, based on this understanding, business intelligence will be perceived as a business partner, acting at eye level with other partners of the organization.

By nature, top management resources are rare, and a "BI strategy" competes for top management attention compared to strategies of other lines of business, such as sales, IT, or finance. The targeted positioning of business intelligence ensures relevancy and priority on the C-level agenda and should include a targeted positioning within the portfolio of corporate strategies, capabilities, processes, and technologies. As we have discussed earlier, it is increasingly common practice in companies to discuss processes with an end-to-end mindset. However, the visionary statements and objectives of becoming a "data-driven" company still often lack commitment, clear assignment of accountability, and operationalization. If companies want to adhere to these objectives, the role of business intelligence should be described as a future target position. Consequently, the positioning of business intelligence should be seen as part of organizational design. We will discuss this in more detail later in Chap. 5.

With the goal of developing a forward-looking BI strategy, this approach of describing a future target position for BI in a specific corporate context will add value, as it allows the establishment of new connections from and to business intelligence. However, from a practical point of view, this ambition needs to be sufficiently tangible and geared toward concrete activities. It is key to act in incremental improvements, striving to become better tomorrow compared to today. We will further detail the concept of closed loops later in Sect. 2.2.

Business Intelligence Strategy—Attractive and Motivating Perspective
Creating awareness of common, attractive, and achievable goals focuses on people's thoughts and actions and thus motivates them. Thus, a clear perspective helps unite forces around a common (shared) goal. The key is to provide a clear, concise, and easily digestible perspective that is attractive enough for others to become part of the journey.

The more attractive a future state scenario is, the more it motivates people to join the journey. Conversely, the less attractive a future state scenario is, the lower the intrinsic motivation. Therefore, for example, if superiors want to enforce such a less attractive future state scenario, a stronger extrinsic motivation is needed. Regardless of an attractive or less attractive future state scenario, we can assume the need for what we call a "strategic impulse." We will detail the idea of a "strategic impulse" later in Sect. 2.2.

With the goal of developing a BI strategy, this approach is particularly valuable because it introduces the ambition to "share" and align views with others in the organization. In other words, if only one person understands a strategy, it will not allow it to scale within an organization. Only the ability to scale will allow us to work together toward a common (shared) goal based on mutual understanding. Sharing, thus communicating a BI strategy, allows the development of a collective perspective. This is a key cornerstone to operationalizing the BI strategy in an organization, as it helps validate that everyone is following and supporting the same goals.

Being attractive and motivating is relevant not only internally but also externally. Imagine that your business intelligence is an independent entity that has to survive in the market on its own. What would be your biggest concerns and constraints? Think in detail about your BI business model, i.e., who are your customers, what are the inputs/resources needed for the BI products and services you want to delight your customers with, and what is your "BI value creation engine" (BI business model in the narrower sense)? Do not forget the people side because in the "war for talent," competing for the same highly skilled professionals is a major challenge for all organizations. This is true not only between countries and companies but also between departments. What makes your BI organization attractive to a talented candidate? Why should a candidate join business intelligence instead of sales controlling or management accounting?

Based on the detailed key aspects, we have now broadened our understanding of strategy in general and business intelligence strategy in particular. Next, we will discuss the high-level essential steps that are needed to develop a BI strategy. For further details, we recommend Chaps. 3 and 4):

1. The first step is discovering the business intelligence strategy based on already performed business intelligence activities. Depending on existing maturity, this might result in a quick exercise or a larger and time-consuming assessment. In any case, the discovered activities will help us draw a *detailed map of the current*

most relevant business intelligence activities. This activity should be done with a clear customer-centric mindset and include a description of the BI customers or BI customer groups as well. It is possible that this first step might also result in a disillusioning or partly confusing picture if we identify activities that are either insufficiently aligned, conflicting, or simply should exist but do not exist in practice. Whatever the outcome of this first step is, it might guide us to the first and essential learning on the "need for change."
2. Once we have understood the critical activities, including the main drivers, we are going in the second step to *understand if there is a performance gap and how large it is*. The performance gap is the difference between the current business intelligence performance of our own organization and the performance level of our peers or our competitors or, even more importantly, the desired performance level from customers' perceptions. These insights can be found in *benchmark* studies, global (business intelligence) standards, or *stated aspirations/interviews*. In some cases, statements about frustrations could also be used as a source to describe performance gaps. A likely outcome of this exercise is that we see multiple performance gaps in more than one area.
3. The third step is to think about *how to differentiate our new business intelligence from the current one*. To do this, we must first shape our view of the features that matter most to our BI customers. The key is to think from the customer's perspective. Do not spend too much time listing the features of a BI service or solution, as this approach can easily become a defense of the status quo with existing tools and services. Instead, try to openly answer the question, "What are the most important features along my journey as a BI customer that could help me do my daily work more efficiently, less painfully, and more enjoyably?"
4. Finally, we enter strategic discussions on *where (which characteristic)* and *to what extent (target ambition level)* we *intend to reshape our business intelligence*. The reshaping itself can be, for example, a setup of regular feedback sessions with BI customers, a change within our services, a decommissioning of a BI solution, the intake of a new BI product or service, or a combination of all. Any of the changes will have multiple implications, such as costs, user satisfaction, and many more. Based on these decisions, a new BI strategy will be created.

It is worth emphasizing that up to now, we have just described WHAT we intend to do and WHY we think this is a good choice. This is still just theory. In addition, we must outline HOW we aim to make this happen. Consequently, we need to bear in mind that nothing has changed thus far in reality unless we act according to our promises and, finally, prove impact.

Let us now try to summarize what we learned in this chapter.

> We can understand strategy as a promise to others to realize the most viable set of activities aiming to achieve the published goals.

With this definition, we emphasize the following aspects within the definition of strategy:

- *The promise*: A strategy is a clear commitment to do our best to execute the set of activities that make up our strategy.
- *To others*: We have a clear target group that we want to attract, such as the organization, individuals, stakeholders, and shareholders. We accept that this target group will ultimately judge whether we have succeeded or not.
- *Most viable*: The set of activities that ultimately define a strategy is not chosen randomly. Instead, in the chosen configuration of possible alternative sets of activities, we have one that is seen as most viable to achieve our strategy. It is a purposeful selection from various options that we have evaluated in advance.
- *Set of activities*: Typically, we need more than one activity or action but a set of activities that ideally belong together and reinforce each other.
- *To achieve*: We do not intend to change our ambition without having fulfilled our promise. We aim to achieve a defined and shared goal.
- *The published goals*: We publish our goals, making it transparent whether we are on track or not and whether we have finally succeeded or not. This publication puts us, committed to achieving the goal, at the center and serves as the basis for judging us.

Essentials of what Strategy is all about. Strategy is …

- Forward-looking and guiding, not backward-looking and describing
- Providing flexibility to adapt, no strict rules to follow one by one
- Open to new emerging ideas and experiments, not constrained by a fixed framework with explicit borderlines.
- Focusing on action intending to change and impact, not on documentation of theories.
- Attractive and motivational for others to join our journey.

Even the best approach to BI strategy development cannot compensate for the immaturity of the corporate strategy. If strategic mindset and understanding are lacking at the corporate or functional level, the BI strategy will also likely suffer.

2.2 Gearing BI Strategy with Other Strategies

A BI strategy is embedded in a business environment and exists to serve a purpose. The purpose is to help the business perform better and make decisions based on facts and reliable data.

However, why is it important to align the BI strategy with other strategies? Strategic alignment aims to add value by identifying commonalities between different strategies, resulting in mutual reinforcement. The idea is to achieve a situation where BI supports strategic business requirements in an "optimal way." This "optimal way" is neither clearly defined nor stable over time. Therefore, strategic alignment should be treated as a journey rather than a destination.

In this sub-chapter, we outline a pragmatic, closed-loop approach to help our readers begin their strategic alignment journey.

In Chap. 4, after gaining a deeper understanding of strategies, we will strengthen the connection between "Business Intelligence" and the business. However, before proceeding, we must establish a shared understanding of the basic principles. For this reason, in this chapter, we concentrate on iteratively aligning business intelligence with corporate and business strategies such as finance, sustainability, and IT.

To do this, we must first agree on a general framework that ideally applies to all types of companies and industries. While we understand that it may not be applicable in any context and not always to everyday practice, we can still illustrate general relationships and make them transparent.

Figure 2.1 presents the four interrelated building blocks of this general framework:

1. Corporate strategy and other functional strategies
2. Deducted BI requirements, which have their source in the previous building block
3. The BI strategy itself and
4. (New or revised) BI services and the corresponding (new) offerings to the business

Why is it essential to begin with corporate strategy and other functional strategies in our framework? Without it, we will struggle to define our target audience, which will ultimately determine whether we have successfully delivered on our ambitions and promises. A clear reference point is necessary to validate BI value expectations and BI value contribution.

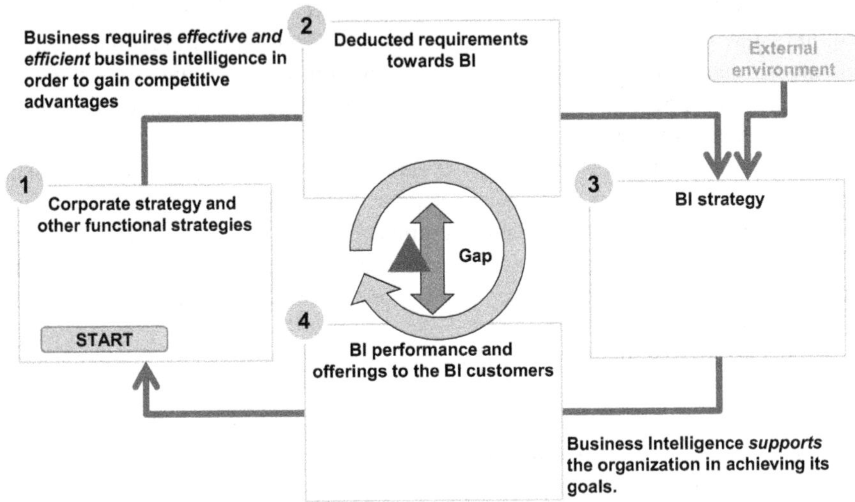

Fig. 2.1 Gearing of corporate and BI strategy—foundation of value-adding BI initiatives (© Exner/Zunic 2024. All Rights Reserved)

It is important to note that our book does not judge the established ways of bridging the corporate vision, mission, and strategy with other divisional or functional strategies and further operationalization. Rather, we assume that such processes are present within an organization already, albeit with varying degrees of maturity. Chapter 3 will further discuss this topic.

Let us initiate the first iteration with the current corporate strategy and other functional strategies, including sales, marketing, production, and finance (referring to number 1 in Fig. 2.1).

Each company entity and decision-making body necessitates effective and efficient business intelligence support to execute their strategies and enhance their competitiveness. This requirement leads us to the first basic needs of BI (number 2). We do not need to specify them yet as we will start with an overview of the working principles.

A BI strategy uses internal customer requirements as input from demand and supplements them, if necessary, with external market trends and data to establish a solid basis for creating or updating a BI strategy that includes new or revised BI offerings (supply) (no. 3). Based on this, the BI strategy prioritizes and outlines the most relevant and promising areas of opportunity to maximize the strategic value of BI (no. 4).

The goal is for the BI strategy to assist the entire company in achieving their objectives and realizing their strategies. Although a commendable objective, it may not always be practical. Thus, the BI customers have the final say in determining the effectiveness of the strategy. If the current BI performance offerings fall short of expectations, the BI customers identify a "gap" between the BI value they demand and the value they receive. Therefore, we must enhance our business intelligence (BI) performance or enrich our BI services to realign with customer expectations. This upgraded support aims to better assist customers with their strategies. Referring to Fig. 2.1, we have now completed the feedback loop.

Within the loop, we must frequently evaluate whether the strategic requirements for BI are aligned with the services and support being delivered (BI performance). In simpler terms, the key to achieving optimal BI is to minimize or in best-case, eliminate, the gap between the requirements and BI performance. The more BI exceeds known business requirements, the more likely it is to become a preferred and valued partner for the business.

From a practical point of view, we see four significant triggers of entering a new iteration:

- Larger number of new requirements
- Emerging fundamentally new needs
- Significant changes in the BI strategy context, such as organizational restructuring, new business models
- Minimum time-based review cycles, for example, every year

The loop in Fig. 2.2 was introduced as a generic framework with the implicit assumption that the boundaries of this model correspond to the organization's boundaries. In reality, these are sometimes blurred, as, for example, new companies become part of the group through mergers or acquisitions, new companies that emerge and disrupt established industry forces and ways of working are acquired, or employees can act as customers buying products from a company they work for.

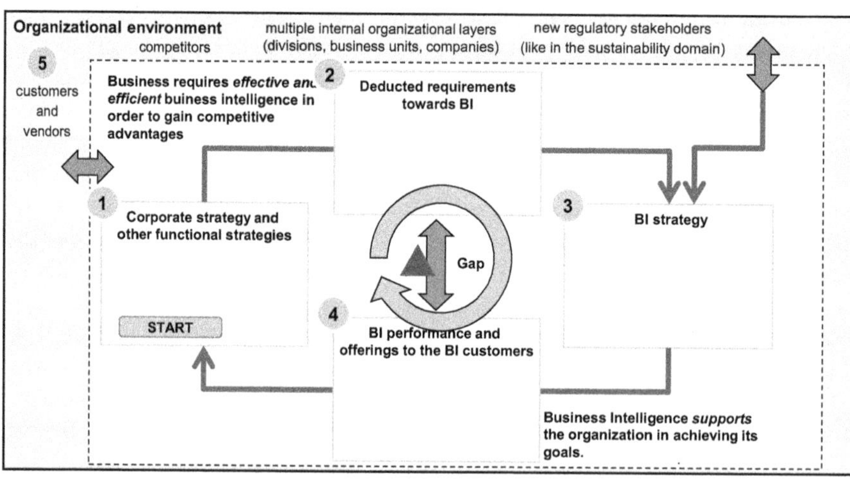

Fig. 2.2 Corporate BI in a wider context (© Exner/Zunic 2024. All Rights Reserved)

Based on this broader view, we can enrich the view by adding (not exhaustive)

- Customers and vendors
- Competitors/peers
- Multiple internal organizational levels (divisions, business units, companies)
- New regulatory stakeholders, such as in the area of sustainability
- Employees

resulting in additional interfaces, as visualized by the two arrows in Fig. 2.2 above. In practice, we could enrich the above model with these dimensions, but we consider this aspect less relevant for the basic understanding of how to develop a BI strategy.

However, the model can still be applied in different organizational contexts, such as:

- Overarching corporate strategy (without existing potentially conflicting sub-BI strategies)
- Divisional BI strategy
- Regional BI strategy
- Functional BI strategies

However, how does the model work in a more complex environment, say three divisions within a corporation where we have a different setup with likely implications toward BI strategy, as illustrated in Fig. 2.3 below.

In our illustrative example below, we assume a group consisting of a corporate headquarters and three divisions. Division A exists from the very beginning of the

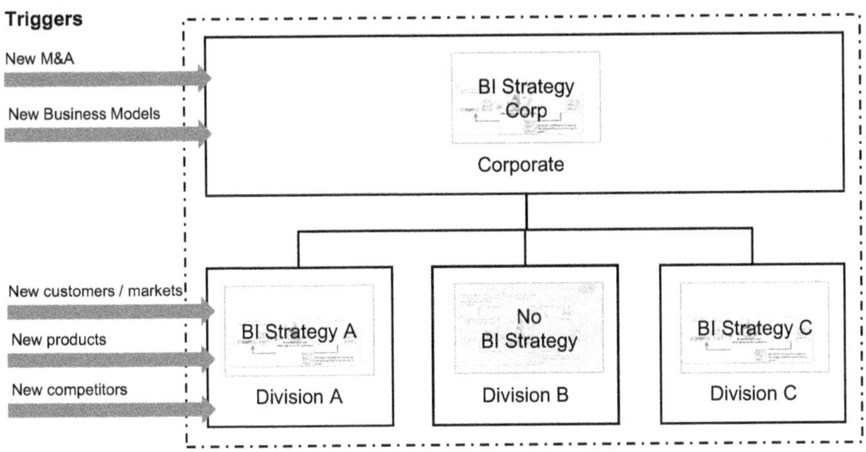

Fig. 2.3 BI strategy in different organizational contexts (© Exner/Zunic 2024. All Rights Reserved)

company with a well-established business model and global operations. Division B entered the corporation due to a takeover of a small company with a unique value proposition and promising digital capabilities and future synergies with the other business models. Finally, division C resulted from a merger between a former business unit with regional operations and another external mid-size company with operations in other regions.

In this scenario, and noticing the divisional development patterns, we can easily imagine that BI strategies look different. However, not only the BI strategy as such might look different, this holds true also for BI strategy development cycles, maturity levels, way of working with the divisions, and many other characteristics as well. The key to successful BI strategy development is to find the right way and balance between central and divisional views, expectations and requirements, which need to be continuously synchronized. From this perspective, the approach to agree on an iterative approach of continuously adjusting and aligning the way of working to gear the different existing BI strategies with a central BI strategy and other divisional and functional strategies in such a complex scenario might be valuable.

In addition, we can see that on the corporate level or for each of the divisions, different triggers exist to revise a new BI strategy release.

2.3 Corporate Strategy

Corporate strategy, to start with, is the ultimate top-level strategy a BI strategy can contribute to and, hence, should be aligned with. Depending on many different factors, the corporate strategy will differ between companies, and so a BI strategy supporting corporate strategy will as well.

During the past several years, the strategy discussion was enriched by business model and business model innovations. Due to multiple factettes of the strategy topic as such, we will focus on this topic.

First, we will briefly explore corporate strategy and set this in the context of data-driven decision-making.

Next, we will introduce the terms business model and customer journey and gear these terms with our corporate strategy discussion.

Based on the aforementioned, we will then extend our discussion about basic options to include business intelligence in this structural design. These options will uncover some choices for alignment between corporate strategy and a new business intelligence executives should consider.

Statutorily regulated figures do not describe corporate strategies like we typically see in IFRS or GAAP-grounded balance sheets and P&L statements. Even a 5- or 10-year projection of revenue on operations does not describe a strategy. It is rather an indication of the level of top-line ambition and growth.

Revenue is the ultimate financial consequence of completed organizational activities in various connected areas like marketing and pre-sales, sales, product-management, procurement, production, logistics, after-sales service, accounting, etc. However, revenue as such or revenue growth is not a sufficiently complete indication of strategic success. Instead, for example, sustainable, profitable growth is such an indicator. Nowadays, especially the attribute "sustainable" calls for detailing.

Sustainability is and remains the ultimate global challenge and "hot topic" to bridge economic well-being with the long-term survival of humans. In this context, sustainability discussions are quite often headlined by "de-carbonization." A definition of "sustainable" can be found in the UN report "Our Common Future" which defines "Sustainable development is development that meets the needs of the present without compromising the ability of future generations to meet their own needs." (United Nations (UN), 1987).

However, in our book, we will use the term "sustainable" mainly by focusing on the dimension of time. There is not a simple answer to the simple question of "what is our common understanding of 'sustainable'?" Our viewpoint will be different depending on the industry, business model, and many other factors. And most likely, even in top management teams, this definition is not necessarily common. For our discussion, "Sustainable" could be understood as being "continuous" and long term. The essence remains that profitable growth does not stay forever.

> Successful strategies for profitable growth are about continuously exploring new future business opportunities and profitable revenue streams. Successful operations are about exploiting the opportunities defined by strategy.

In practice, questions in this context arise, like

- How do we determine if a strategy will likely be projected as equally successful and sustainable?
- How do we translate an assumed successfully designed corporate strategy into more tangible operations? and
- What makes a corporate strategy finally come true?
- How are we going to measure if we are on track in terms of strategy operationalization?

To answer the above questions in a fact-based manner, executives aim for data-driven decision-making. It typically requires a wide variety of data and Key Performance Indicators (KPIs) from the entire company and needs to put the customer at its center.

Key Performance Indicators (KPIs) represent measurable business performance of an organization as a whole or of parts of an organization. However, to achieve a desired level of business performance, a multitude of underlying processes must first be executed effectively and efficiently. To be able to measure, control, and manage processes, it is necessary to define Process Performance Indicators (PPIs). While KPIs are typically used at a more strategic level, PPIs are typically used at an operational level. Successful process execution is a prerequisite for achieving the desired results. In this context, we can further distinguish between the so-called leading indicators, typically PPIs, and the so-called lagging indicators, typically KPIs. Both serve the purpose of decision support by providing a comprehensive overview of the business situation.

Customer centricity is more than just offering an additional "online channel" or a more convenient shopping experience. Customer centricity is a fundamental view of the customer journey, including true end-to-end experiences. By nature, this end-to-end must not end with successfully placing the order or get the delivery in time. Deluging customers with endless feedback surveys along their journey might be able to collect some data but, on the backside, it could cause some unintended frustration, leading to refused surveys or intentionally wrong feedback. From this perspective, "customer centricity" must not be reduced to just completing the transactional activities. Instead, all factors, including soft ones after product or service delivery, must be considered. This helps improve customer perceptions of being shepherded, strengthening customer loyalty and potentially leading to recurring revenues.

Collecting data is the starting point, and it needs to be carefully balanced between the ambition of becoming data driven and the overambition to get any single interaction completed by a feedback survey and respective data set. Which manager would deny the attractiveness of acting and deciding "fact-based" as this is sometimes a welcomed means to reduce one's own risk of wrong decision-making?

Let us explore the customer journey and business model in more detail. What is a business model, and what are the interrelationships with a customer journey?

> A business model is a unique combination of business processes to serve customers attractively and profitably (Fig. 2.4).

The unique combination of business processes refers to critical processes translating key resources into superior products and services. "Key resources" can be understood, for example, as highly skilled people, superior technology, innovative research and development facilities, engineering equipment, and others. The level of "attractiveness" depends, among others, on customer perception and available alternatives to fulfill customer requirements. Due to high confidence in own strengths and superior competitiveness, executives sometimes overestimate their capabilities, thus underestimate warning signals from their customer base.

Finally, the "profitability" makes it attractive for a company to continuously offer the products and services to achieve its own profitable growth ambitions. If this

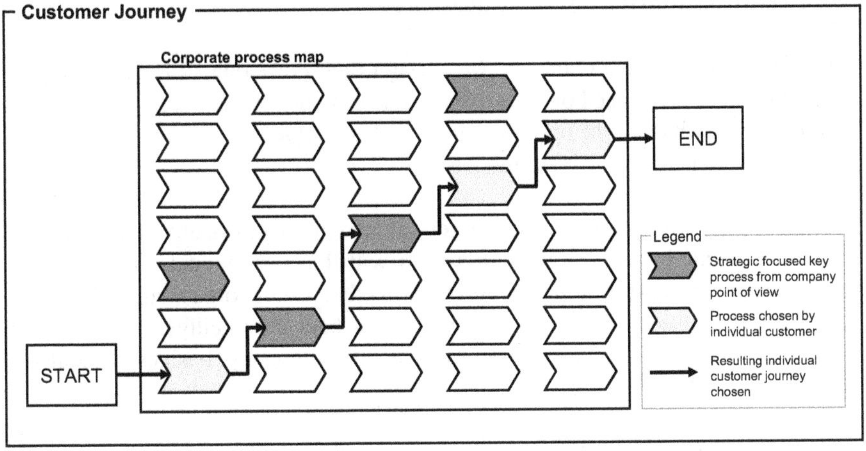

Fig. 2.4 Customer Journey (© Exner/Zunic 2024. All Rights Reserved)

attractiveness were not fulfilled, a company would typically double-check and potentially ramp down the respective products and services.

The notion of "unique combination of business processes" refers to key processes and key resources which finally translate into superior products and services. The intended repetition of 'key' should explain that not all processes or resources are equally important from a strategic point of view. However, we must not forget, that in practice often the little "easy to forget" elements are important to keep the business model engine up and running.

> The customer journey can be understood as a series of activities and interactions between a customer and a company during which the customer typically experiences several business processes.

If the landscape of business processes is designed well, all its elements add value individually but provide further value as an entirely consistent and mutually reinforcing value-adding system. A well-designed process landscape is typically characterized by sustainable, multi-year growth, indicating that operations are both able to scale with demand and adapt to changed business needs.

An existing business model should not be assumed to be stable over time. As we described earlier, business models are unique combinations of business processes. Consequently, these elements are continuously challenged and impacted by many internal and external factors like changing customer demands, disruptive innovations, new technologies, emerging competitor products, and services, etc. For this reason, business models should rather be perceived as objects which follow a life cycle. Based on this understanding, a business model is by nature not endlessly "sustainable."

The above leads to the following questions:

- How should executive managers (re-)design their corporate strategy to support customer journeys based on attractive business models sustainably?
- And further, what are the options to gear such strategic decision-making requirements with changing business models?

The need to develop a suitable target setup within an organizational design, including considering steering requirements with business model innovations in parallel, becomes evident. In this context, we need to discuss organizational options for alignment between corporate strategy and new business intelligence.

When embarking on a strategy assessment of a company, business executives have questions like:

- How mature is our current business model?
- Is our business model still sufficiently attracting our customers, or are we falling behind our competition?
- What indicators provide us early warning signals to mitigate business model related risks before potentially existing downside trends materialize?
- What are our options to sustain profitable growth, and which one is the best? Do we need to improve our current model, do we need an additional one, or do we fundamentally need to transform our entire company to a new business model?
- How do we ramp up a new business model within our (one business model) company? Shall we operate this integrated within our existing model, treat this as a start-up within our company, or loosely coupled as a joint venture?
- What kind of data do we need to ground our strategic options reliably and finally our decisions?

The optimal organizational design depends on the factual interdependencies between business models, their relevancy to management deciders, and the impact on organizational performance. In case relevance of interdependencies is transparent to management, typically different options exist, and organizational separation can be a justifiable choice. However, the performance implications at the entity but also at the group level should be thoroughly assessed in a concrete organizational context. This includes the possibility that at a later point in time, once an entity has grown into a more mature business, a reassessment may lead to a different, but then still optimal, organizational design decision.

Assuming we start our journey of organizational design with a one business model company and intend to add a second business model as illustrated in Fig. 2.5. At least initially, the new business model will be a smaller but growing business compared to the well-established one. We symbolize this in Fig. 2.5 by a smaller box. We need to decide how to support the two business models by a suitable business intelligence setup, separately or combined.

Let us assume significant synergies between the two business models (top row of Fig. 2.5). In this scenario, an obvious option might be to support both business

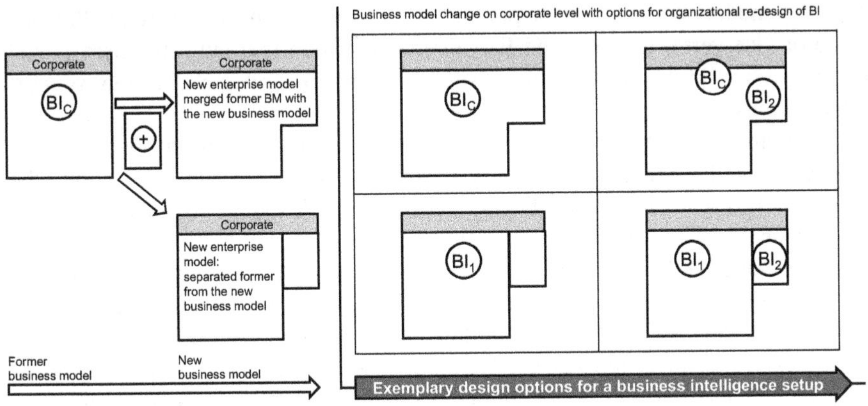

Fig. 2.5 Exemplary design options for a business intelligence setup in a multi-business model enterprise (© Exner/Zunic 2024. All Rights Reserved)

models based on the very same (existing corporate) BI (BI_C). The capital "C" indicates one central "Corporate" BI. Another option could be that the new business model should be supported by a dedicated BI (BI2) in case of future divestitures or outsourcing decisions. However, let us now revert the assumption above and think about little to no synergies between the two business models (bottom row of Fig. 2.5). Even in such a case, we could decide against a dedicated BI for the new business model, for example, due to cost considerations. Of course, the option to split the BI support in BI_1 and BI_2 still remains. As shown in Fig. 2.5, organizations can decide to design their business intelligence setup in very different ways depending on their business models and corporate structure. We are just sketching some scenarios here on a high-level, but the key finding is the following:

> If we assume these basic options of multi-business-model configurations within a company, we need to think about the best choice for organizational (re-)design of business intelligence as well.

A second business model in a separate unit will still require reliable data and business intelligence support. In consequence, whatever option a company chooses, different complexities need to be considered, which arise from the decided design of the business models, the overarching collaboration model between these, and the visibility of the interdependencies.

The objectives of minimizing overhead complexities with resulting costs and exploiting synergies are valid in any case to support the path of profitable growth.

Organizational design includes, among others, task and decision allocations, target-setting principles, incentive systems, and communication channels. It consists of the choice of the business model as such, but even further, it must also include the design of an optimal business intelligence setup. Just focusing on business model redesign but neglecting the impact on the business intelligence setup or vice versa, the expected BI value contribution to a multi-business-model enterprise would be a strategic mistake and harm strategic decision support requirements.

Assuming the company will enhance the organizational design, including the business models, it should be clear how this new organizational setup should be strategically aligned with a new business intelligence. It sounds obvious, but we see much room for discussion and alignment in practice.

Organizational design is one of the critical levers to influence how the different business models of a company attract customers. As companies typically aim to benefit from the speed of decentralized decision-making to exploit new opportunities quickly, executives must carefully balance these expected benefits with risks of inadequate inter-business-model alignments. It is advisable to make strategic decisions on organizational design early but still properly grounded, monitor intended synergies and alignment between different business models over time, and adjust the multi-business model setup of a company if needed.

Decision-making support within such multi-business model organizations is not a one-time decision. Instead, it should be an ongoing top management concern and will remain essential to shape continuous profitable growth. For this reason, it should be a regular topic on the executive management agenda.

Within the context of organizational design, it should be well decided how business intelligence is considered. The development of a BI strategy can be seen as an invitation to executives to assess the current situation and to take necessary steps to improve the strategic value contribution of BI for all business models of the entire company. We will further discuss the topic in our Chap. 5 Organizing BI Strategy.

2.4 Strategy for "Going Digital"

The term "digital" is the centerpiece of many strategies and innovations. However, some "flavors" exist, like "digitalization" or "digitization." Due to the high relevance for companies in general and business intelligence in particular, for which digital data is of utmost importance, we will introduce the different meanings and supplement them with further implications. Finally, we will introduce how the concept of "digital" relates to a new BI mindset and BI strategy.

For a few years, the term "digitalization" must not be missed in any discussions and publications about strategy. While for many companies, digitalization comes with disruption of the well-known and tremendous opportunities for other companies, digitalization is associated with the need for change. Consequently, companies are urgently searching for answers and strategies to the uncertainties and challenges ahead.

This topic is not only relevant for single companies but for entire economies. In the EU, the Digital Economy and Society Index (DESI) shows the relevance of "going digital" on the country level and that some countries are more successful than others (European Union, 2023). In other words, this is a call to action to improve and accelerate the pace of "going digital." However, organizations follow their individual path of "going digital." Some are fast and innovative, some are lagging. Some follow a clear and well-designed path to a visionary target, while others still try to find the best starting point to increase their digital maturity or even struggle to take the first steps. Whatever your status in this rallye, any company should think about a roadmap toward an ambitious but achievable target state. This requires a fact-based steering model with a reasonable set of KPIs to measure the progress on the journey to become truly "digital."

It is advisable that BI strategies evaluate and incorporate maturity levels to provide tailored value add to the companies going for "digital." By supporting this ambition, BI should raise self-critical questions about its current maturity level and develop a clear path forward. This questioning should be seen as an integral part of each BI strategy.

Despite frequently using the term "digitalization," there is no common understanding. Quite often, variations of terms like "digitization," "going digital," or "digital transformation" are used without noticing the different meanings. To avoid misinterpretation, we will first introduce these and highlight the main differences.

For this purpose, we plot in Fig. 2.6 below the different activities related to "digital" against the axis organizational coverage and maturity level.

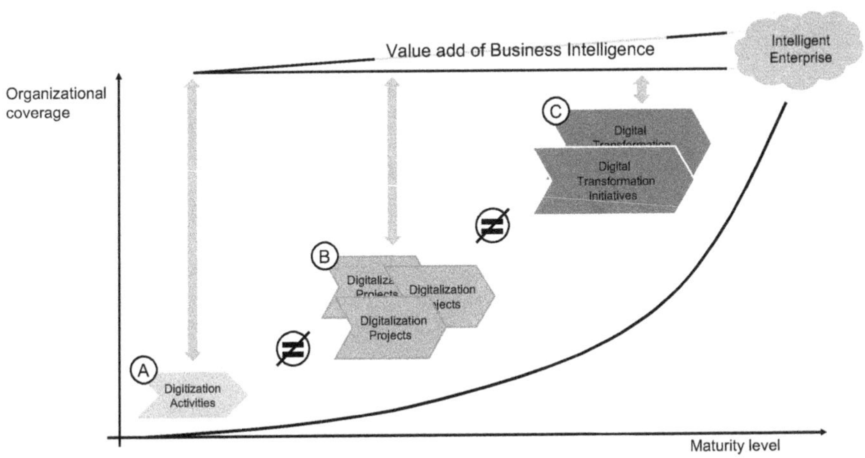

Fig. 2.6 Value add of business intelligence growths with each stage of the digital journey (© Exner/Zunic 2024. All Rights Reserved)

The horizontal axis called "maturity level" describes qualitatively the achieved level of being "digital." The more we move from groundwork activities to sophisticated initiatives, the higher the maturity level.

The vertical axis, called "organizational coverage," describes the reach of a particular activity within a given organization. The more a specific activity becomes relevant for other departments, corporate functions, or ultimately the entire organization, the higher the organizational coverage of being "digital."

Within Fig. 2.6, we assume an exponential growth pattern of "becoming more digital" as each of the activities, projects, or initiatives fuel and reinforce subsequent ones. Once companies are on their journey of identifying analog processes and trying to replace them with digital ones, it increasingly becomes transparent where the digital bottlenecks are. At the same time, the value add of business intelligence will rise. This journey ultimately points to the visionary target of becoming an "Intelligent Enterprise" (for further details, please refer to Sect. 1.2).

Let us now detail the different stages:

- Digitization
- Digitalization
- Digital transformation

Digitization

For any organization, digitization is nowadays a prerequisite for dealing with (former analog) information in an efficient, reliable, predictable, and scalable way. "Paper-based" processes are quite often used as synonyms for analog information. Let us think of the daily processes still carried out today in analog and paper-based form, in whole or in part. How could a first step of improvement look like? Scanning a document, for example, is digitization. In an assumed rudimentary approach, we are just replacing a paper with bits and bytes.

It is not yet digitalization as the scanning does not typically change the process, and it does not or is very limited to providing additional opportunities.

Digitalization

Picking up the scanning example from above, combining the scanning with an OCR (Optical Character Recognition) functionality can add value by reading or enriching content. This again allows, for example, to automatically forward documents after scanning based on a pre-defined workflow to responsible people in a company. As this creates new opportunities for process acceleration and removal of manual tasks, it adds value, hence we do digitalization.

Let us assume that you operate a front office desk that cares about any kind of customer requests, physically, by mail, or still paper based. Even if your company is already saying 70% digitalized, you can gain more efficiency by going the remaining 30%. Obviously, the earlier in the process you shift from analog to digital, the more opportunities and synergies you will be able to exploit later throughout your operations.

This leads to certain conclusions:

- You should particularly pay attention to the external boundaries to your surrounding eco-system, such as customers, vendors, but not to forget internally the colleagues sitting next door. If the HR department is asking you to fill a paper-based leave request, the purchasing department is asking for the physical signature of your boss to approve buying a new laptop and many more. Certainly, you experience a lot of other examples in practice.
- The earlier in the process you move from analog to digital, the bigger the opportunities for subsequent functions, people, and managers to benefit from digital data.
- Only the availability of digital data provides the opportunity to use state-of-the-art tools for further processing. Some tools will support efficient process execution, while others will provide better transparency on workload, efficiency metrics, and other indicators.
- Once digital data is available, we achieve the first significant milestone in getting equipped with improved transparency to analyze our current status and remaining journey to become truly digital. However, we need to be careful with this milestone, as "getting equipped" does not necessarily mean that all requirements are met just by having sophisticated tools implemented or some processes improved here and there. To develop a digital mindset, you must invest considerably in training, change management, cross-departmental collaboration, and continuous optimization.

Digital Transformation

Digital transformation is the next stage of evolution. Whereas in digitalization, we are still focusing on single processes even if they are cross-departmental, in digital transformation, we enlarge the scope of change to the entire organization or even beyond to a network economy. Digital transformation aims to ultimately simplify and digitalize business operations from an end-to-end perspective. If a company starts to thoroughly assess its processes and challenge its value proposition, quite often, these companies also question strategically if a process allows differentiation toward the competition or not. In case not, it is seen as a candidate to outsource or for radical simplification, standardization, and finally, automation.

As illustrated in Fig. 2.6, we can summarize that digitalization is a prerequisite for digital transformation. In addition, digital transformation must not be reduced to technology change; it contains all the various areas a company consists of, such as operating model, business processes, organizational setup, steering, way of working, culture, innovation mindset, and so much more than the sum of several digitalization projects. We symbolized this in the above figure with the "≠."

> … we digitize information, we digitalize processes and roles that make up the operations of a business, and we digitally transform the business and its strategy. Each one is necessary but not sufficient for the next, and most importantly, digitization and digitalization are essentially about technology, but digital transformation is not. Digital transformation is about the customer. (Bloomberg, 2018)

As companies ultimately aim for profitable growth, the bottom line is that they aim for business processes that are efficient, reliable, predictable, and scalable at competitive cost. This drives companies to continuously search for levers to identify and exploit digital opportunities. Technology is not only an essential tool for digitizing a company, it is a prerequisite. Without technology, it is not reasonably possible to decode analog information into bits and bytes to connect business processes and gain transparency on business process performance.

Based on the definitions above, we can now conclude:
In the discussion of "digital," the terms digitization, digitalization, and digital transformation must not be confused as they describe different states of evolution.

As the main challenges and opportunities are related to "digitalization" and "digital transformation," we will focus on those definitions only. We assume that companies have already achieved a level of digitization.

But how does the aforementioned contribute to BI strategy?

One of the key contributions of business intelligence is to help companies to succeed. If a digital transformation is seen as a critical strategic lever for companies to sustain, business intelligence is asked to support decision-making in this context.

A typical objective of digital transformations is to simplify, standardize, and automate. Hence, the same goal should also be valid for business intelligence. This means that BI strategy must not stand aside from the game. Instead, BI strategy is about outlining how to continuously optimize the value contribution of BI based on:

- Helping companies to identify, understand, root cause, and finally remove bottlenecks to become truly digital.
- Breakthrough boundaries between fragmented processes and organizational entities, internal and external.
- Environmental screening of emerging, potentially valuable new digital data assets.
- A self-critical consideration of which of the beforementioned optimization approaches are also valid for the own area of business intelligence.

If BI itself cannot prove its value add clearly and continuously, it might be at risk of being questioned.

How to Measure the Progress of "Going Digital"

"If you cannot measure it, you cannot manage it." This quite well-known statement is valid for the journey of "going digital" as well. But what should be measured, and what kind of status quo and progress indicators exist?

There are different views and dimensions on the term "digital," thus it is advisable to consider the slightly different definitions. Please also note the various terms introduced related to "digital" in this chapter.

For example, Roland Berger defines "the digital transformation as the seamless, end-to-end connectivity of all areas of the economy, and as the way in which the

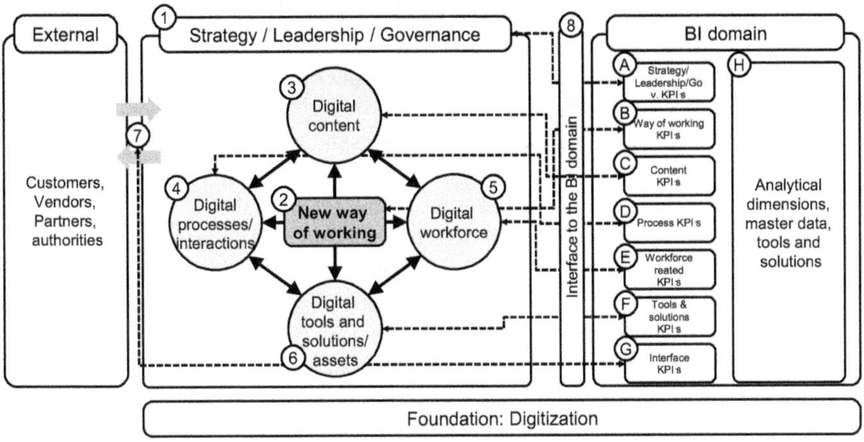

Fig. 2.7 Relationships between the corporate digital stage and BI domain (© Exner/Zunic 2024.)

various players adapt to the new conditions that prevail in the digital economy." This definition highlights dimensions such as digital data, automation, connectivity, and digital customer access. (Roland Berger Strategy Consultants, 2016).

If we now try to generalize the various elements and combine them into an overarching model for companies, it could look as shown in Fig. 2.7. The centerpiece of this model consists of the following elements:

1. *Strategy/leadership/governance:* Strategy describes the way to improve coverage and maturity of digitalization within a given organization. Leadership focuses on the people side, thus, the executive management making the organization move in an intended and strategy-compliant direction by setting appropriate targets. Governance describes the ruleset by which the leadership acts, defines target-setting principles, and monitors progress toward defined objectives.
2. *New way of working:* This is the very core of the change. If everybody agrees, but nothing changes, you have not successfully implemented a new way of working. But you can also turn this around. If you cannot describe the changes of your way of working in a clear, understandable, and tangible way, you are most likely talking about your intentions but not translating ideas into concrete actions.
3. *Digital content:* Every digital representation of a physical/hardware object is digital content. Furthermore, digital content is any kind of computer-based software object, even if it exists only in the digital world. Even more, content like news, pictures, stories, chat messages, subscriptions, digital currencies, and others are digital content.
4. *Digital processes/interactions:* Processes entirely executable on computers are fully digital. Processes, which are not wholly, hence end-to-end executable on computers, are not fully digital. They require humans to bridge and complete specific process steps, provide additional human intuition, experience, side information, or a combination of all these factors.

5. *Digital workforce:* A workforce that can be described as "digital workforce" is typically characterized by blurry characteristics like digital experience, know-how with proficient usage of developing digital content, executing, and improving digital processes, tools, and solutions.
6. *Digital tools and solutions/assets:* These tools and solutions are sometimes confused with being "digital," however, as we have previously learned, there are many more elements required and contributing to "digital."

   Let us now extend our view and turn to the external environment.
7. *Interfaces to the outside world:* Any kind of interaction with customers, suppliers, partners, and other external stakeholders is only possible via interfaces. Typically, these interfaces are digital to speed up information exchange and to enable a direct interaction and engagement channel.
8. *Interface to the BI domain:* The inherent role of the BI domain is to support all areas of strategy, leadership, and governance with data and facts to support decisions. This goes beyond traditional performance management and extends to measuring the strategic contribution of the BI function itself toward a digital intelligent enterprise. It becomes clear that different categories of KPIs and metrics are needed to support such a transformation which help to report, monitor, and provide decision support to transition into a "digital" enterprise space. However, it is not necessarily trivial to define and focus on the right KPIs.

Table 2.1 shows an exemplary list of metrics per category. These KPIs should be viewed as illustrative rather than a ready-to-consume set of indicators.

From a practitioner's point of view, even agreeing on suitable units of measure for each of the above metrics seems not to be trivial.

Communicating the ambition of improved digitalization is a typical pattern for nearly any company, regardless of industry or size. The very same applies to authorities. However, executing this strategy thoroughly and sustainably typically turns out to be much more complicated than expected. Consequently, we often notice a mismatch between the formulation of strategic intent and execution.

Any kind of "digitalization strategy" should be treated as integrated with other strategies. Let us neglect this view for a moment. The opposite approach would be to treat "digitalization strategy" as a separate strategy, hence with its own ambition for execution. If we think about, for example, a finance strategy and a separated "digitalization strategy," this separation will result in executing a finance strategy without any operationalization of digitalization as this would be part of the "digitalization strategy." This artificial separation is, from a practicability point of view, useless. Consequently, any functional business strategy must include its "digitalization strategy."

As we have seen, the use of IT technology is essential to digitization. But to conclude the opposite would be misleading. The use of more IT technology does not necessarily mean that a company is moving toward digitalization. Rather, a company's various capabilities need to be redesigned, combined and, in some cases, completely reimagined. These changes should be fundamentally customer centric.

Let us return briefly to the visionary view of the Intelligent Enterprise as outlined in Sect. 1.2. The characteristics of an "Intelligent Enterprise" are based on an

Table 2.1 Different KPI categories in the "going digital space"

#	KPI category	Exemplary metric/KPI
A	Strategy/ leadership/governance	• Number of digital strategy items defined and confirmed by executive management • Organizational coverage and penetration of digital objectives as part of management by objectives (MbO's) • Existence and number of regular meetings per year for further discussion and improvement of managing digital target setting and monitoring
B	New way of working	• The number of process flows that have been changed due to new digital capabilities. • Number of e-learning participants • Number of papers used for printing • Number of executive meetings with complete digital agenda/presentations (no paper-based handouts or minutes) • Share of use for self-services (procurement, reporting, etc.) within a given threshold
C	Digital Content	• The number of digital representations of a physical/ hardware (digital twin). • Any kind of computer-based software object with a cost and/or price tag, even if it exists only in the digital world. • Newly created content like news, pictures, stories, chat messages, subscriptions, digital currencies, and others Number and updates of central customer records • Number of articles/blogs published
D	Digital processes/ interactions	• Number of fully digital processes. • Number of processes which are not entirely, hence end-to-end fully digital. • Number, duration of human interaction required to bridge process steps, provide additional human data or experience or others, or a combination of all these factors.
E	Digital workforce	• Share of job descriptions referring to digital content, processes, and technologies • Spend of training dedicated to enhancing digital know-how on an employee basis.
F	Digital tools and solutions/assets	• Money spent and quantities of computers, software, and subscriptions. • Money spent and quantities for collaboration tools and telecom equipment. • Number of users regularly accessing digital tools and solutions • Number of users providing feedback on the usability of digital tools and solutions • Share of assets such as smart buildings, smart parking, and others
G	Interfaces to the outset	• Use seamless integrations with customers, vendors, intercompany, and partners without regular human support. • Number of IT tickets related to interfaces

enterprise that uses digital data extensively in all its processes and functions, as described above. However, to conclude that this automatically leads to an Intelligent Enterprise would be a simplistic and misleading view. As we have learnt, an Intelligent Enterprise encompasses further advanced characteristics, such as highly automated decision-making and execution processes, and a way of working and thinking that extends to a cross-company business network.

Defining priorities and making choices is an ongoing task for any executive. There is no difference for business transformations. It was and still is essential to even better predict upcoming changes in customer demands, industry developments and respond to those changes to keep the company ahead of the competition.

Key considerations for developing a BI strategy

- Changing business models require a new way to steer, thus new Key Performance Indicators (KPIs) along with new business processes measured by new Process Performance Indicators (PPIs).
- Today, digitization seems like an anachronism. However, some companies and government agencies still do not know where they stand regarding being "digital."
- Executives must treat digitalization and data-driven decision-making as two sides of the same coin. You simply cannot have one thing without the other.
- A new portfolio of products and services will emphasize the need to continuously challenge the existing historically grown structures based on an outdated data design. If these structures persist unchanged, it is no wonder that companies face challenges adapting corporate structures agilely and, for example, managing their margins on the latest products, service offerings, and bundles.
- Think BI organization as an "Innovation think tank." If BI is about "insight to action," fuel the innovation pipeline with the best possible data and get your workforce trained and equipped. The "best possible" data means relevant and high-quality data breaking historically grown organizational boundaries and "silos".
- Do not confuse digital maturity with digital strategy. Digital maturity models typically aim to simplify complex questions by providing an apparently logical path toward increased maturity. However, increased maturity does not necessarily translate into increased customer satisfaction or competitive offerings.
- The very same applies to BI: first, think about the primary conditions and (customer first) culture. Do not start a BI tool discussion and wonder why the business is not embracing the provided solutions, hence not likely returning the investment.

2.5 Finance Strategy

Quite often finance landscapes are historically grown, fragmented, and call for redesign. Due to in-depth integrations with logistics, this turns out to have lots of implications.

Financial reporting and analysis was and still is one of the key areas within finance. It is about providing stakeholders with accurate and timely information about the organization's performance. This includes, but is not limited to preparing financial statements, conducting financial analysis and providing guidance, and steering relevant recommendations to management based on financial and increasingly nonfinancial data.

"Information about the organization's performance" must not exclude finance performance. Self-reflecting analysis of own finance related process bottlenecks and opportunities for further improvements needs to be considered as well.

Within the finance strategy chapter, we will broaden our view to understand possible changes within finance that might become opportunities or challenges for BI. This will allow us to reflect these insights in developing a reliable and resilient BI strategy.

In addition, we will take a look to highlight those finance subareas, which might in particular be impacted by potential outsourcing including their resulting complexities for alignment with a BI strategy.

One of the common denominators of all companies is the finance function. Quite often, finance landscapes are historically grown, fragmented, and consequently include a vast number of local or regional processes and decentralized ownership based on complex systems. In addition, sometimes the finance processes are highly siloed either by countries or by organization but often, with limited end-to-end process ownership and transparency. Corporate steering in such environments is slow, cumbersome, error-prone, and hence not able to support corporate strategies and competitiveness.

Exemplary functional ambitions for finance could look like

- Fact-based decision-making
- Forward-looking planning and decision-making
- Operational excellence
- Evolving finance disciplines
- Etc., etc.

Any project in such an environment is asked to contribute to strategies and objectives to help the organization meet these ambitions. And obviously, any project needs to contribute to the overall objectives of cost reduction to support competitiveness, while at the same time, the project is asked to harvest opportunities toward state-of-the-art innovations such as machine learning and robotics. This is true for any project, thus for a project aiming for renewal of finance as well.

Looking into strategic ambitions, these sound sometimes quite trivial "Improve transparency on profitability by products, regions and market."

However, what is the challenge? Or even more important, what is the root cause of this challenge, why does it hit us? As mentioned before, finance landscapes are often historically grown and fragmented. For decades, implementing finance was seen as the necessary evil to supplement the core processes of producing and selling to the customer. Consequently, implementation projects in former times focused mainly on the core business with its revenue-generating processes, which led to lower priorities for sustainable, reliable, and resilient finance processes. In addition, finance was widely perceived as a mere supporting process, and it was common practice to add just another single-purpose finance process for the sake of not harming revenue-generating processes. Finally, for quite some time, the companies felt well equipped, as they were able to successfully surf on the wave of globalization. Since globalization is reaching its zenith for many industries, stakeholders are increasingly asking for new value growth opportunities. These opportunities lead to new customer segments, new products, software and services and bundles, stabilizing revenue streams by moving from one-time sales to continuous delivery and ultimately to streaming of service delivery and, quite logically, revenue generation by subscriptions.

If we think about companies with current regional or global operations, many plants, warehouses, points of sale, many stakeholders, and decision-making bodies, so a significant organizational complexity, we can see that in those companies, for example, the definition of products and services is no longer trivial. Instead, if a company grows based on selling machines and equipment, all the related master data are perfectly designed to serve this particular service: selling machines. If customer demand is increasingly driving the sales force to sell complementing software and services and ideally to bundle these in a flexible way, we can imagine how this could end up in a patchwork situation. Of course, who would refuse a customer's order and instead help the competition by simply arguing that the internal processes, the underlying master data, and the subsequent record-to-report processes are not yet ready to meet all the requirements? No one would do that.

However, does this neglecting remove any of our challenges? Of course not.

Looking at implementation projects and their key objectives, they aim to implement the latest software technology, which is sometimes treated as a welcomed anchor and vehicle to a business transformation that holistically involves processes including master data, people, organizational setup throughout the entire enterprise (considering end-to-end value chain and value flows), and technology. In other words, there is a "window of opportunity" to get rid of the grown complexities.

With the implementation of a new IT system, companies intend to eliminate nonvalue-adding activities and varieties in the IT systems, processes, and data within the entire organization on a local, regional, and global level. The same applies for finance. However, the ambition of reducing or even better eliminating nonvalue-adding activities should be seen as an everlasting priority of any management and not relying on a particular IT implementation. These nonvalue-adding activities occur in practice in many flavors, such as

- Mapping from chart of account A to chart of account B
- Redundant analytical dimensions for the same use case
- Slightly different data structures and KPI definitions between business units C and D
- Different data structures between solutions E and F
- And many more

What is the impact on BI strategy? BI is about data-driven, fact-based, and reliable decision support. From this perspective, any kind of mapping should be treated as a call for action. Mapping means that two views exist, which are strong enough to individually justify its logic. However, from a bigger point of view, it means that two versions "of the truth" exist in parallel. This again contradicts our abilities to provide clear guidance or to make clear decisions.

For example, let us assume a product structure based on profit centers. From a finance perspective, it might be sufficient to report financial KPIs on a certain level of granularity from a P&L perspective, while for sales, the structuring and granularity are seen as insufficient to support customer engagement. Sales as representing the core business process consequently require a different, generally much more granular view of products and services.

Opportunities for BI value contribution

When structural inconsistencies are identified, BI can be a valuable business partner in initiating discussions to address these issues with a cross-domain perspective. In principle, BI can act in two ways—either ad hoc on a case-by-case basis (reactive) or taking ownership of these types of improvements in a more proactive and holistic way.

Assuming that such a previously mentioned implementation project is not just focusing on a particular business unit but the entire company, there are multiple additional areas that companies want to improve, such as (not exhaustive):

- Strategy on a corporate level—cost leadership, differentiation, or a mixture?
- Finance strategy and objectives—focus areas to contribute to corporate strategy?
- Maturity of the current finance landscape (processes, organization, IT systems)?

- Target Operating Model—how will finance operate in the future?
- Steering Model—how to successfully steer in an increasingly competitive environment? What are the "single source" and "single version" of the truth?
- Sustainability—how can zero-carbon emission targets be measured and controlled?

To translate such business questions into IT implementation projects in a meaningful way, companies basically have two options: Either they technically convert their existing financial systems to a new solution, if they are quite satisfied with the current situation. This option is often referred to as "brownfield." Alternatively, companies that are significantly dissatisfied with their current processes could decide to build a new financial system from scratch. This option is often called "greenfield," just to name two extremes of a possible approach. There are, of course, other scenarios in between, all of which have different implications.

By nature, any kind of decision with this magnitude has many implications and typically requires a thorough assessment upfront. From one perspective, these changes and their implications might be seen as obstacles, risks, and enormous investments; from another perspective, these can be seen as catalysts, accelerators, and enormous opportunities for further and sustainable growth.

What is the impact on BI strategy? In the case of targeting data-driven decision-making, BI as such must not be seen as sidelined. Instead, it must be an integrated part of any process (re)design activity right from the beginning. Covering reporting as a separate work stream within a larger program or project is simply not enough because this setup tends to solidify siloed thinking. A common way how these silos manifest themselves in project and operational governance is an organizational separation of responsibilities between transactional process design and analytical process design. Due to this decoupling, analytics is often asked to "make the best out of previously designed process and data structures" resulting in reduced efficiency in BI. The reason is that BI is either not involved in business process design decisions at all or insufficiently. This includes decisions related to data creation, origination, and use. Consequently, BI is requested to design reporting based on already cemented processes and data.

> BI strategy has the big opportunity to shape awareness on deciding to follow historical practices or to align on a more integrated approach with all its opportunities.

Organizational Patterns in Finance

For many years, an increasing number of companies have decided to implement shared service centers (SSCs) in finance. This means that the SSC takes operational responsibility for process execution centrally, while at the same time, decentral units get rid of their operational workload. What is the impact? The process execution of the central SSC on behalf of the decentral unit means that internal charging takes place. There needs to be an intercompany invoicing process implemented. In addition, both parties need to replan their workload. The SSC needs to consider additional workload, including peak times, while on the other hand, the decentral entity needs to plan to downsize their capacities and to decide how to utilize the new free capacity in the best possible way. Obviously, both plans need to be kept continuously in sync. To achieve this, meaningful collaborative planning needs to be designed and implemented as well. From a corporate perspective, it is not sufficient just to keep the overall costs as before. Instead, quite often is the common goal to reduce overall cost. However, this is just one example, there are many more.

The same applies if a company aims to implement a Center of Expertise (CoE). A Center of Expertise is not mainly aiming for benefits by economies of scale due to handling an enormous number of transactional processes within an SSC. Instead, the key objective of a CoE is to share rare, costly expertise within an organization to avoid redundant local or regional expertise and resulting costs.

What is the impact on BI strategy? Should BI be seen as a Shared Service Center, or should it be organized as a Center of Expertise? Whatever the design is, it should be closely aligned with other corporate functions, and the design should be sustainable and robust to avoid unnecessary disruption. We will pick up and detail this topic further in Chap. 5.

Ownership of Finance Domains and Implications for Data Provisioning

From production, we know the concept of "vertical integration." It describes the portion of in-house production, thus the ratio between "make" or "buy." The same applies to finance organizations. What is the optimal level of finance for in-house production or service provisioning? How does this evolve? Today's sufficient level of finance in-house service provisioning might not be sufficient in the future. Consequently, companies need to think beyond historically grown organizational boundaries where "finance" was and often still is seen as only "make." Instead, if broadening the thinking, decision-makers come to a new finance landscape, wherein some, not differentiating cases, finance functions go external, while others will be kept internal. If companies, based on this mindset, think about a state-of-the-art steering model with planning, executing, and reporting of the internal and external process, it is quite obvious to see the relevance of designing a Target Operating Model (TOM) for finance.

For many years, companies have increasingly valued the availability of historical data for decision support. However, what is the value of 2–5 years of manufacturing data in a specific differentiating process, such as electronics or high-tech manufacturing, when a company is forced by competitive pressures to move to reduced vertical integration? What is the new value of this type of data in corporate memory?

Up to now, a possibly implicit assumption was that we are considering the same business model today as well as in the future. Let us now challenge this assumption as well. What, if again due to the high level of competition, we are forced to change the business model from a production company to a retail company? Therefore, instead of producing machines, the company is buying these from suppliers. The complete value chain will transform significantly. Within a certain period of time, a complete corporate transition with an enormous magnitude needs to be managed. To strategically contribute to changed circumstances, finance and business intelligence most likely are asked to contribute by new KPIs, provisioning of new relevant information and not to forget cutting costs. One lever of cutting costs is to further standardize processes and to automate wherever possible. "Wherever possible"—what does this mean in detail and again, how does this impact BI?

What is the value of 10 years of manufacturing data if the company strategically decides to change the business model from manufacturing to retail? What is the value of corporate memory? This question leads to another interesting question: How can industry-specific data volume be monetized? One key aspect will be still valid: Balance of demand and supply. The more specific, thus individualized data volumes are due to a high level of individualization, the smaller the niche of possible prospects. In contrast, the higher the level of standardization within the data pattern, data structures, etc., the more likely a potential buyer might value structural similarities to own data structures, hence, will be interested in buying.

In most companies, the following finance domains are seen as "the core" of finance:

- Financial accounting
- Group reporting
- Treasury (Cash, …)
- Controlling and profitability analysis
- Financial planning
- Analytics & reporting

To further detail ownership of finance domains with its implications for BI and data provisioning, let us look at typical finance functions and which of them are possible candidates for keeping in-house or outsourcing (up to business process outsourcing), as shown in Table 2.2.

The table columns classify different finance functions from a "make-or-buy" viewpoint:

- Column (A) Potential of differentiation against competitors/peers. We distinguish between H high, M medium, and L low
- Column (B) Strategic intent to keep finance function either inhouse (key), outsource candidate, or, in case we are not sure on any option "To be assessed"
- Column (C) First describes initial thoughts of potential implications for BI

The more likely a finance function is to be outsourced, the more recommendable it is to (re)assess the effectiveness of a given BI strategy regarding its overall BI delivery process. It makes a difference if you are able to talk to a colleague or if you need to collaborate with somebody from a completely different company. The more we have to consider third party involvement, the more we have to deal with interfaces. These interfaces not only have technical implications but also organizational, process-related, and governance aspects.

Table 2.2 Illustrative "make" or "buy" example with BI implications for finance functions

Finance function	(A) Potential (H ǀ M ǀ L)	(B) Strategic direction Finance	(C) Implications for BI
Accounting			
Accounts receivable	L	Outsource candidate	Interface to third party
Accounts payable	L	Outsource candidate	Interface to third party
Asset accounting	L	Outsource candidate	Interface to third party
Tax accounting	M	To be assessed	Get involved in decision-making
…			
Controlling			
Overhead controlling	M	Outsource candidate	Interface to third party
Profitability analysis	H	Inhouse (key)	Partner with business
Group costing	H	Inhouse (key)	Partner with business
…			
Treasury (Cash, …)	H	Inhouse (key)	Partner with business
Financial planning	H	Inhouse (key)	Partner with business
Front ends/user experience	L	Outsource candidate	Interface to third party
Analytics & reporting	H	To be assessed	Get involved in decision-making
Legal group consolidation			
Finance master data (integrated end-to-end view)	M	Inhouse (key)	Partner with business
"Green"/"ESG reporting"	H	Inhouse (key)	Partner with business

Within the same company, it is not a big deal to align and to collaborate. However, what if the finance area is scattered in multiple areas in-house and/or partly outsourced? How will it be possible to adjust processes and KPI definitions according to the situation while simultaneously being able to provide BI services at a lower cost?

The BI strategy is asked to design a robust and resilient organizational setup that supports data-driven decision-making at competitive cost. This ambition needs to be operationalized on all levels.

In recent years, it has been observed that corporate sustainability reporting moves to the core as well. "On 5 January 2023, the Corporate Sustainability Reporting Directive (CSRD) entered into force. This new directive modernizes and strengthens the rules about the social and environmental information that companies have to report. A broader set of large companies, as well as listed SMEs, will now be required to report on sustainability—approximately 50,000 companies in total." (European Commission, 2023). The CSRD calls for companies to take action on reporting, which will impact business intelligence. Any state-of-the-art BI strategy should rethink its value contribution to help steer a company not only based on financial KPIs but also on nonfinancial and increasingly important sustainability KPIs. We will further detail this topic in Sect. 2.6.

All companies have a steering model based on financial KPIs, including P&L, balance sheets, cash, or cost-related KPIs. However, due to historic developments such as the introduction of balance scorecards and learning based on economic crises caused by, for example, the coronavirus pandemic, many companies have broadened their steering model beyond pure financial KPIs. One of the main reasons for doing this is to improve insights into driving factors (leading indicators) for the targeted strategic KPIs.

The abovementioned finance domains and functions, which should not be treated as exhaustive, are closely interrelated within a corporate steering model, which is in short a framework for operationalizing corporate strategies and objectives into measurable targets. A steering model is by nature a top management concern and hence is owned by the board, CEO, and most commonly by the CFO.

What have we learned thus far for BI strategy development?:

Key considerations for developing a BI strategy

1. BI strategy should provide guidance and recommendations on removing structural inconsistencies and redundancies to strengthen corporate efficiencies. This should be done in a holistic way which is a prerequisite of seamless data-driven decision-making.
2. Organizational redesign of finance function might have a significant impact for the operation and collaboration model. In further consequence, data access and the capability to seamlessly provide data-driven decision support might become a challenge. To ideally anticipate impacts caused by revised finance strategies, a continuous strategic alignment between finance and BI is necessary.
3. BI strategy should design a robust and resilient organizational setup, which supports data-driven decision-making at competitive cost.
4. A steering model should not be solely based on financial KPIs but include nonfinancial KPI's as well. Overarching ownership for data-driven decision-making and getting the infrastructure (processes, solutions, governance, etc.) in place needs to be defined.
5. BI strategy can be seen as a "call for action" to provide answers to beforementioned topics and to strategically align between the functions.

At the beginning of this chapter, we explained the business intelligence ambition to provide "information about the organization's performance." However, what does this mean in more detail? Performance typically means the level of achieving financial and operational performance measures (KPIs) and specific (additional) objectives defined by key stakeholders.

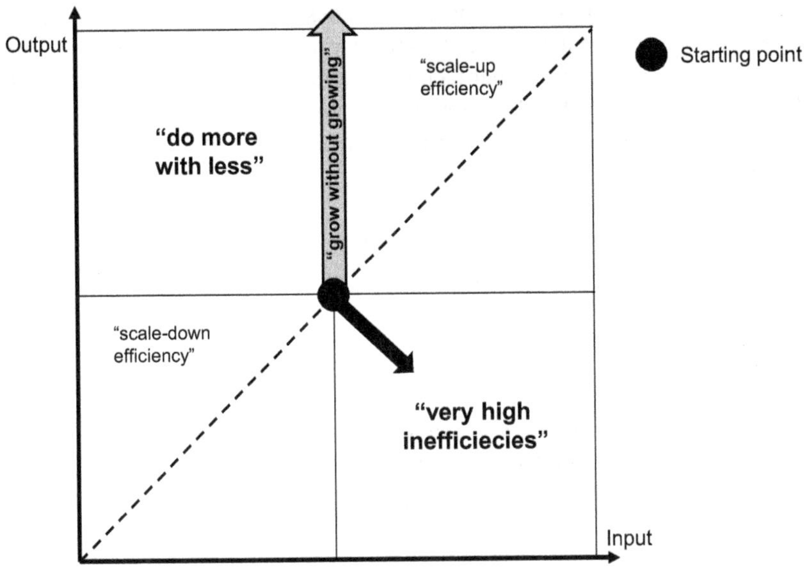

Fig. 2.8 Views on efficiencies (© Exner/Zunic 2024. All Rights Reserved)

In the context of performance, we need basically to consider two sides: a more strategic side toward sustaining long-term growth of the business (effectiveness) and an operational side oriented toward steering business performance according to key performance indicators (KPIs) in the most efficient way. For additional information, please refer to Sect. 2.3 Corporate Strategy.

The everlasting challenge and duty of any executive is to "do more with less." The "Do more" addresses the value aspiration toward improving value add as a company, in more detail, improving the share of value-adding activities. This holds true in general, but specifically for finance and is in our context even more relevant for business intelligence.

As the term "do more with less" sounds quite catchy, let us explore this in more detail. For this reason, we illustrate the line of thoughts in a matrix with two dimensions: input (x-axis) and output (y-axis), as illustrated in Fig. 2.8. We assume that the starting point is right at the intersection of the matrix. Let us now think of different developments.

- If we are able to achieve more output with less input, which would be the ultimate goal, we would be able to "do more with less" (upper left corner).
- If we are able to achieve more output while keeping the level of input constant, we can describe the pattern as "grow (in output) without growing (input)."
- Let us now further assume that we are still able to produce more output, but we have to accept slightly more input; this scenario we can describe as "scale-up efficiency." In other words, we are improving our performance, but we need to invest more.

- The previous example showed a positive business development resulting in more output. However, recent crises such as the coronavirus pandemic, global disruptions of supply chains, and other factors have caused economic downturns. How does this scenario look like? We now assume that we have to produce less output. If we are able to reduce input even higher than the output declines, we overall still gain more efficiency.

What are the implications for decision support of business intelligence?

In the context of business intelligence, these activities could be illustrated like in Fig. 2.9 (not exhaustive):

- Decision support in general "What are the options and what is the best one?"
- Planning and forecasting "What will happen next?"
- Analytics and reporting "How to extract and communicate the facts?"
- Root-cause analysis "Why did it happen?"
- Scenario analysis "What are our best options?"

The "… with less" addresses the ambition to achieve the improvements with less input, typically associated with working in a smarter way. This may include the following (not exhaustive):

- Less repetitive manual tasks
- Less nonvalue-adding activities
- Less cumbersome, stupid work
- Less number-crunching
- Fewer unnecessary iterations

Very often, the overall objective to gain efficiency is combined with a reduction in head count measured in full-time equivalents (FTE). This is typically associated with nonvalue-adding activities. In addition, when we talk about headcount

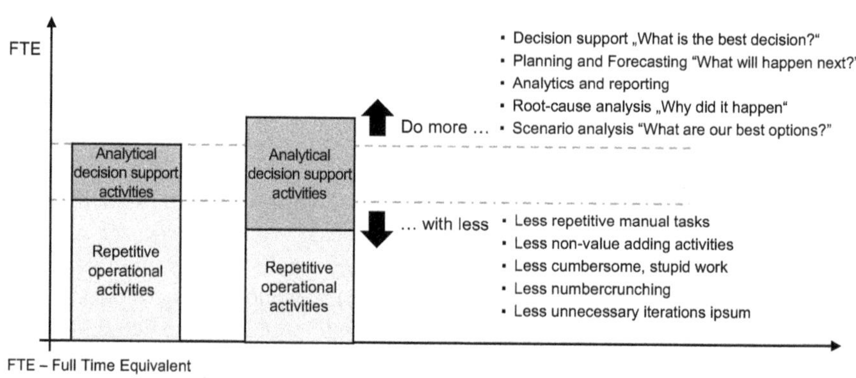

Fig. 2.9 The everlasting challenge of any CFO—"do more with less" in business intelligence context (© Exner/Zunic 2024. All Rights Reserved)

reduction, the first impression is usually negative, as we assume that we are talking about cutting jobs. However, the "with less" can also be achieved by reducing efforts required to produce the same or an even better output. Demographic changes in Western countries, where low birth rates are leading to fewer skilled workers of working age, are increasingly forcing companies to develop strategies to meet this challenge. As a result, "doing more with less" is becoming part of the strategy to survive in these market conditions.

2.6 Sustainability Strategy

Sustainability is a new growing topic for many organizations. This new topic is looking for a strategic home. Due to various reasons, however, there is no obvious link with other functional areas, since this topic must be considered very far reaching and comprehensive (from the procurement of (pre)products, services to the finished end product, or service provision including a usage phase of the end customers).

Due to this overarching importance and the need to record the environmental impact in a precise and structured manner along the entire value chain, the question arises as to where and how this can be done most effectively and efficiently. This is where the finance function comes in, since historically, accounting recording processes have been established in all companies along the value chain.

In this respect, it is almost obvious that sustainability reporting, with its specific requirements that will have to be further developed in the future, is based on the financial system.

In the following chapter we describe

(a) The strategic relevance of the topic (it is an ongoing topic)
(b) The role of BI in measuring and controlling the topic

Key question: What's in for BI Strategy? From a BI strategy perspective, we can (a) ignore this new topic or (b) take it up in full or (c) define some kind of middle ground. A BI strategy takes up this new design space and answers the question of how a company should deal with these new information requirements and how the chosen path can be designed into an optimal overall construct, taking into account the interactions with other BI target groups.

Drivers and Barriers of Sustainability Management
In recent years, many companies have become active in the field of sustainability management. Increasing pressure from customers, investors and not least regulators have forced organizations to provide higher levels of transparency on their sustainability ambitions and practices across all ESG (Environment, Social, Governance)

dimensions. This has led to extensive disclosures on sustainability related issues to external stakeholders, for example via regulations such as the Non-Financial Reporting Directive (NFRD) or more recently the EU Taxonomy and European Sustainability Reporting Standards (ESRS). Yet from a strategic perspective it often remains unclear how sustainability is embedded into and/or connected with other business strategies. Rather, the impression persists that while sustainability issues are being tracked and communicated more consistently, they are not yet cohesively integrated into an overall strategy.

Several barriers stand in the way of taking a strategic approach to sustainability.

1. Unclear boundaries of sustainability
   Sustainability (similarly to business intelligence) is a broad concept with fuzzy boundaries. It has a relevance in many business domains and at the same time requires a broad stakeholder-oriented perspective. This includes, for example, an understanding and measurement not only of the organization's own performance but also the impact it has on society and the environment at large. Furthermore, sustainability requires a new look at the end-to-end value creation process to consider not only the economically value-adding aspects but also societal, environmental, and behavioral value.
2. Unclear organizational ownership
   The traditional paradigm of measuring organizational success was purely based on economic criteria like profit, loss, and efficiency without necessarily accounting for negative outward impacts and externalities. This mindset often clashes with the more holistic, balanced, and long-term perspective on company success propagated by sustainability. As companies are still typically organized and rewarded based on financial accountability alone, they struggle to adopt accountability for non-financial performance, which often cannot be influenced directly because cause-effect chains are complex. Hence, it is quite often challenging to cascade corporate sustainability targets and performance ownership down to the operational level.
3. Data availability challenges
   Many companies suspect that the non-financial figures they are disclosing externally are not an accurate reflection of the "real" situation, because either data is unavailable and needs to be estimated/extrapolated or averages are used instead of actuals. This makes data-driven decision-making and strategy development challenging because a trustworthy underlying data foundation has not yet been established for allowing steering on a monthly or even more regular basis.
4. No established performance metrics aligned with strategy
   In addition to data availability challenges, sustainability performance measurement is also complicated by a lack of generally accepted value measurement and accounting methods for sustainability. Such concepts have evolved in the finance domain over centuries ranging from accounting standards to corporate valuation concepts. So it is no surprise that it takes time for such frameworks to

be generally adopted. However, the absence of standard approaches can have far-reaching consequences. It can lead to a situation where ESG ratings from different providers disagree substantially for the same company and hence compromise a company's ability to attract capital. In consequence, a methodology for measuring and reporting sustainability consistently and reliably in the different ESG domains is a necessary prerequisite both for formulating internal sustainability ambitions and targets but also for accountability and incentivization to drive action.

5. Cultural barriers
   Sustainability has a lot to do with changing behaviors and potentially questioning and rethinking established business practices. This can range from strategic considerations like, for example, cutting manufacturing of energy-intensive product lines, replacing or enhancing products with less resource-intensive services down to more operational initiatives like integrating circular-design principles in product design, transitioning the car fleet to e-mobility, or cutting business travel. All of these changes will typically lead to some form of resistance in the organization, especially if the change is implemented by force and no personal financial benefits and rewards can be expected.

Critical Success Factors

Increasingly, a key strategic success factor is striking a new balance between a short-term profit maximization motive and a longer-term sustainability motive which also takes into account externalities. This new approach avoids burdening future generations with the negative consequences of exploiting natural resources and human capital. However, it requires a comprehensive strategic transformation that encompasses all areas of a company.

Some common characteristics of successful sustainability initiatives can be observed, all of which require data and an understanding of data relationships.

- *Customer and stakeholder awareness*
  The most successful sustainability strategies start with the customer and end user. This includes questions like: who is using my products? who is the "real" end-consumer? What are usage patterns and what happens at the end of product use? How can the share of products that is recycled be maximized? How strongly is demand shifting to "green" products? This starts with a deep understanding of customer needs and expectations and translating them into material topics and sustainability priorities from which strategic initiatives and unique customer offerings can be derived. All of this should and increasingly must be supported with data and analytics like, for example, quantitative materiality assessments, horizon scanning (structured process to systematically identify trends, emerging topics, and events that could be highly relevant to the environment), scoring models, behavioral analyses (like, for example, buying patterns) and involve multiple stakeholders. Data-driven communication to external stakeholders has

also become a key priority like, for example, sharing de-carbonization goals and targets, sustainability programs, product transparency, transparency in supply chains and others.

- *Investor focus on sustainability performance*
  Increasingly investors take sustainability criteria into account when making investment decisions. They are looking for companies with resilient business models and long-term viability which includes a balanced, environmentally, and socially responsible portfolio of products and services. The basic assumption here is that there is no contradiction for companies to act sustainably, on the one hand, and to strive for economic success on the other.
- *Operational efficiency and energy economics*
  Efficiency is an obvious additional focus topic of sustainable transformation as it has a direct bottom-line impact. It essentially means minimizing the deployment of resources in relation to the realized output. This is traditionally achieved through product and process optimization ("lean management") which reduces waste and input energy in the production process. More recently, it is being reinforced by circularity concepts in product design and produce use, for example by substituting conventional materials and product designs with lightweight structures and using increasingly recyclable materials or materials that have lower pollution potential.
- *Policies and regulations ("license to operate")*
  ESG essentially means making non-financial, sustainability-related business efforts measurable and quantifiable. External stakeholders like investors, communities, and regulators increasingly demand the disclosure of reliable performance data in an accountable and transparent manner—assured by external parties. The scope of disclosure meanwhile goes far beyond the company's own boundaries and includes the entire value chain down to individual product level. This requires new approaches, new data, and new way of steering to account for, measure, and manage business performance holistically. Some prominent examples include the GHG protocol for carbon accounting, double materiality concepts, value balancing, and climate risk management.

Embedding Sustainability in the Organization

To tackle the pressing challenges of sustainability, a collaboration of different business domains is absolutely essential. Figure 2.10 below illustrates how a sustainability strategy can be integrated with other functional strategies including business intelligence.

Typically, sustainability will not be driven alone by a central sustainability department or function. It needs to be embedded into the core business processes ideally accompanied by a coordinating central team which sets a global direction and shares guidance and expertise on regulatory sustainability requirements, reporting and data requirements as well as program and project management.

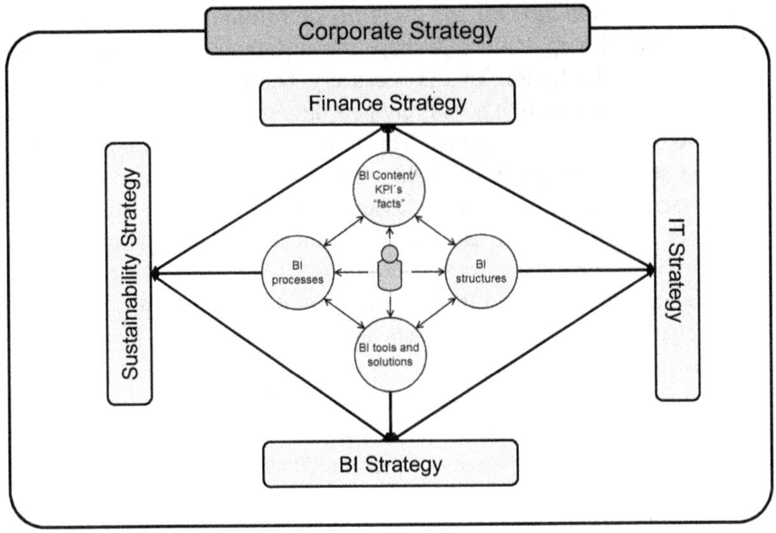

Fig. 2.10 Interrelations of sustainability strategy with other strategies (© Exner/Zunic 2024. All Rights Reserved)

The Role of Business Intelligence

As sustainability becomes increasingly relevant on executive level as a topic of strategic concern, it is increasingly necessary to understand, quantify, and account for sustainability performance. Therefore, companies have already for some time started to establish cross-functional ESG data and reporting programs to coordinate the process of data collection and reporting to achieve an enterprise-wide view of environmental and social performance in addition to economic performance. Typically, finance and accounting play a key role in this activity. Leading companies have already gone far beyond the boundaries of their own organization and include data from suppliers, customers, and third parties along the entire value chain.

Essentially, effective sustainability management requires an enterprise-wide effort to collect, manage, and enrich data from various internal and external sources. This calls for a close alignment with business intelligence, which plays the key role in providing the underlying data foundation and organizational alignment.

A BI strategy can add value in the following areas:

1. *Synchronization and consolidation of sustainability data demands*
   BI strategy should pick up the data demands arising from sustainability and give guidance and recommendations to ESG programs and teams regarding the best data management approaches, data sourcing, and governance. If this is not done, sustainability risks to become yet another silo with an own, ungoverned data environment detached from other corporate data.

2. *Extending data foundation for sustainability performance management*
   BI strategy should help define and shape the sustainability data foundation and data footprint of the future. This is necessary, because sustainability reporting might require the integration of entirely new data sets and governance structures which were not available in the past. This might include, for example the integration of climate risk data (types of risk, probabilities of risk, risk ownership), climate scenario models, qualitative assessments of material topics, supplier performance scores related to sustainability indicators, new sustainability-related attributes of corporate assets such as buildings or vehicles. BI strategy can particularly contribute by setting the reporting and data boundaries, evaluating the need and cost of external reference data and understanding the fit/gap (re-usability) of existing data artifacts.
3. *New BI opportunity to offer "Sustainability-as-a-Service"*
   Finally, as the central data authority in the organization, a BI strategy can facilitate data-driven alignment across different departments in the organization. Typically, an ESG program or department is not aware of the entire corporate data foundation that is already available. BI strategy can help avoid silos, improve the understanding of available data and its meaning, and help assess data gaps and how to overcome them. This provisioning of guidance and advisory service can be headlined as "Sustainability-as-a-Service." Sustainability can be seen as a window of opportunity to position the BI organization as a strategic partner to provide guidance in orchestrating this new domain.

As sustainability becomes an integral part of any business, business intelligence should be envisioned toward "sustainability intelligence." This vision and strategic evolution path should be considered in the BI strategy discussion.

2.7 IT Strategy

For many years, IT is said to be struggling not only to justify its existence but also to prove value contribution to corporate strategy and other lines of businesses. One of the most often mentioned key requirements from the IT outside is "improve IT performance at lower cost" and "improve flexibility" to cope with everchanging competition.

During the recent years, "going cloud" and "... as a Service" got increasingly important answers to those requirements, thus can be found in close to any IT strategy regardless of size, region, or industry of a company. What does this mean for BI strategy development?

In the first part of this sub-chapter, we will explore the reason and need to continuously innovate in information technology. We will introduce the Kano model which helps to understand customer perception on product and service features. Based on this understanding, we will then learn about the underlying reasons for continuous innovation. The pressure to continuously innovate leads us to a development called "exponential growth," which increasingly can be illustrated as "tornado of exponential growth" with foreseeable consequences on future work share between humans and IT. To make this more tangible, we will highlight these consequences by some impressive examples and further recent innovations in conversational artificial intelligence (AI).

Finally, we will provide some food for thoughts regarding levers to improve BI performance at lower cost, some further input for developing a BI strategy.

The everlasting challenge remains to provide IT services at lower cost which is the final part of this chapter. We translate the "going cloud" and "Everything as a Service" (XaaS) in the last years into "Business Intelligence as a Service" and follow this line of thoughts to a layered model describing the huge bandwidth of business intelligence ranging from IT infrastructure, on the one end, to the execution of fact-based decisions made on the other.

Despite today's widely recognized importance of information technology to a company's competitiveness, the value of IT was perceived very differently about 20 years ago. At that time, some people provocatively asked, "What is the value of IT?" and questioned the very existence of IT. Today, certainly, nobody would think about a world without any IT. Many IT devices are so much embedded in our daily private or professional lives, that we hardly can draw the line between private and business. Roughly 20 years ago, the idea of "Bring Your Own Device" (BYOD) was born to even eliminate this borderline.

From a business perspective, managing global supply chains in increasingly interconnected ecosystems requires collaboration among colleagues and partners around the world in real-time from any place at any time. This ranges from video-conferencing, instant messaging, chat to social media and AI-supported chatbots. In this business environment, a global economy without IT is almost inconceivable.

Based on the current maturity of information technology, it is still valid to raise the question of the strategic value contribution of IT. What are the distinguishing factors that make us think of low IT value contribution, while on the other hand some "lighthouse" examples prove that high performing IT is strategically contributing to competitive advantage? Strategies are designed to get or stay ahead of the competition. But when everyone in the market is using the same IT, the same processes, the same technology, in short, the same core IT functions, it is hard to find a starting point for true competitive advantage.

One systematic approach of analyzing value contribution from customer point of view refers to the Kano model. The Kano model was developed by Noriaki Kano in 1984 on product development and customer satisfaction and classifies customer preferences or requirements basically in three key categories. Depending on source these categories are named slightly different, however the underlying principle remains.

- Must-have requirements
- One-dimensional requirements and
- Attractive requirements

Must-have requirements describe the solution feature expectations, which are perceived as being existing even if not explicitly requested. In consequence, customers feel very disappointed if this feature is not existing; however, if the feature does exist, customers feel quite neutral as their unexpressed expectation was met. In other words, no need for being delighted. For example, we expect our analytical applications running smoothly every time we are using them, our Internet access should work without interruption at high-speed ("business intelligence at your fingertips"), etc. Having any of these will not make us delighted but lacking them will definitely make us complain on the product or service.

The category one-dimensional requirements describe another pattern of customer reaction. In this case, the level of customer delight grows with the level of presence of a feature. The underlying pattern is like "the more … is given … the more I'm delighted as customer." When you are investing in an analytical application, the number of in-build statistical or data visualization features or the number of standard interfaces to other solutions could be a one-dimensional attribute. The more you have of those features, the greater your satisfaction.

The attractive requirements now do not cause disappointment in case the feature expectations are not met, but they will boost satisfaction and happiness in case they exist. One example could be, for instance, the first time we interacted with a bot in a conversational way on how to proceed in a specific context. Think of the first time you used truly real-time analytics, where you notice instantly recorded order entries in your dashboard with the availability of all the details of products, margins, pricing details, quantities, delivery dates, outstanding approvals, and many more. You might remember that feeling you get when experiencing something beyond your imagination, what you know and expect from similar products or services.

The Kano Matrix can be used to evaluate product features and feature prioritization from customer point of view in a structured and standardized way.

Key considerations for developing a BI strategy

- How do you describe the value contribution of your BI services from internal customer point of view?
- What are the must-have requirements in reporting and analytics, planning and forecasting of your customers?
- What are the one-dimensional requirements in analytics, which impact customer satisfaction in a traceable way, and
- Have you ever thought about attractive requirements in, for instance, your planning processes and solutions? If so, how would you characterize them?

Unfortunately, or luckily customers get used to features. They want more, even better functionality and performance, simplicity, and usability of their tools. Kano predicted some kind of feature gravitation, which turns attractive requirements over time into must-have requirements (Yadav, 2015). In Fig. 2.11, this feature gravitation is visualized by the arrow starting from the attractive requirements in the upper left-hand quarter and pointing to the must-have requirements on the lower right-hand quarter.

In simple terms, we are getting used of a certain feature and are no longer excited. Example: many years ago, there was existence of a touch screen very new and innovative. In today's environment no mobile device would be sold in case it would not offer a touch screen handling. Another example: at the beginning mobile devices were designed to offer remote calls from anywhere and that was it. Nowadays, all mobiles have among other features sophisticated camera features which in some cases outperform normal smaller dedicated cameras, they can translate verbal speech into written text, and so on.

The option in BI applications to root cause certain anomalies in any analytic dimensions down to line-item level could be an analogy example of attractive requirements for business intelligence. Many years ago, and coming from an outmoded paper-based reporting, a simple IT supported "drill-down" capability was a great innovation to get into the details. Nowadays, it is quite common for end users to be able to explore huge amounts of data and this feature is perceived as a "must-have requirement."

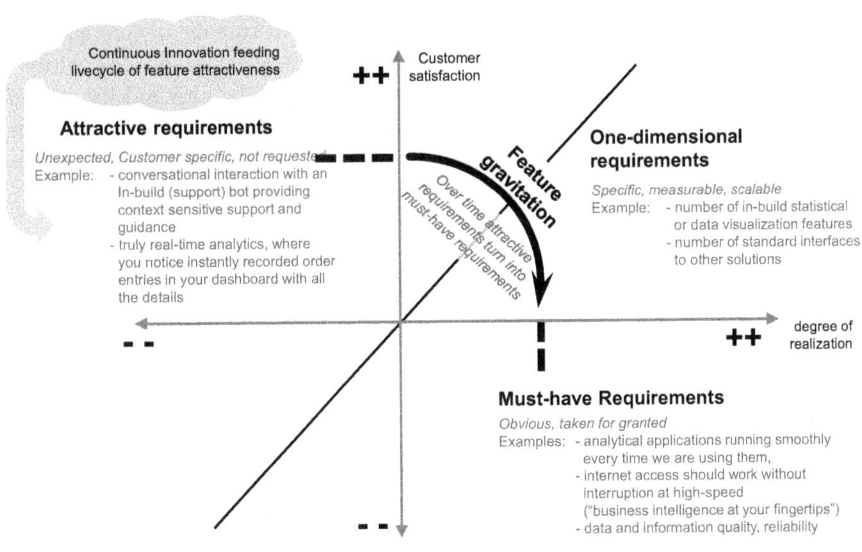

Fig. 2.11 Gravitation pattern of customer expectations, based on Kano, adapted from Yadav (2015) (Visualization adapted from: Yadav, S. (2015, December 18). The Kano Model—A tool to prioritize the users' wants and desires. Interaction Design Foundation—IxDF. https://www.interaction-design.org/literature/article/the-kano-model-a-tool-to-prioritize-the-users-wants-and-desires, last checked 16.10.2023)

The underlying mechanic of feature gravitation is applicable to strategic resources as well. Starting from a scarce innovative resource with potentially strategic value typically only a few companies are willing to invest and pay high skimming prices without having a clear path for returns on their investments. The more initial promises materialize, thus prove to come true, the more the (obvious) attractiveness growths and the more companies will invest in these resources. As the time goes by, the market for these strategic resources becomes more and more saturated, hence the remaining (former strategic) value of owning this resource will decrease unless this resource becomes a "Must-have" or in other words, "commodity."

What have we learned so far?

> "Value" and "value contribution" in general, but also valid for business intelligence, is not a level of achievement that is stable over time. Even if this sounds quite disillusioning, it should motivate us to continuously rethink what matters most:
>
> Value perception of our customers of BI services, data analysts, and BI users.

What is feeding the Kano model? It is continuous innovation! To survive in an increasingly saturated and global economy in the digital age, the only way to sustain and protect the own survival is to invest in unique selling propositions which is in other words continuous innovation. This leads to high pressure on any company to invest in new products, new services, new ideas to be perceived as a value contributor from customer point of view. Due to this everlasting pressure and the global availability of information, Internet-based collaboration and innovations, the lifecycle of products and services is becoming shorter and shorter. Regardless, where the innovation is locally "born," it will be deployed globally in an increasingly shorter timeframe.

The pattern of exponential growth originates to Gordon E. Moore, the co-founder of Intel, in 1965, who observed that the number of transistors on computer chips doubles approximately every 2 years. This pattern was double-checked several times and still holds true since many years. As of now there seems to be no limit how computer technology is changing with high-speed. In Fig. 2.12 below, this exponential growth is visualized by the bold line.

Digital data is fueling the ability to combine and recombine new technologies including their exponential growth patterns. Thus, the available and still growing amount of digital data could be seen as the "big bang" of the Exponential Growth tornado.

In contrast to this, we see organizational capabilities of companies, which are constrained by hierarchical setups, clearly structured responsibility centers, and defined ways of working. In other words, on the contrary to the technological progress, organizations cannot keep pace with this speed.

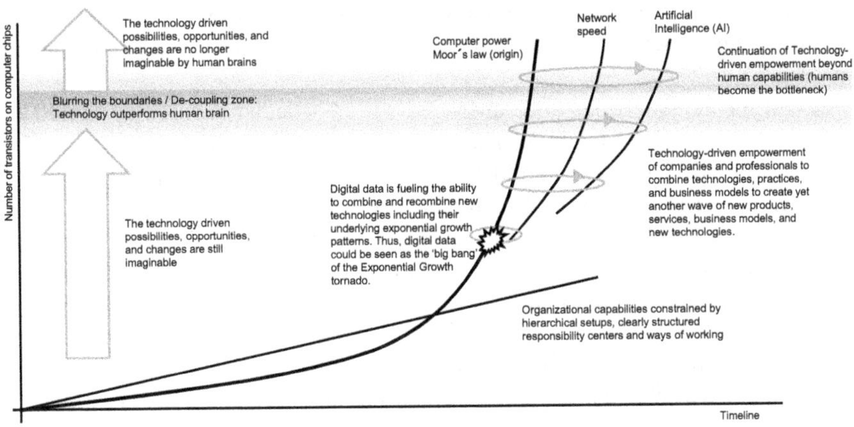

Fig. 2.12 The "Tornado of Exponential Growth"—infinitely fueled (© Exner/Zunic 2024. All Rights Reserved)

Next to the exponential growth of computer power in a narrow sense, we see similar developments in other technological areas, which are grounded on this power like network speed, artificial intelligence (AI), digital twins to name just a few. Due to this, we can assume that these technology areas are following a similar exponential growth pattern. Computer power of chip technology, network speed, AI, and other is not existing in isolation. Instead, breakthrough innovations in one area will fuel other areas. In consequence, companies and professionals will increasingly be empowered by technology to combine latest technologies, practices, and business models to create yet another wave of new products, services, business models, and again new technologies and innovations.

Where does these developments lead us to?

Nowadays, the technology-driven possibilities, opportunities, and changes are still imaginable and controllable. But the steeper the curve of the innovation speed, the more clearly the question of the possible bottleneck of the equation arises. There is no indication yet that somewhere in the nearer future the ground rules will break such are:

- Ambition for sustainable profitable growth of companies
- Companies competing globally and increasingly we see inter-system competition
- The willing to continuously invest in innovations, many of them tightly connected with information technologies and data
- Customers, which are hungry for the latest features and at the same time increasingly faster bored by commodities
- Increasing difficulties of organizational structures to keep pace with the multi-dimensional exponential change patterns

And even if it looks disillusioning to humans, on the mid- to long-term there will be increasingly less room for human value contribution in business processes, which are to a large extent relying on digital data. In consequence, we will enter a “de-coupling zone” where technology outperforms human brain and human performance.

One of the key questions to be answered will be whether technology should be deliberately decoupled from human capabilities to provide further opportunities for profitable growth. Of course, the lines are blurred, but for more than 20 years, we have seen increasing evidence of such scenarios. One of the most prominent areas, where the development has become transparent to the public in recent years, has been the machine–human competition in various games, such as chess, Go (which is said to be the most complex strategy game), and others. Based on these examples, we can conclude that artificial intelligence has already reached a high-end level of capability, which allows to follow highly sophisticated and superior strategies even in unknown environments. But even further, the level of capabilities has already reached a level that unsupervised learning is possible without the need to be told the underlying rules. In other words, there is no need for a machine to wait for humans to “teach” rules of a game.

> Consequently, and whether we as humans like it or not, the former scenario of deliberately decoupling technology from human capabilities is already a reality.

What’s ahead of us? Winning games against humans is one thing. But of course, the logical next step is to apply these capabilities to the huge range of complex problems in chemistry, bioengineering, climate change models, and many others. If we see decision-making in the context of enterprises and competition, it seems likely that these kinds of algorithms will support or potentially even replace human decision-making in the foreseeable future.

Let us now bridge the technological capabilities with another recent innovation. The above examples describe very complex learning algorithms which outperformed human world class champions in their fields. However, the human–machine interaction was and still is focused to quite specific use cases, which are not covering typical working environment in companies, for example, in discrete industries. But we can increasingly imagine that the area in which physical machines can be clearly distinguished from their digital twins is becoming increasingly blurred.

What if we would have a human-like conversational way of interacting with a computer algorithm? The question is intentionally rhetorical as in 2018 another innovation was born in the field of conversational AI combining natural language processing (NLP) with machine learning.

Key considerations for developing a BI strategy

- BI strategy development should aim for a clear and recognizable uniqueness and value contribution. Otherwise, BI will increasingly struggle to prove its relevance and value compared to the typically transparent costs. As a result, BI runs the risk of being sidelined.
- The ubiquity of digital data should be seen as an opportunity to gain value and competitive advantage.
- Customer satisfaction drives buying behavior and the likelihood of recurring sales. However, customer satisfaction is the result of a multi-faceted, multi-variable race for success and growth. What is valid for external customers should be valid for internal BI customers as well. The BI strategy should in both scenarios provide guidance and a promising path for the organization to benefit from and adopt the latest technologies and breakthrough innovations.
- As we have learned, the speed of innovation curve is getting steeper and steeper. Speed is king, and every organization should strive to remove barriers to acceleration. What is true for organizations in general should be true for BI in particular. Consequently, a BI strategy should self-critically evaluate opportunities to learn faster, innovate faster, develop and deploy faster.
- If we agree that speed is important, the BI strategy should be transparent about how that speed is measured.

One of the main drivers to "improve IT performance at lower cost" is a consequence of IT facing challenges to convince its customers on its strategic value contribution. If information technology is increasingly perceived as commodity, one of the remaining differentiators is price/cost.

Among the various options to further reduce IT spent is one to challenge the "make or buy" strategy. Once it becomes clear, that further opportunities of pure internal IT cost cuttings are not sufficiently existing, companies need to rethink their purchasing strategy of IT as such. This covers the whole bandwidth of an IT portfolio including hardware, software, services, etc. And it will cover staff as well. Is it necessary to buy servers, operating systems, and business applications, providing services and taking care of all the required background activities like IT resourcing, continuous upskilling, and training of IT staff, just to name a few, by your own company? Wouldn't it makes more sense to buy just what is needed at a certain point in time?

During the recent years, "going cloud" and "Everything as a Service (XaaS)" got increasingly important answers to those cost-cutting and flexibility requirements toward IT. XaaS is an umbrella term that refers to the delivery of anything as a service typically via the Internet. Instead of buying complete infrastructure, hardware, software licenses and run the IT on-premises within an enterprise, companies use just the products, tools, and technologies, which are currently needed, nothing more and nothing less. This means that companies can link their purchase of IT performance with the dynamic requirements they have in their businesses. From commercial point of view, one of the often-used key arguments is that companies will be able to move high Capital Expenditure (CapEx) to more predictable and flexibly adjustable operational expenses (OpEx). The are of course some pro's and con's, but more and more elements can be found in nearly any IT strategy regardless of size, region, or industry of a company.

If we now broaden "Everything as a Service" to include "Business Intelligence," we see that it is basically just a small step to open a line of thought that ends with "Business Intelligence as a Service." Let us continue this line and think about Business Intelligence based on a layered architecture in a broader sense. By doing so, we will be able to explore how underlying arguments can create value, and thus could be considered as a BI strategy element. We consider a structure consisting of five layers, as shown in Table 2.3 below. Within this table, we express the assumed level of IT contribution in the second column as Harvey balls. The more the Harvey ball is filled black, the higher the assumed IT contribution.

1. Starting from the first layer IT Infrastructure as "home ground" of IT. The key task is to provide basic infrastructure components and services as a foundation capability. This layer needs to aim for reliability, scalability, security, and others and is very similar to the provision of IT infrastructure for other business areas like procurement or finance. The ownership is typically solely IT. For further details, please see Sect. 6.6.5.
2. The next layer might be the data layer. In this layer, we are talking about provisioning of data by feeding data in IT systems, either manually or supported by functionality, internal and external data. A lot of well-known tools around Extract Transform Load (ETL) are typically positioned in this layer. The ownership is mixed as we typically see that data ownership or responsibilities for data quality reside in the different businesses, where the data in most cases is created, not in IT or in BI. For further details, please see Sect. 6.6.3.
3. The previous one is followed by a business intelligence layer. In this layer the provisioning of analytical and reporting, planning, and forecasting capabilities to the users is done. IT typically contributes by analytical tools and solutions close to the specific use cases of the end users. For further details, please see Sect. 6.6.4.
4. If we enter the decision-making layer, we see that we now need to change our view. Decision-making requires fact-based options, which have been provided by the previous layers. But the existence of these options does not necessarily constitute what decision is the very best option to choose. In essence, decision-making is still mainly a human activity, as in addition to facts, experience, learning, contextual and non-fact-based information such as gut feelings and other factors contribute significantly. But, as we learned before, the artificial intelligence with its unsupervised learning techniques and new conversational AI starts to blur the boundaries.

Table 2.3 Layered architecture of business intelligence-as-a-service

Layer	IT contribution	Technical layers	Key purpose
Layer 5—Execution focus/mixed ownership	○ → ◐ due to unsupervised learning techniques and conversational AI	Execution "stack"—how to turn decisions made into concrete activities, to change. Without execution, the best decision will not materialize.	"from insight to action," i.e. translating transparency on what is going on and where is the root cause to a set of key activities with highest probability to succeed in eliminating cause for missing the target/intended business performance level
Layer 4—Decision-making focus/mixed ownership	○ → ◐ due to unsupervised learning techniques and conversational AI	Decision-making "stack"—defined guiding principles how decisions are made and how they are grounded based on facts (data) and documented, to make them repeatable or provide a baseline for later review in case of missing the intended outcome. Success rate of decision-making	
Layer 3—BI focus/ownership	◐	Business intelligence stack/layered scalable architecture	Provisioning of analytical and reporting, planning, and forecasting capabilities
Layer 2—mixed ownership	◔	Data "stack"	Provisioning of data by feeding data in IT systems (manually or supported by functionality, internal and external data)
Layer 1—IT focus/central ownership	●	IT Infrastructure stack	Providing basic infrastructure components and services as a foundation capability

5. Finally, we see the execution layer. Even if we know fact-based arguments in a certain situation, if we further know all the basic options for decision-making and even if we have somehow made our decision on the most preferable option, still one piece is missing: execution. Unless we are not able to turn the decisions made into concrete activities, nothing is going to change. The best decision will not materialize into any change if we do not take any action.

From historical perspective, we see that IT contributed in the past mostly on layer 1 and 3 due to a technical focus on tools, solutions, and IT architecture. This implies that specifically in those areas we can assume a higher cross-dependency between BI strategy and IT strategy if we reduce BI strategy to a more technical focus. Consequently, corporate strategies on Infrastructure-as-a-Service (IaaS) or Software-as-a-Service (SaaS) will impact Business Intelligence most likely.

The closer we move business intelligence to businesses or trying to position BI to be perceived as business partner, the more we consequently need to enter the decision-making space within the business. In this case, we are more focusing on layers 2, 4, and 5 in the above table. Due to this, we increasingly need the alignment between IT strategy and BI strategy and, even more important, with BI strategy and business strategies.

In a nutshell:

If BI is perceived as mainly IT technical function, BI strategy needs to be very closely aligned with IT strategy up to the extreme that there is seen no room for a dedicated BI strategy. If, however, BI is perceived as key element to support steering the business by accelerating "SPEED TO IMPACT" then BI strategy must include strategic alignment with the businesses. Decision-making, execution and ultimately intended impact still will be the key differentiator between theory and practice.

Let us come back to the ambition "improve performance at lower cost" in the context of business intelligence. What are some key levers to achieve this target of Business Intelligence at lower cost?

Key considerations for developing a BI strategy

- Reduce complexities by simplification of BI solution portfolio and adopt more standard BI solutions.
- Improve transparency on day-to-day BI activities (baseline) and improve the level of automation end-to-end.
- Challenge the very end, as it should not suffice to provide reports but ignore the range from having KPI's at hand up to making and executing a decision for change.
- Improve transparency on data quality issues like inconsistencies or missing data. If data quality is perceived as must-have requirement from BI customer point of view to what extent is BI mandated, willing and/or able to improve data quality? Or, in contrast, is BI perceived as the "guilty" but without any means to improve the situation at its source?
- Improve report creation and analytics by a more agile way of working, introduce "agile" or self-services in BI. "Speed is key!" and in many cases perceived as one-dimensional requirement: "the faster—the better."
- Establish a value-based management methodology as a basis for BI service delivery. If speed is key, do not ask for "how fast can I create my report or my dashboard" rather than asking, how can I quickly find what is already existing and adapt the remaining to meet my needs.

Finally, let us complement some ideas which might be helpful to reduce the overall cost or increase flexibility of business intelligence.

- To what extent do we need to own BI related hardware by ourselves?
- How quickly will we need to scale-up or, if needed, scale-down our BI infrastructure capacity? Is this flexibility already contracted with the vendors and does it include scenarios in both directions?
- What kind of BI activities can be outsourced? What are our arguments to keep certain activities inhouse and for both scenarios, what are the overall implications and risks?
- How do we want to scale-up or, if needed, scale-down business intelligence with the business? Is our BI landscape sufficiently prepared for this from technical but also from organizational point of view? Is this preparation sufficiently grounded by facts or is it just by hope that the situation will never occur.
- Should our BI landscape be on premise, in the cloud or do we prefer a hybrid landscape? What timeline do we have in mind for designing our BI landscape.

Of course, the before mentioned ideas are by no means complete. However, they should be treated as starting point for further discussion and development.

History showed that IT can be outsourced to a large extent. But BI as well? We increasingly see the need to get clear how to use the existing data and information assets for strategic steering and decision-making. In addition to this, we need to discuss and shape awareness who should in future take what decision as such. Will it still be humans in any case like in the past or to what extent are we willing to delegate decision-making to algorithms, which outperform human brain. It certainly will not be a black and white discussion.

3 Tool Kit for Strategy-Aligned BI

In some cases, organizations face a situation where BI responsibilities are not known, not defined, or not sufficiently involved in (business) strategy development. Even when such BI responsibilities are defined, those responsible may not be sufficiently informed about the business strategies, their underlying goals, and appropriate performance measurement criteria. As a result, the ability to consistently provide effective support through tailored business intelligence is likely to be weak, or at least only incidentally aligned with business strategies.

How can this situation be remedied? Undoubtedly, the best scenario would be to achieve an improved situation of continuous close collaboration between all relevant stakeholders. However, if for some reason this is not sufficiently possible, the next best option is to strengthen the ability to interpret the business strategies and their key components and to develop a basis for deriving the strategic business requirements for business intelligence. This does not necessarily mean that this interpretation and the resulting proposals will be valid in all facets, but it still provides the opportunity to contribute to business decision-making in a collaborative way.

In this chapter, we will present a tool kit on how this could be done in practice. Keep in mind that this is still a second-best option, but it is typically quite common.

In order to link a BI strategy to other business strategies, a structured approach is advantageous, allowing business intelligence requirements to be derived in a logical, transparent, and standardized manner. Logic and transparency again aims to allow backtracking to prove the value contribution of BI against the original strategic requirements. The criteria of standardization support a repetitive execution of activities and allow to gain experience. Such an approach is not only beneficial for

R. Exner, A. Zunic, *The Path to an Intelligent Enterprise*, Future of Business and Finance, https://doi.org/10.1007/978-3-031-69914-6_3

a business intelligence use case. Rather, it is typically implemented to serve a broader set of strategy operationalization and performance measurement purposes in other areas of an organization.

In the first sub-chapter, we present an approach that helps us better understand how strategies and strategic objectives can be linked in a consistent way. It should be noted, however, that we do not intend in our book to discuss other approaches or every single detail. Instead, the reason for starting with this topic is to provide an anchor for the subsequent alignment of a BI strategy with other business strategies.

In the second and subsequent sub-chapters, we will present a methodology for deriving BI requirements in a structured format. Our focus here will first be on the unfiltered collection of business requirements. Based on this, we typically have a high level but still complete set of business requirements. Next, each captured business requirement is decomposed into different dimensions and described in more detail. Within these different dimensions, we will be able to identify patterns, commonalities, ambiguities, and contradictions or even conflicts across all the detailed derived requirements. This provides the requirements backlog for defining a BI strategy. The usage of this framework and methology in an iterative closed loop will be introduced in Chap. 4.

3.1 The Strategy House Concept

The Strategy House concept is an approach that focuses on two key dimensions in a discussion about strategy. The first dimension is about answering the question "What needs to be done?" and the second dimension is about answering the question "For whom are we going to do this activity?" The idea is to focus the discussion on these key questions.

In the context of our book, the introduction of this concept should not be confused with the idea of developing a BI strategy as such. The reason for this is that the original idea of the Strategy House is primarily about corporate strategy. In other words, we do not aim to use the Strategy House concept to develop a standalone BI strategy. Instead, we want to provide a starting point for understanding some of the key aspects of the strategy discussion.

From a BI strategy perspective, we need to provide guidance, so we also need to answer the question "What needs to be done?" And from a BI delivery perspective, we need to translate the answer to the previous question into a concrete set of activities and delivery commitments to BI customers. But "BI customers" does not mean that this group, with all its requirements and preferences, is a homogeneous group of individuals that can be satisfied by just a few products and services. Consequently, the second question, "For whom are we going to do this activity?" emphasizes the need to clearly identify the internal customer. This is particularly important because, in the end, it is the customer who decides whether we have done a good job in meeting their requirements.

In this chapter, we will introduce some basics of the Strategy House Concept. In the subsequent chapters, we will develop and tailor this concept further to decompose a given strategy top-down.

The House of Strategy approach was introduced by Dr. Herwig Friedag and Dr. Walter Schmidt (Friedag & Schmidt, 2016). They combined the balanced scorecard approach with stakeholder theory into a matrix with two main dimensions:

1. Dimension: What needs to be done? The answer will be the "strategic tasks"
2. Dimension: For whom? What are the most relevant stakeholders we are "selling" the benefits of conducting our strategic task to? The answer will be the "target groups"

At each of the resulting cross points the strategic tasks are linked to the stakeholder and their requirements.

The above approach was visualized by a house, subsequently called Strategy House. To visualize a simplified house, it needs a foundation, a body of the house, and a roof (see Fig. 3.1 below).

Each of the three key components is serving a specific purpose.

- First, the foundation contains all the underlying grounding factors like culture, way of working and communicating and many more. This area is assumed to be stable, and a given factor, and we will not discuss this further.

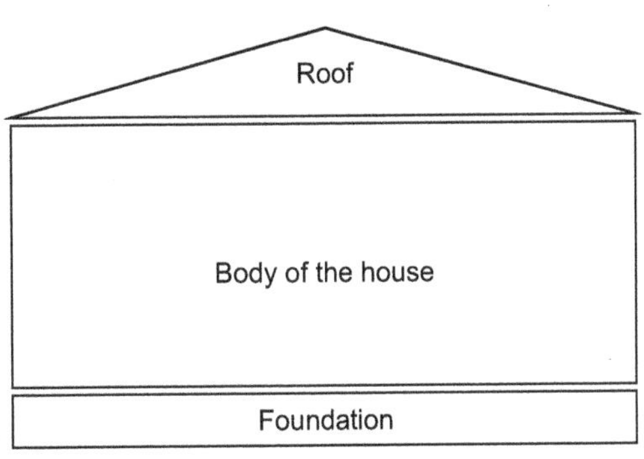

Fig. 3.1 Key components of a house—very simplified

- Second, the body of the house contains all the rooms we are typically living in. Hence, this is the centerpiece of the house, and we will focus on this on the next pages.
- Finally, the roof of the house which spans across the beforementioned other components.

Let us start with the roof. According to the Strategy House approach, the roof contains the top-level corporate framework of success which is the ultimate guiding objective (mission), guiding vision with a clear Unique Selling Proposition (USP) and a guiding KPI, that is the most relevant criteria to judge all strategic decisions for value contribution.

Each of the floors (levels in Fig. 3.2) of the house represent a certain type of stakeholder or stakeholder group with individual characteristics, ambitions/goals, who should do or avoid something to make the company even more successful. For each of the stakeholder groups such as, for example, owners, shareholders, staff, a goal needs to be defined as well as a KPI to measure progress toward the goal. It is advisable to keep the number of stakeholder groups below six to stay focused.

Each of the vertical columns contains strategic tasks. These are the most important requirements for fulfilling the guiding goals. Also here: for each of the strategic tasks, a goal needs to be defined and a KPI to measure progress toward the goal. To stay focused, a reasonably small number of strategic tasks (3–5) should be considered.

At the intersections, stakeholder expectations connect with the strategic tasks of the company. To stay with the analogy of the house, we can refer to these intersection points as "flats" or "strategy rooms." Finally, we see for each of the "strategy rooms" a clearly defined objective and a KPI to measure success, in total we develop

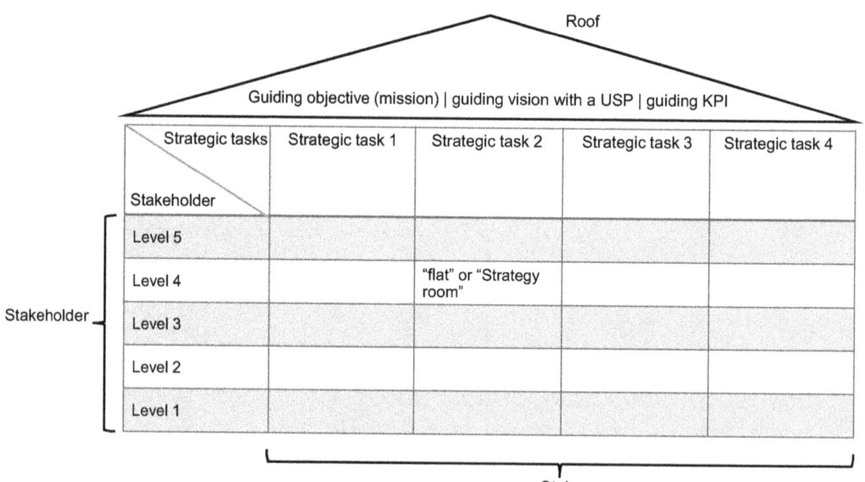

Fig. 3.2 House of Strategy, adapted from Friedag and Schmidt (2016)

an interconnected system of objectives. This big picture again provides guidance through the house as such but can still be improved.

Let us take an example of "Operational excellence" to make it more tangible. "Operational excellence" as such is very general and does not provide sufficient guidance. Therefore, if we take this statement as a "strategic task," it does not clarify the objective. However, if we combine "operational excellence" with a specific stakeholder's perspective and a specific KPI, such as "quote conversion rate," it becomes more meaningful and guiding.

Let us be a bit more concrete and start again with the roof. In practice, we all know of course that a real house will be build up starting with the foundation. What are the core corporate drivers for success and how do we get them verified? We need to ask ourselves some basic questions:

1. Mission:

   (a) What is our unique and ultimate objective for the next years?
   (b) What is most important to our customers? How do we want to be seen by them?

2. Vision:

   (a) What does our guiding vision, our internal goal with a clear (USP) look like?
   (b) What do we need to do to make us unique compared to our competition?

3. Key indicator:
   (a) What is our ultimate guiding KPI expressing corporate success or failure?

Let us consider the above questions as proof points. If we are not able to answer the above questions right away, or only after a long time of thinking, asking colleagues or peers, etc., this can be taken as an indicator that there may be some fundamental uncertainties that need to be clarified beforehand.

Mission:

- A mission explains in simple and understandable terms the purpose of a company's existence.
- The first question "how do we want to be seen by the market, your customers" seems to be a simple question. However, even for practicioners, it is not that easy if you start on a white sheet of paper. Do you really know what matters most for your customers?

Vision:

- A vision is an inspirational statement of an idealistic future of a company.
- The same applies for the next question "guiding vision with a clear internal goal (mostly, but not always a USP)." With an USP the company can achieve better prices on the markets, a higher market share or a better reputation.

Key indicator:

- The question regarding the ultimate key success metric allows us to focus on the most relevant topic to become or to stay successful. The advantage of this guiding KPI is that it forces us to be specific.

By answering above questions, we can understand and describe the "roof" of the strategy house as illustrated in Fig. 3.3 below:

With the roof as a starting point, we now begin to build the house itself, or rather the body of the house. The first activity is to answer the question of strategic tasks. In other words, "What are we going to do strategically?" The strategic tasks are highly relevant to the execution of the strategy. But even more important is the accomplishing of the tasks. Realized strategic tasks, true strategy execution, is the difference between theory and practice. Walk the talk.

Each of the strategic tasks can be seen as an "elevator" (vertical "stairway") in our house. By nature, the elevator in our house has a vertical movement, so we touch all floors/stakeholders. The number of strategic tasks should be reasonably small. Limiting the number of strategic tasks to about four is a helpful approach to maintaining focus. However, it is important to view this limitation as a guideline rather than an absolute rule. Combining the strategic tasks with different stakeholder groups yields a total of 16–25 rooms, which is well in line with the motto "twenty is plenty" and reflects a focused and efficient approach. Furthermore, we can easily imagine that in larger organizations, we would need to adjust this approach.

In a slightly changed visualization of the House of Strategy the different floors of the house could also be interpreted as balanced scorecard perspectives as illustrated in Fig. 3.4 below.

A further detailing of this approach leads us to even more granular insights which according to Friedag/Schmidt can be described by O-A-R which is Objective–Action–*Ratio* (Friedag & Schmidt, 2016). A first connection to Business Intelligence can be imagined by the "ratio," which can be understood as a metric or a key performance indicator.

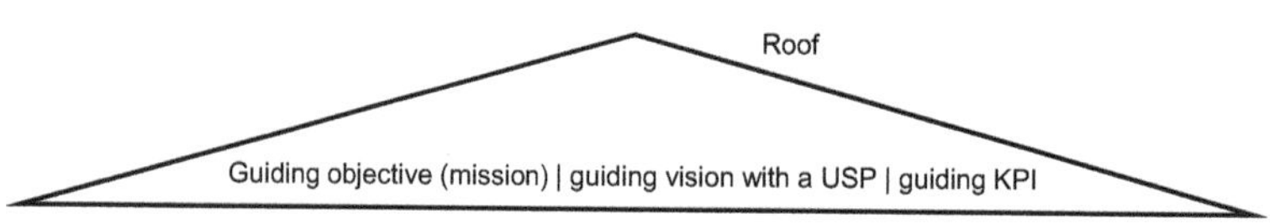

Fig. 3.3 Roof of the House of Strategy, adapted from Friedag and Schmidt (2016)

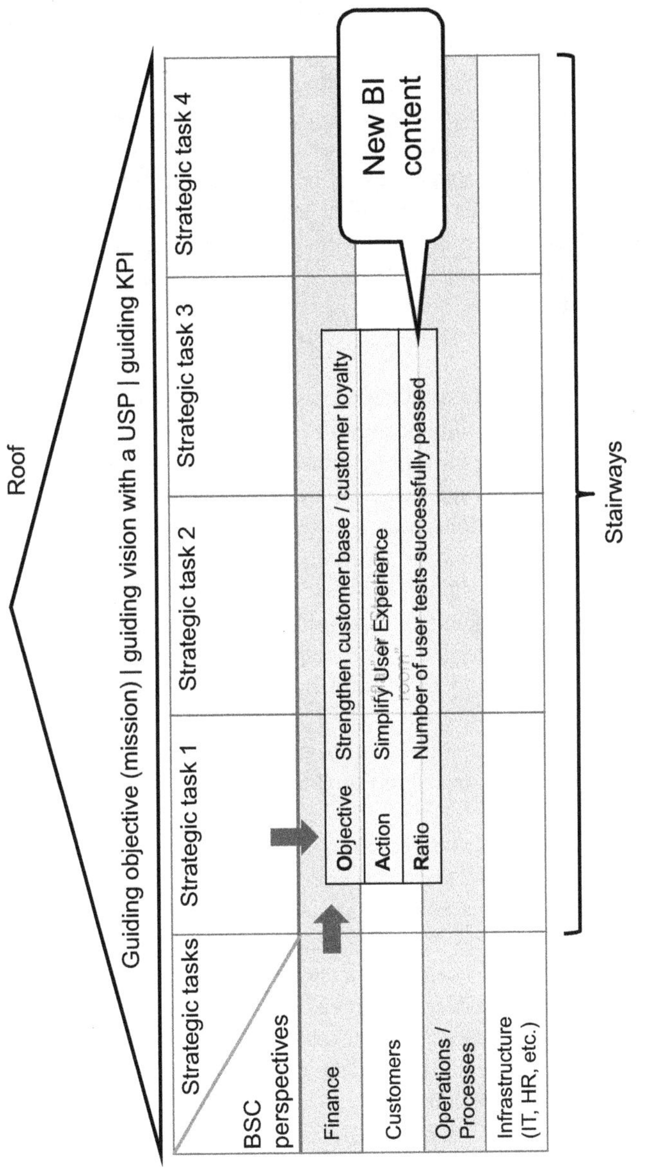

Fig. 3.4 O-A-R—Objective–Action–Ratio, adapted from Friedag and Schmidt (2016)

3.2 How to Decompose a Given Strategy

In the previous sub-chapter, we were introduced to an approach for describing a strategy in a structured way, and we learned how strategic business requirements can affect business intelligence based on ratios.

In this section, we will use some selected parts of the approach and develop it further to facilitate the subsequent decomposition of given business strategies. The ultimate aim of this decomposition is to create a single source of requirements that supports tracing back to the business strategies. This single source will later allow us to discover similar requirements from different business functions such as finance, supply chain, procurement, and others.

We will learn that these similarities can be seen as an opportunity to leverage synergies for future BI services.

The introduction in the previous sub-chapter was intended to provide a first starting point. However, today's complex organizations often face the challenge of managing strategic goals along multiple dimensions simultaneously. In such scenarios, the above approach may not be sufficient. Complexity arises, for example, from many international locations, management styles, working methods, and employees from different cultures. In addition, the IT systems in such organizations tend to be historically grown and not very standardized. One of the key challenges in such a complex landscape is to develop a strategic balance between (a) decentralized degrees of freedom to better exploit customer proximity and (b) overarching synergy potential to ultimately increase efficiency throughout the entire organization.

To even better support a later translation to new BI requirements, we will now adjust our guiding structure illustrated in Fig. 3.5 as follows:

- Column 1: We will rename the strategic tasks "strategic cornerstones." A "strategic cornerstone" is a high-level anchor that provides the answer to "WHAT needs to be done?" Strategic cornerstones provide guardrails to improve strategy interpretation, communication, and operationalization of a strategy in the intended direction. The existence of strategic cornerstones allows strategies to be further detailed and enriched with additional targeted facets without compromising the strategy statement itself. The reason for the renaming is that we want to strengthen the ability to reasonably decompose the top-level strategic objective throughout multi-layered complex organizations.
- Columns 2 and 3: We know that our BI customers are our target group. We typically find our BI customers throughout the entire organization, regardless of hierarchy level, span of control, role within the organization, or any other criteria. From this perspective, even the term "stakeholder" can be ambiguous and

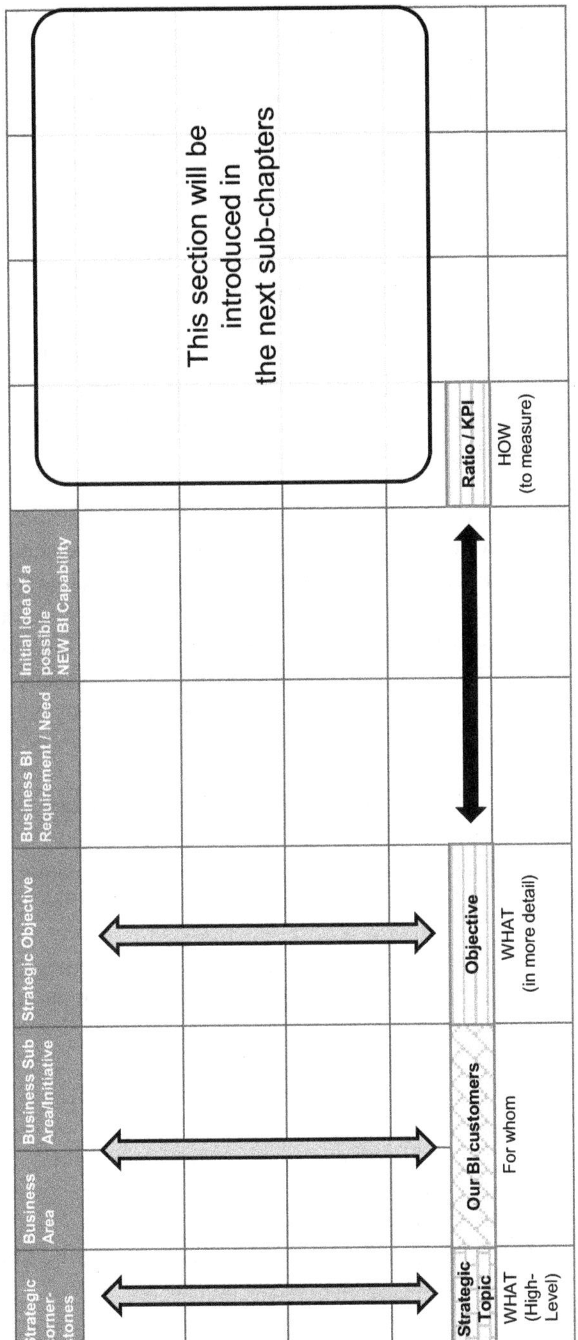

Fig. 3.5 Adjusted guiding structure for strategy decomposition (© Exner/Zunic 2024. All Rights Reserved)

potentially misleading, so we replace it with Line of Business (LoB) or Business Area/Business Subarea. We acknowledge that this renaming may lack some guidance, but the idea of this replacement is to be even more neutral toward any kind of organizational structure.

- Column 4: In the next column, we record the given "strategic objectives," ideally with a clear traceability to their referencing strategic cornerstone. In other words, a strategic cornerstone for a particular line of business or business area might consist of several strategic objectives, all of which help to operationalize the top-level strategic objective.
- Column 5: Each line of business or business area is typically represented by a manager. If the managers are able to describe their "Business BI requirements and needs," we will also record this in our table.
- Column 6: In the next column, we start to think about potential new BI capabilities needed to meet the beforementioned business BI requirements we have recorded. This can initially be done in a very pragmatic way. Simply describe what seems obvious from a BI perspective.

Based on the concept introduced earlier, we are able to decompose a strategy into a tabular structure. This allows us to transparently link the BI requirements identified so far to the strategy with its strategic cornerstones, and at the same time trace back to prove the value contribution of BI. It is advisable to follow a top-down approach. This means that the various "strategic cornerstones" are identified and captured first. It also helps identify where potentially strategic statements are not sufficiently grounded in operations. The reason of this is to provide early guidance and anchors for the details that follow. In this approach, we start at a high level and go into further details step by step.

Our sequence of steps, based on the structure above (Fig. 3.5), is as follows:

1. First, we capture, analyze, and understand the given top-level corporate strategy or strategies. These strategies can also be expressed by multiple strategic cornerstones.
2. Second, we need to understand how business area or business subarea strategies are intended to support the corporate strategy. How do they impact on each other? What are the causalities?
3. Third, we identify existing or emerging initiatives within each business area. Some of them might exist for quite a while, some of them might be just in discussion.
4. Fourth, we capture the strategic objectives of each of these initiatives. We do this as accurate, detailed, and comprehensive as possible but at the same time aiming to maintain a transparent traceability to the top-level strategy.
5. Fifth and finally, we request (if not yet given) and record the (resulting) business requirements toward BI to support given strategic objectives.

Table 3.1 below describes typical activities to decompose given strategies and provides additional practical considerations.

Table 3.1 How to decompose a given strategy—sequence of activities

Step	Area	To be further considered by practicioners
1	Corporate strategy, sometimes expressed by multiple strategic cornerstones	Replace strategy vocabulary, sometimes buzzwords, with meaningful action-oriented descriptions. If this proves difficult, ask the strategy owners to explain what should change and what should stay unchanged.
2	Business area strategies	Same as above
3	Initiatives within each business area	Validate that there is a reasonable and meaningful cause-and-effect relationship (logical trace of arguments) between each initiative and the business strategies that the initiative is intended to support. Don't be discouraged if this proves difficult. Our goal is not to improve strategy development and maturity, but to understand the essentials.
4	Strategic objectives	Validate against S-M-A-R-T characteristics of objectives: S-pecific M-easurable A-chievable R-easonable T-ime-bound
5	Description of business requirements toward BI	This is typically done using business language and terminology, so don't expect IT language, specific tools, etc., at this stage. Just keep asking questions like "If you want to make this happen/be successful strategically, how can business intelligence support this even better?

It is advisable not to make any prematurely judgements or conclusions at this stage. This is not the intention of this phase. Rather, the aim is to gain transparency about the multitude of strategies, their decomposition into different business areas and the corresponding underlying strategic objectives. A first and intended outcome is a strategic overview, the big picture as a starting point.

If you find that some elements look strange, congratulations. It is not a bug, it is a feature of this approach, and we will come back to that later. One result of this exercise may be to identify "white spots" within the overall big picture table that has been developed. This will be an advantage because it will allow us to take steps to reduce or even eliminate these white spots through improved communication and collaboration.

By its very nature, the structure of the second column Area in above Table 3.1 may be different in different companies. It is not black or white or just one version.

What do we generally expect at this stage? Let us take an example. For ease of understanding, we will underline the relevant items in this example. This approach allows us to focus on the different steps, but of course it does not provide a complete picture.

At the corporate level, the idea is not to expect very detailed descriptions, but rather statements that provide first and fundamental guidance on the intended strategic direction the company should take. As mentioned earlier, for the sake of simplicity, we will focus on only one or two exemplary items, for example, the top level (Step 1) of the first corporate strategy, "Improve Operational Excellence" (as shown in Table 3.2).

Table 3.2 How to decompose a given strategy—sequence of activities and example

Step	Area	Typical examples and level of description
1	Corporate strategy	• *Improve operational excellence* • Capture the full potential of the service business • Grow profitably in mature and emerging markets
2	Business area strategies	•
3	Initiatives within each business area	•
4	Strategic objectives	•
5	Description of business requirements toward BI	•

At the next level, we look at the different business areas. Most likely, these areas and their names will vary from company to company because of different organizational setups, but they should not be confused. At a very high level, however, it is assumed that these business areas are at least similar.

- Corporate
- *Finance*
- Human resources
- Supply chain planning, construction, and transport
- Sourcing, logistics, and warehousing
- Production/manufacturing execution
- Research and development
- Sales and marketing
- *Global IT*

As you can see, in our example, we will focus on finance and global IT.

It might be generally applicable to split business areas in sub-business areas or straight into initiatives; however, the methodology will remain unchanged. In finance, we might find strategic objectives such as (not exhaustive)

- *Ease the budgeting process*
- Increase level of process standardization and automation
- Reduce number of overall headcounts in finance
- Optimize BI operation in finance ownership, governance, and requirement capturing

In Global IT, it could be like for example (again not exhaustive)

- Actively bring opportunities for digital services
- *Deliver ongoing insight into the performance of business processes*
- Engage and participate in business planning
- Master Data reporting and analysis

In some of the examples above, such as “Ease the budgeting process” for finance or “Deliver ongoing insight into the performance of business processes” for global IT, we can identify at least some (business) guidance on the direction of improvement needed.

With this level of information, we are now able to formulate some guiding questions that will help us to better understand and decompose the strategic requirements, such as

- How satisfied are you with the overall budgeting process?
- What are the key drivers of business satisfaction?
- What are the pain-points? What exactly is missing?
- What KPIs are used to monitor the current performance and which ones help to track improvements in the budgeting process?

Following this approach, the decomposition will lead us to a potentially very large table with many business requirements that might look similar to Fig. 3.6 below. This is an achievement of high value.

> By using our top-down decomposition methodology, we are now able to clearly link business requirements for BI with business strategies and even corporate strategy, improving our ability to explain the value contribution of business intelligence. This new ability to tell a consistent strategic story is of great value to many BI departments.

To complete our exercise, we need to further decompose and translate the collected business requirements in a way that allows us to identify patterns and commonalities. The reason for this is that, as business intelligence professionals, we naturally strive for effectiveness and efficiency. In other words, we want to remove redundancies and eliminate elements that distract from the most valuable focus points.

From a practitioner’s point of view, is it realistic to assume that we will be successful if we only consider a top-down approach? Certainly not. There are many other patterns of strategy development, as illustrated in Fig. 3.7. In addition to the classic approach of top-down strategy ideation and initial development, strategy ideation can be initiated by middle management or, in rare cases, bottom-up by the workforce. Business transformation projects, in particular, can act as strategy incubators (project-driven). All of the above cases have one thing in common: the timing. They all refer to an early stage of strategic ideation, not to a final decision on strategy, strategic funding or operationalization of strategy, or monitoring and performance management.

It is at least when the question of “who is going to pay” arises that top management gets involved. Formally adopting, publishing, and communicating a strategy is usually a board matter. Once the decision is made, the next step is to operationalize

Strategic corner-stones	Business Area	Business Sub Area/Initiative	Strategic Objective	Business BI Requirement / Need	Initial idea of a possible NEW BI Capability
Capture the Full Potential of the Service Business	Service	Continuous Improvement Management	Discover patterns in failures on the main components of the turbines, making it possible to use this in preventive maintenance thereby minimizing turbine downtime.	Analyse patterns in failures on the main components of the turbines and report to preventive maintenance.	People: Data model development, new competencies/resource allocation Technology: DW Integration with CIR. Self service data analysis
Grow Profitably in Mature and Emerging Markets	Sales & Marketing	Market intelligence	Market intelligence available to enable differentiated value added services to various segments	Market intelligence available in Sales cockpit	Tech: Integration of Market data in SAP BW. Dashboard. People: DW Data model development. Process: Self service data mashup and analysis ?
Improve Operational Excellence	Global IT	Initiative to implement Process Performance Indicators (PPI´s)	Deliver ongoing insight into the performance of business processes	Business process performance measurement and BPP analytics capability	Improve Operational Excellence
Improve Operational Excellence	Finance	Budgetting and Planning	Ease the budgetting process.	Reporting assistance e.g. to consolidate department budget versions and fore-casting consequences of a budget draft.	People: Consultancy for budget process optimization

This section will be introduced in the next sub-chapters

Fig. 3.6 Collection of information—strategy-driven approach at a glance (© Exner/Zunic 2024. All Rights Reserved)

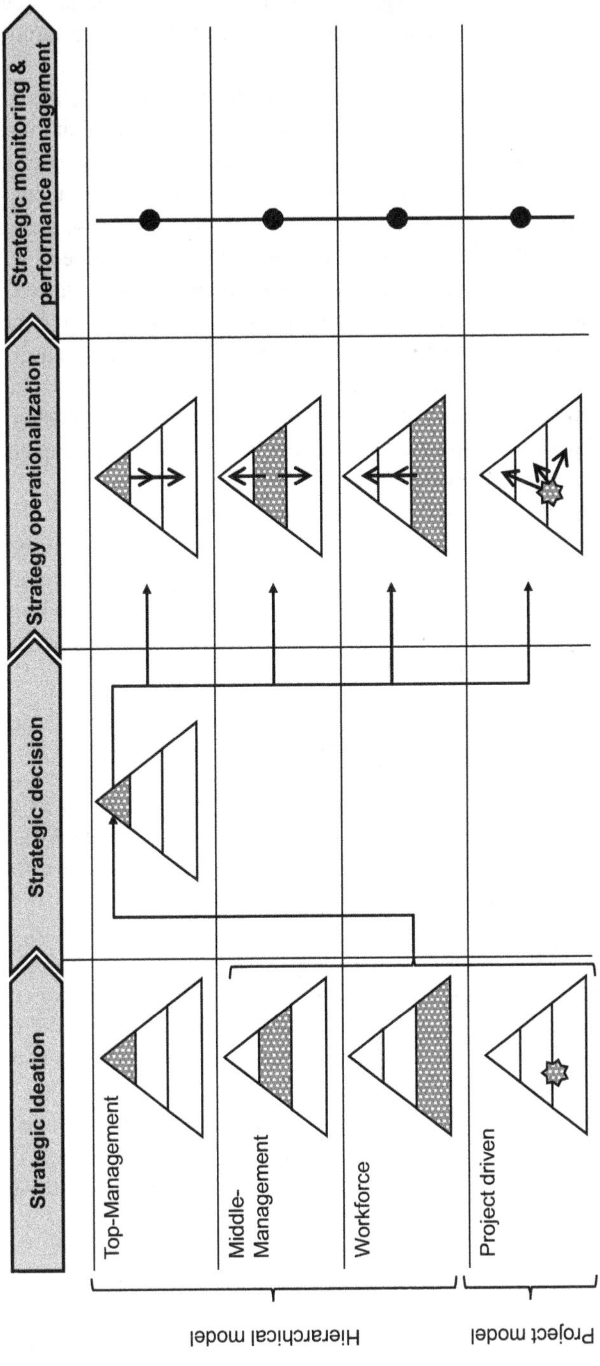

Fig. 3.7 Different paths from strategy ideation to strategic monitoring (based on Müller-Stewens & Lechner, 2005)

the strategy, which typically involves all levels of the organization. In addition, it is often done not only by the line organization, but also by some projects within a broader project portfolio. We also see activities around strategic monitoring and performance management.

Let us briefly discuss a project-driven approach. For example, in the case of a large project or transformation project, we can typically assume that there is a thoroughly developed, and therefore existing project charter with clearly defined project objectives. These kind of projects typically span multiple lines of business, such as manufacturing, supply chain, sales, accounting, and others. In these projects, which require a significant budget, the question of how value will be added to the various strategies must be answered up front. In addition, to get a project started, a steering committee and stakeholders must be defined to ensure that project costs are invested in the right way to maximize strategic value for each of the business units involved. Therefore, strategic ideation and strategic decisions are most likely to occur in such project-driven approaches. Strategy operationalization and monitoring is ideally integrated into the value realization management of such large projects and supported by project management standards.

In the next chapters, we will discuss the top-down approach.

With the above activities, we will most likely not end up with a fully populated table. However, based on our records, we will have sufficient input at all levels of detail with sufficiently clear descriptions of the requirements for each item. As such, it will be a source for valuable further analysis, which we will present next. In addition, we will be able to expand and enrich this structure next time.

Key considerations for developing a BI strategy

- It is advisable to break down a strategy into a tabular structure to transparently link the BI requirements identified so far to the strategy with its strategic cornerstones, and at the same time to trace back to prove the value contribution of BI. It is also advisable to follow a top-down approach.
- Don't be confused if some strategic statements look odd, or if you see "white spaces" that should have been filled but aren't.
- Aim to clearly link business requirements for BI to business strategies and even corporate strategy, as this will improve the ability to explain the value contribution of business intelligence. If this results in a consistent and easily digestible strategic story, it is of great value.
- Try to further decompose and translate the collected business requirements in such a way that patterns and commonalities can be identified. This will allow you to identify possible synergies and thus opportunities for efficiency gains.

3.3 How to Consolidate BI Requirements in a Meaningful Way

In the previous chapter, we learned how to further decompose a given strategy.

In this chapter, we will now take the next step and structure our recorded requirements in a way that allows us to even better identify similarities. This will be our single source to detect patterns, commonalities and provide us opportunities for later effective and efficient determination of new BI solutions and services. Idea: develop a new BI service once, serve many businesses.

One simple and effective structure is to decompose, translate and finally consolidate requirements into four sections:

New BI content (KPIs, master data, analytical dimensions, hiearchies, etc.)
New BI processes (capturing requirements, service delivery, monitoring, etc.)
New BI structure (organization, goverance, etc.)
New BI tools & architecture (analytical tools, integrations, backend, etc.)

First, the "new" should indicate to the reader that we are not talking about maintaining a current situation as it is. The reason for this is that the business obviously requires something additional or different, in short, something new that does not currently exist.

For each row of the table we introduced in the previous subchapter, we now reflect the existing business requirement descriptions and try to translate the business terminology into BI language. In other words: What does the business requirement mean to us as BI professionals? What is new? What should be changed? Usually, we can expect these descriptions to touch not just one of the four sections above, but several or even all of them.

How does this look in detail?

In the next example, we will translate the requirement "Business process performance (BPP) measurement and BPP analytics capability" into these sections as shown in Table 3.3. To ease readability, we removed the leading columns of our larger table but bear in mind that they still exist.

The example above needs to be conducted for each row in our table. This means that we analyze the business requirement such as "Deliver ongoing insight into the performance of business processes" and decompose the requirement into meaningful requirements for each of the four sections. Don't get discouraged if you have trouble filling in a column. Just move on to the next column or move on to the next business requirement. As you gain experience, you can go back to the previous requirement and you may have an idea. Keep in mind that at the enterprise level, we will have quite a large table, so this exercise will take some time to complete.

Table 3.3 Structure for decomposing a strategy—example

[…]	Original requirement	New BI content	New BI processes	New BI structure	New BI tools & architecture
[…]	"Deliver ongoing insight into the performance of business processes"	New BI content: Process performance data like • time to close books • first time pass	New process for process perfomance measurement and analysis like • From separated to embedded reporting • Define process stages with quality gates and data points	New skills required to perform process analytics like • New roles and authorizations • New target setting principles • Definition of process governance • Clarifying areas of responsibilities	New BI tools and corresponding architecture with new functionalities regarding BPM analytics and advanced analysis like • Process mining • Workflows • Alerting

However, once you are done, you will have a solid foundation for the future and you probably will not need to do this in this level of detail too often.

Once you have completed this exercise to the level described, there are several benefits:

1. We can identify patterns and potential commonalities, such as new analytical content or new analytical process support.
2. We have a solid basis for identifying synergies across different user groups within business units and/or initiatives. This, in turn, will help us avoid "reinventing the wheel."
3. The improved visibility will help us leverage existing or new solutions, thereby increasing our level of standardization of BI solutions and services.
4. The increased level of standardization will support overall efficiency goals.
5. We will have opportunities to reduce overall costs

3.4 How to Improve Captured Input

In the previous chapters, we decomposed a given strategy and connected strategic requirements with tangible BI requirements.

However, what if we identify some anomalies like white spots, areas where we were not able to deduct our BI requirements? In this chapter, we will detail some examples of such patterns and support the reader with approaches on how to deal with these anomalies.

Let us assume that the achieved tabular outcome looks somewhat incomplete, as illustrated in Fig. 3.8 below. We now want to look into this overview from a quality management point of view. Possible questions are as follows:

- In which areas do we see anomalies unexpected patterns or incompleteness?
- What (standardized) strategies do we have at hand to address these issues?

There might be several anomalies at the same time. Therefore, let us approach them step by step. Let us start by looking at Fig. 3.9.

Potential findings

- In Fig. 3.9, we detect that for some strategic objectives given by the business, the resulting business requirements for BI are not specified (A).

What is the likely challenge of the scenario?

- It is not possible to describe requested expectations toward the improvement of BI capabilities to offer even better BI value-contributing services to the business.

Strategic corner-stones	Business Area	Business Sub Area/Initiative	Strategic Objective	Business BI Requirement / Need	Initial idea of a possible NEW BI Capability	New BI Content	New BI Processes	New BI structure	New BI tools & architecture
Improve Operational Excellence	Finance	Budgetting and Planning	Ease the budgetting process.	Reporting assistance e.g. to consolidate department budget versions and fore-casting consequences of a budget draft.	People: Consultancy for budget process optimization	*None*	*None*	*None*	*None*
Capture the Full Potential of the Service Business	Service	Boosting service competitiveness	France turnaround is key to reach FC profitability in the service business Service business will aim to capture the value from the service business turnaround in Italy			*None*	*None*	*None*	*None*
Capture the Full Potential of the Service Business	Service		Supply Chain Operations aim to improve the delivery performance of spare parts through optimization of distribution network, better FC and local sourcing Service business will prepare for scale and expand component FC on transactional business			*None*	*None*	*None*	*None*
Reduce Levelized Cost Of Energy	Sourcing, logistics and warehousing		Analysis on the 'quality' of a vendor, including - ability to meet deadlines - quality of deliveries			*None*	*None*	*None*	*None*

Fig. 3.8 Structuring results of analysis (© Exner/Zunic 2024. All Rights Reserved)

Strategic corner-stones	Business Area	Business Sub Area/Initiative	Strategic Objective	Business BI Requirement / Need	Initial idea of a possible NEW BI Capability	New BI Content	New BI Processes	New BI structure	New BI tools & architecture
Improve Operational Excellence	Finance	Budgetting and Planning	Ease the budgetting process.	Reporting assistance e.g. to consolidate department budget versions and fore-casting consequences of a budget draft.	People: Consultancy for budget process optimization	*None*	*None*	*None*	*None*
Capture the Full Potential of the Service Business	Service	Boosting service competitiveness	France turnaround is key to reach FC profitability in the service business Service business will aim to capture the value from the service business turnaround in Italy	None specified	Unknown	*None*	*None*	*None*	*None*
Capture the Full Potential of the Service Business	Service	Supply chain delivery performance	Supply Chain Operations aim to improve the delivery performance of spare parts through optimization of distribution network, better FC and local sourcing Service business will prepare for scale and expand component FC on transactional business	None specified	Unknown	*None*	*None*	*None*	*None*
Reduce Levelized Cost Of Energy	Sourcing, logistics and warehousing	Vendor Intelligence	Analysis on the 'quality' of a vendor, including - ability to meet deadlines - quality of deliveries	None specified	Unknown	*None*	*None*	*None*	*None*

Fig. 3.9 Looking into the details—example of improvement potential (1/3) (© Exner/Zunic 2024. All Rights Reserved)

How could some small steps of improvement look like?

- One option is to come back to key business stakeholders and to ask for explanation. There might be several and simple reasons for this. However, unless this is not clarified, we only can speculate.
- Another option could be to deepen existing discussions with business stakeholders and strategy owners to achieve a sufficient level of understanding.

Let us take another example. Our table could look like described in Fig. 3.10 (B) Potential findings

- For certain business areas, no subarea/initiative could be assigned. In other words, what is the plan to operationalize the strategy in the particular business area? Who is responsible?

What is the likely challenge of the scenario?

- It is hardly possible to track progress and align operational execution across all activities at the top management level. In the above scenario, business area "Global IT" has no business sub-area/initiatives assigned (see section B). This means that, for whatever reason, it is not possible to cascade the strategic objective down to the next organizational level, and hence the responsibility for it's implementation remains at the level of Global IT. As Global IT (considered a top management function in this example) will most likely not be able to deal with the details of implementation, there is a high probability that the strategic BI requirements will not be implemented at all on operational level. This example shows how BI initiatives can get stuck due to a disconnect between strategy and execution.

How could some small steps of improvement look like?

- Assign responsibilities to operational people.
- Complete as best as possible with an "initial" proposal and ask explicitly for review and feedback from the business. If there is no better counterproposal provided, proceed with the existing one.

In practice, there might be other anomalies, but after these two exercises, we now will have a look at a "best practice" example, as illustrated in Fig. 3.11, in which we see a good filling of the various sections.

Findings

- Good content and structured input to further detail requirements toward new BI capabilities.

Strategic corner-stones (1)	Business Area (1)	Business Sub Area/Initiative (1)	Strategic Objective (1)	Business BI Requirement / Need (1)	Initial idea of a possible NEW BI Capability (1)	New BI Content (2)	New BI Processes (3)	New BI structure (4)	New BI tools & architecture (5)
Grow Profitably in Mature and Emerging Markets	Sales & Marketing	Profitability calculation	Improve speed and reliability of price setting through historic sales data.	Historic sales data available for analysis. Enable standardization of price setting.	Grow Profitably in Mature and Emerging Markets	*New BI content: Historic sales data*	*None*	*None*	*None*
Improve Operational Excellence	Corporate	Business Process Management (Supply chain)	Enable BPM analysis for process performance optimization	Facilitate BI competencies for Business specialists and platform for doing BPM analysis	Impro Operational Excellence	*New BI content: Process performance data*	*New process for process performance measurement and analysis*	*New skills required to perform process analytics*	*New BI tools and architecture with new functions regarding BPM analytics and adv. analysis*
Improve Operational Excellence	Global IT		Actively bring opportunities for digital services	Actively bring opportunities for analytic services to the bus and collaborate in service development	Improve Operational Excellence	*New BI content: Data for analytical purpose*	*New BI processes for analytics engagement*	*New skills required to engage actively in analytic development*	*New front end analytic/visualization tools and corresponding architecture*
Improve Operational Excellence	Global IT	(B)	Deliver ongoing insight into the performance of business processes	Business process performance measurement and BPP analytics capability	Improve Operational Excellence	*New BI content: Process performance data*	*New process for process performance measurement and analysis*	*New skills required to perform process analytics*	*New BI tools and architecture with new functions regarding BPM analytics and adv. analysis*
Improve Operational Excellence	Global IT		Engage and participate in business planning	Engage with business and IT business partner to capture BI requirements		*None*	*New process to Optimize engagement model for Data & Analytics*	*New skill required to engage and do business requirement capturing*	*None*

Fig. 3.10 Looking into the details—example of improvement potential (2/3) (© Exner/Zunic 2024. All Rights Reserved)

Strategic corner-stones	Business Area	Business Sub Area/Initiative	Strategic Objective	Business BI Requirement / Need	Initial idea of a possible NEW BI Capability	New BI Content	New BI Processes	New BI structure	New BI tools & architecture
Grow Profitably in Mature and Emerging Markets	Sales & Marketing	Profitability calculation	Improve speed and reliability of price setting through historic sales data.	Historic sales data available for analysis. Enable standardization of price setting.	Grow Profitably in Mature and Emerging Markets	*New BI content: Historic sales data*	*None*	*None*	*None*
Improve Operational Excellence	Corporate	Business Process Management (Supply chain)	Enable BPM analysis for process performance optimization	Facilitate BI competencies for Business specialists and platform for doing BPM analysis	Impro Operational Excellence	*New BI content: Process performance data*	*New process for process performance measurement and analysis*	*New skills required to perform process analytics*	*New BI tools and architecture with new functions regarding BPM analytics and adv. analysis*
Improve Operational Excellence	Global IT	Global solution architect community	Actively bring opportunities for digital services	Actively bring opportunities for analytic services to the bus and collaborate in service development	Improve Operational Excellence	*New BI content: Data for analytical purpose*	*New BI processes for analytics engagement*	*New skills required to engage actively in analytic development*	*New front end analytic/visualization tools and corresponding architecture*
Improve Operational Excellence	Global IT	Initiative to implement Process Performance Indicators (PPI´s)	Deliver ongoing insight into the performance of business processes	Business process performance measurement and BPP analytics capability	Improve Operational Excellence	*New BI content: Process performance data*	*New process for process performance measurement and analysis*	*New skills required to perform process analytics*	*New BI tools and architecture with new functions regarding BPM analytics and adv. analysis*
Improve Operational Excellence	Global IT	Global solution architect community	Engage and participate in business planning	Engage with business and IT business partner to capture BI requirements		*None*	*New process to Optimize engagement model for Data & Analytics*	*New skill required to engage and do business requirement capturing*	*None*

Subsequent consolidation of interim results

Fig. 3.11 Looking into the details—example of improvement potential (3/3) (© Exner/Zunic 2024. All Rights Reserved)

What is the likely challenge?

- None, as a transparent and traceable link of new BI delivery to given strategic requirements is provided.
- None, as transparent value contribution of BI improvements to given business strategies does exist.

How could some small steps of improvement look like?

- None.

Based on Fig. 3.11, the resulting content of each of the three sections BI content/KPIs, BI processes, and BI structure will again be input for discussion of the other areas, such as BI architecture. In other words, the key is to treat the pillars not isolated but as tightly integrated, as illustrated in Fig. 3.12. Ideally, the sequence is to start with content/KPIs, then process, structure and finally BI solutions and architecture. However, in case the recorded requirement points straight forward to a specific section, do not get confused, just question how this relates to the other sections. Typically, the items are not isolated.

Let us discuss the four sections. Similar to the Balanced Scorecard with its perspectives, the four sections provide a good approach to investigating the essential relationships.

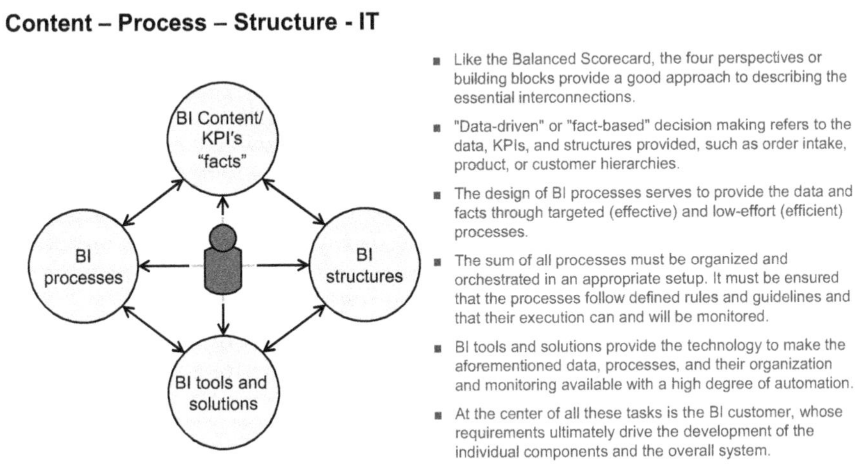

Fig. 3.12 Interconnectivity of BI Content, BI processes, BI structures, BI tools and the BI customer

- The section "BI content"/KPIs "facts" refers to the data, KPIs, and structures provided, such as order intake, product, or customers along different hierarchies, such as sales channels, responsibility centers, and others.
- The design of BI processes serves to provide the data and facts through targeted (effective) and low-effort (efficient) processes.
- The sum of all processes must be organized and orchestrated in an appropriate setup. It must be ensured that the processes follow defined rules and guidelines and that their execution can and will be monitored. In Fig. 3.12, all the organizational aspects are considered in the section "BI structures."
- Finally, BI tools and solutions provide the technology to make the aforementioned data, processes, and their organization and monitoring available with a high degree of automation.
- At the very center of all these tasks is the BI customer, whose requirements ultimately drive the development of individual components and the overall system.

The outcome of the discussions in one section might lead to change requests and needs for further optimization in other sections as well as in BI organization (→ BI architecture advisory board/governance) or BI processes (processes/governance). Even if as a first result for a given row in the table one of the sections might be empty, double-check if there are truly no relationships or cross-dependencies to the other sections. Ask yourself, why this is the case and what good reason would support this specific pattern.

During the decomposition of business strategy, the practitioners know which topics will be touched quite regularly: It is governance. From a big picture perspective, we must distinguish between overarching governance, "strategic" business governance, and BI governance, as illustrated in Fig. 3.13. If we face challenges in sharing and bridging business requirements and objectives with BI or difficulties in aligning strategies as such, one reason may be that different governance views or philosophies coexist.

Due to the high relevance of the governance topic, we will not explore this topic within this chapter. Instead, we refer to Chap. 5 Organizing BI Strategy.

To summarize into a transparent and structured overview of all requirements, it is a good idea to record the content in a table. This table becomes quite big, hence tends to become very busy and very detailed. This is still good and serves its purpose. However, having our ambition to develop a BI strategy in mind, we also want to attract our target group of stakeholders, so we have to focus on key topics that matter most. Obviously, such a table is not a good option for communicating BI requirements on a strategic level.

Aiming for better support of communicating BI requirements, their origin and, most importantly, the conclusions on a BI strategic level, it might be worth thinking about developing a wiki-page on a collaboration platform or simply a word document next to the large table (Fig. 3.14). This will support easier reading and consumption.

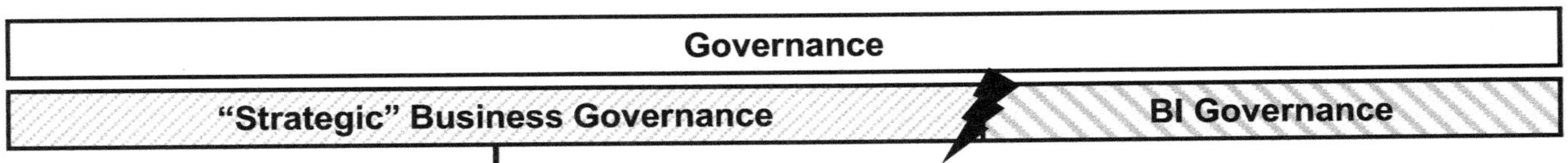

Strategic corner-stones	Business Area	Business Sub Area/Initiative	trategic Objective	Business BI Requirement / Need	Initial idea of a possible NEW BI Capability	New BI Content	New BI Processes	New BI structure	New BI tools & architecture
Capture the Full Potentia of the Servic Business	Service	Continuous Improvement Management	iscover patterns in ailures on the main omponents of the urbines, making it ossible to use this in reventive maintenance hereby minimizing urbine downtime.	Analyse patterns in failures on the main components of the turbines and report to preventive maintenance.	People: Data model development, new competencies/resource allocation Technology: DW Integration with CIR. Self service data analysis	*Component Inspection Report component failure data*	*Support getting access to relevant data, plus how to use tools for analysis*	*Appropriate governance required to protect data against misuse*	*New BI analysis tools and corresponding holistically new BI architecture*
Grow Profitably in Mature and Emerging Markets	Sales & Marketing	Market intelligence	arket intelligence vailable to enable ifferentiated value added ervices to various egments	Market intelligence available in Sales cockpit	Tech: Integration of Market data in SAP BW. Dashboard. People: DW Data model development. Process: Self service data mashup and analysis ?	*New BI content: Market data*	*None*	*New skills required in order to design & implement sales cockpit (analytic/visualization application)*	*New BI tools and corresponding holistically new BI architecture including new integration capabilities for external data.*
Improve Operational Excellence	Global IT		ngage and participate in usiness planning	Engage with business and IT business partner to capture BI requirements	People: Engagement and requirement capturing skill	*None*	*New process to Optimize engagement model for Data & Analytics*	*New skill required to engage and do business requirement capturing*	*None*
Improve Operational Excellence	Global IT	Master Data Management	aster Data reporting nd analysis	Platform for doing MD quality reporting/analysis. Self service capable		*New BI content: Master Data for all objects*	*New BI processes: Data quality KPI process for definition, measure and operation.*	*New skills required to develop and support master data quality analysis/reporting*	*New MD quality tools and corresponding architecture*

Fig. 3.13 Area of conflict between different governance views or philosophies (© Exner/Zunic 2024. All Rights Reserved)

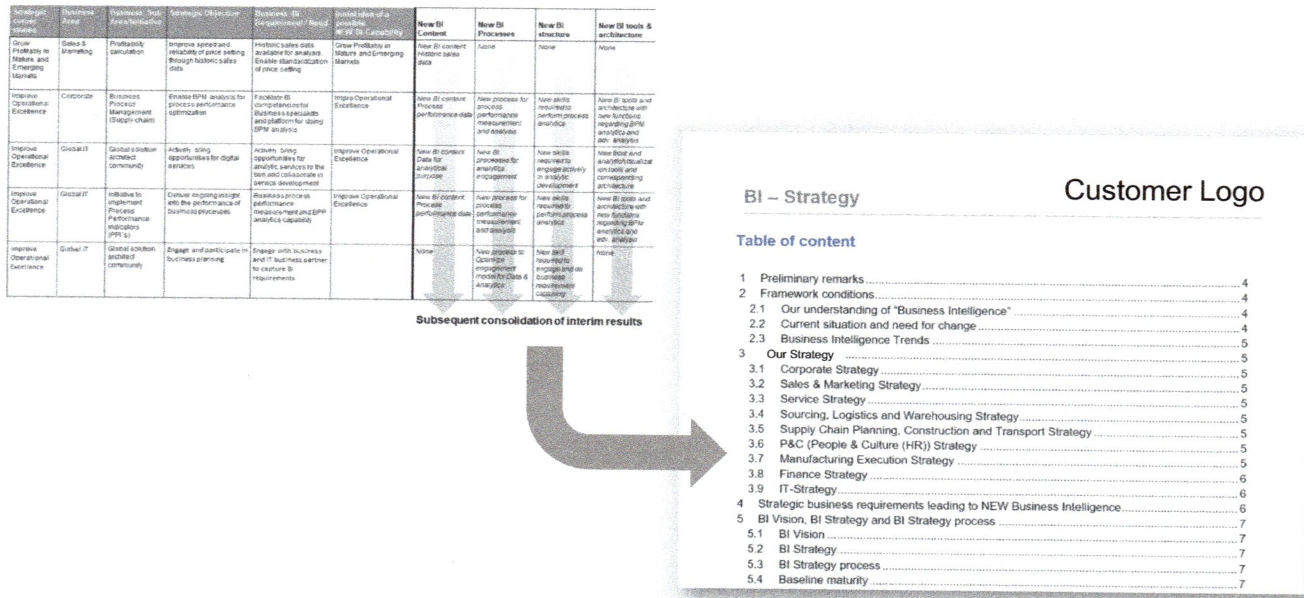

Fig. 3.14 BI strategy development—embedding results into overall BI strategy document (© Exner/Zunic 2024. All Rights Reserved)

How to get started? In this chapter, we introduced the principle of decomposing BI requirements from given corporate or business area strategies.

Key considerations for developing a BI strategy

- Be careful with the input you collect, as it may show some areas with missing information or insufficient quality. Develop strategies to address these issues in general, rather than investing in improvements on a case-by-case basis.
- Be aware that a summary of all requirements will result in a very large, very busy, and very detailed table. Aim to find an appropriate tool setup to handle such large structures in a collaborative multi-user environment.

3.5 How to Improve Strategic Alignment Maturity

Based on a decomposed given strategy and bridged strategic requirements to a tangible level of BI requirements, we now have achieved a significant milestone. However, this achievement could be easily perceived as final instead of a part of a journey. We should aim for a stable process which enables us to sustain and to continuously improve. In other words, we are talking about climbing up a ladder of maturity including a regular assessment of current BI maturity (BI maturity assessment).

In the following sub-chapter, we will introduce some benefits coming with a usage of maturity model. We first will explore the approach of different maturity levels and bridge these generic levels to a more BI-related context. Second, we will describe, how an exemplary BI maturity model could work to provide further guidance for practitioners.

One possible starting point for improving business intelligence is to assess current BI maturity. As many maturity models exist, we will only highlight those aspects that most of these models have in common. The basic idea of this approach is not to be exhaustive but to provide first hands-on guidance to get started.

The intended outcome of a BI maturity analysis is first of all a determination of the status quo. This enables to quickly focus on the most relevant issues instead of wasting time and money. The emphasis is on "quick," not on thoroughly assessing all real-life details. They of course still exist; however, typically in assessments, the most relevant issues will be mentioned first, regardless of the audience.

In Sect. 3.3, we took a very simplistic maturity assessment approach: There, our "maturity model" consists of just two levels:

- "Green" = Pain-point is not existing or is not perceived as relevant
- "Red" = Problem statement is perceived as valid

Of course, it is not a true maturity model because it does not provide further guidance like a true maturity model does. However, its value should not be underestimated in the early stages of assessment, when the goal is to capture the most relevant areas for improvement quickly. Let us now have a look into typical maturity models.

A BI maturity model (BI-MM) typically covers several areas for evaluation, such as information needs/KPIs, governance, processes, and IT architecture areas, like applications and technology. These areas are combined into a structured overall BI maturity framework. Based on the BI maturity framework, either a self-assessment or a consulting-supported assessment can be conducted.

The assessment compares the current situation and corresponding maturity level with a target maturity level that is perceived as both attractive and feasible. This comparison results in the determination of a gap, which ideally indicates the first areas for improvement and the direction of change.

In addition to the discussions during the assessment itself, it is advisable to question the underlying assumptions and reasons for judgments. In particular, the full responses should be recorded. The advantage of this approach is that hidden arguments may surface and become transparent. Be prepared for possibly unknown or even strange answers to be put on the table. All of these items are relevant and should be noted and, more importantly, considered.

As the assessment topics are different, so are the gaps. Either small gaps will be identified in areas where the current maturity is quite close to the target maturity or larger gaps may be identified in areas where the target maturity is significantly higher than the current maturity. Either way, the results will allow you to identify the most relevant areas for improvement.

Key benefits at a glance

- The overview of maturity will guide straightforward to the main areas for improvement.
- Based on this information prioritization of main fields of activities will become possible and transparent.
- Resource allocation to the right areas allowing to exploit highest potentials is supported.
- One deliverable is a structured profile of the BI-related processes and other areas.
- Based on the information gathered the potential for BI improvements will be shown.

As mentioned earlier, there exist a vast variety of maturity models. Many of them have been designed to serve a specific purpose or target audience, such as information technology, enterprise architecture, project management, and quality management.

Nevertheless, there are some commonalities. They all provide a pre-defined set of different maturity levels, typically starting with a lower numbering indicating a low maturity to a higher numbering indicating a higher maturity level. Some maturity models introduce different terminologies indicating the different maturity levels, but this is less relevant for a basic understanding. Each level is designed to measure how well certain KPIs, processes, governance rules, and solutions have been implemented. Typically, a certain level is assumed to be reached when the requirements of this level as well as all the previous maturity levels is met.

All maturity models are based on observation. Therefore, there is no neutral instance for the assessment to have the exact same results independent of the respondents. In other words, if you perform an assessment based on a certain maturity model, you may get different results from different groups of respondents.

Most maturity models provide between four and six different maturity levels. Depending on the origin of a maturity model and the target group of the maturity assessment, the definitions of the different maturity levels differ. However, it is generally advisable to use a maturity model that is based on an equal number of maturity levels, as this forces respondents to make a decision about whether they perceive current maturity to be above average or below average. Since the average maturity level is not available for selection, such maturity models tend not to produce averages and therefore less meaningful results.

We do not claim that the maturity level definitions introduced below, will be a perfect fit to all real-life scenarios. However, they should provide sufficient transparency on the current situation, describe a desired target maturity level, and finally identify hotspots of most relevant improvement potential. Following this approach, maturity models allow to systematically define interim targets and monitor progress toward goals as (interim) target maturity levels.

A maturity framework can be used to record observations about where your company is on the improvement journey. You can develop a strategy that addresses specific burning issues by identifying the gaps between the current and target maturity levels.

- *Maturity Level 0—Inadequate*: This maturity level is typically the lowest, indicating that very basic fundamentals are not in place or are so incomplete or error-prone that they fail to meet basic requirements.
- *Maturity Level 1—Basic*: This level first shows that very basic fundamentals are in place. However, the achievement of specific results is highly dependent on current circumstances. The work results are difficult to predict and are only satisfactory when the conditions are good.
- *Maturity Level 2—Stabilized*: At this next level of maturity, the work results are satisfactory, even if the conditions are challenging. They are no longer difficult to predict because the production of results follows a standardized approach. In

addition, the execution of this standardized approach is planned, monitored, and compared to the plan.

- *Maturity Level 3—Extended*: In the aforementioned maturity level, the underlying assumption was to assess maturity at, say, the departmental level. In this next maturity level, we extend the reach of maturity to the entire organization. This is valuable because most results are based on cross-departmental collaboration and coordination. To achieve sustainable, stable results, new standards must be introduced, trained, and established, and thus extended into the daily work of the entire company.
- *Maturity Level 4—Data Driven*: The next level of maturity can be characterized by replacing potentially subjective judgment, including potential bias, with a fact-based decision-making approach. In other words, the production of results within the entire enterprise is based on a standardized, cross-departmental way of working, considering end-to-end performance aspects that are continuously monitored based on numbers and underlying data. Thus, the organization can be described as "data-driven."
- *Maturity Level 5—Intelligent Enterprise*: The highest level of maturity is achieved when not only all the previous criteria are met, but the entire organization is built on continuous and reinforcing agility and innovation based on established closed-loop thinking and acting. This includes the systematic root-cause analysis of identified variances between actual and target performance levels throughout the entire value chain. The options for decision-making, the best option chosen as the final decision, and the resulting realized actions ("data to impact") to overcome the deviations are recorded. The success rate of achieving the intended impact is determined, continuously monitored, and recorded to serve as a basis for similar decision scenarios. In addition, this way of working and thinking is no longer limited by organizational boundaries but is extended to an even broader, cross-company business network. In this way, the organization can be described as an "Intelligent Enterprise."

Figure 3.15 illustrates such a BI maturity model.

The approach we have taken so far has been a specific one, as we have introduced a rather generic description of maturity. It is worth mentioning that in addition to this approach to assessing process maturity, there is another approach that focuses on the expected results. Therefore, before conducting a maturity assessment, we need to decide if we are going to assess the process itself (A in Fig. 3.16), which is necessary to achieve a certain result, as mentioned before, or if we are going to assess the result itself (B in Fig. 3.16).

In the first case A, we can ask ourselves to decide on the process-related maturity levels observed. In case B, it is essential to have a high-quality overarching BI process model available. This BI process model needs to clearly describe for each of the maturity levels not just a generic level of minimum achievement, but it needs to document concrete deliverables explicitly and completely per maturity level.

Let us now have a look into more concrete guiding questions, which may help us to determine a BI maturity level based on case A, thus we focus more on the

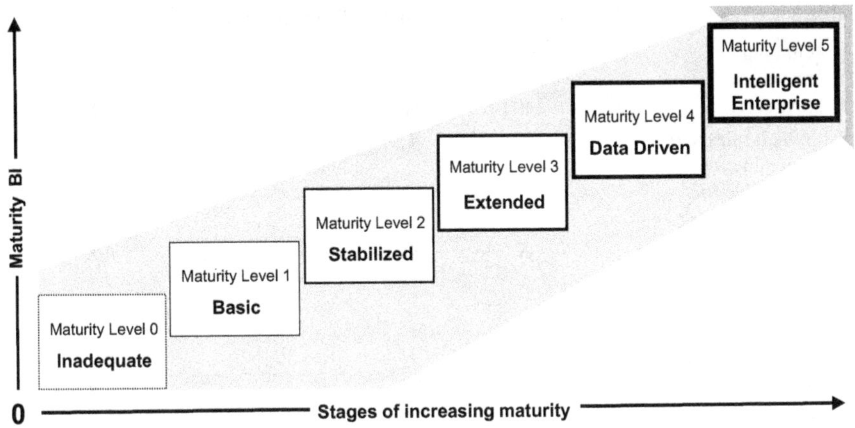

Fig. 3.15 BI Maturity model—path to the Intelligent Enterprise (© Exner/Zunic 2024. All Rights Reserved)

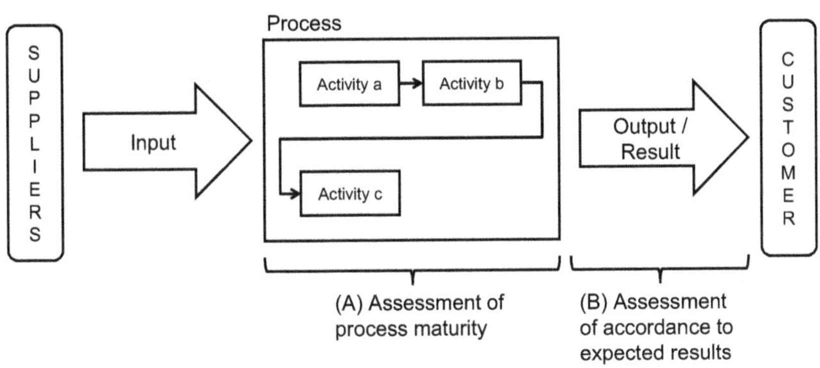

Fig. 3.16 Simplified process model illustrating different assessment types (© Exner/Zunic 2024. All Rights Reserved)

processes. Please note, that in order to keep this example crisp and clear, these guiding questions are not complete. Quite independent from an individual BI process, we can, for example, ask the following questions as illustrated in Table 3.4. Based on the observed level of satisfaction with the results, we determine the appropriate maturity level M0 to M5. Let us take an example.

Why is there no cross in the "M0" column? We assume that according to our definition, the process does not exist as such, or it is missing its target. We cannot describe any rules or purpose of the BI process. In other words, if nobody is able to describe which rules and guidelines apply to a BI process, we assume the lowest level of maturity (M0). If we find somebody, who is able to describe which rules and guidelines apply to a BI process and, in addition to this, is able to explain the purpose of the BI process, its target and proves that the process targets are achieved, we

Table 3.4 Exemplary guiding questions for determining BI process maturity

#	Guiding questions (extract)	M0	M1	M2	M3	M4	M5
1	Which rules and guidelines are applicable for the BI process?		X	X	X	X	X
2	What is the purpose of the BI process? Is target clear and achieved?		X	X	X	X	X
3	Who is explicitly responsible for the BI process execution?			X	X	X	X
4	What processes precede the BI process?			X	X	X	X
5	Which products/ services/ resources are required to run the BI process?			X	X	X	X
6	Which processes follow the BI process?			X	X	X	X
7	How do you determine satisfaction of BI customers related to the process?				X	X	X
8	How many people (FTE) are regularly required to execute the BI process?					X	X
9	Based on which methods do you continuously optimize the BI process?						X

are now on the next maturity level, which is maturity level 1 (M1). Assuming that we can satisfactorily answer all questions up to and including question 6, but not question 7, we would conclude that we have reached maturity level two (M2) based on the table above.

Let us now have a look into a case B example. As we learned before, it is essential to have a high-quality overarching BI process model available, which allows comprehensible judgement by its clear descriptions of the different achievements per maturity level. In this case, we need to define the expected results per maturity level as a stable reference prior to the assessment. What sounds like a pretty obvious approach turns out to be challenging in practice. The reason for this challenge is the pace of innovation, which results in new technologies, approaches, and methodologies being introduced. For further details, please refer to Sect. 3.4. If you do not know what is coming in the near future, it is hard to outline a stable reference on which to base a maturity assessment. Especially in situations where such an assessment is planned the first time, it is an additionally challenging exercise, as it is hard to find a well-established framework that serves all requirements. In such scenarios, it may be advisable to call for consulting support.

It is worth mentioning that it is possible to have different levels of maturity in different areas at the time of the assessment (also applies to the previous MM approach).

To illustrate what an exemplary BI maturity model could look like, please refer to the next Fig. 3.17.

If we now take the above exemplary scenario, the main reasons for the maturity judgment could be as follows:

- No vision and tangible BI strategy of future state BI landscape.
- Limited overall valid guiding principles/governance (only in IT).
- Numerous side reports, partly limited drill-down capabilities alongside various unharmonized dimensions.
- Limited consistency of information due to many different views.
- Many ad hoc requests, acceptance of insufficiencies, no integrated holistic concepts, side reporting.

These observations may indicate a current maturity level that is Level 1 in some areas and Level 2 in others. Using these as a starting point, we can now develop reasonable recommendations for improvement toward Level 3 maturity, such as

- Main key financial data are reliable, such as revenue and EBIT, which can be seen as a good starting point for extending the KPIs and Analytics which must be used in a highly standardized way.
- First improvements within context of current projects evolving (i.e., Key Users, shaping of roles and responsibilities). These improvements aim to strengthen the business governance and aim to establish a BI-Competence Center in future.
- Components already exist, but lack an overall BI strategy and BI organization to provide clear guidance. This can be seen as a call for action to develop a holistic BI strategy.

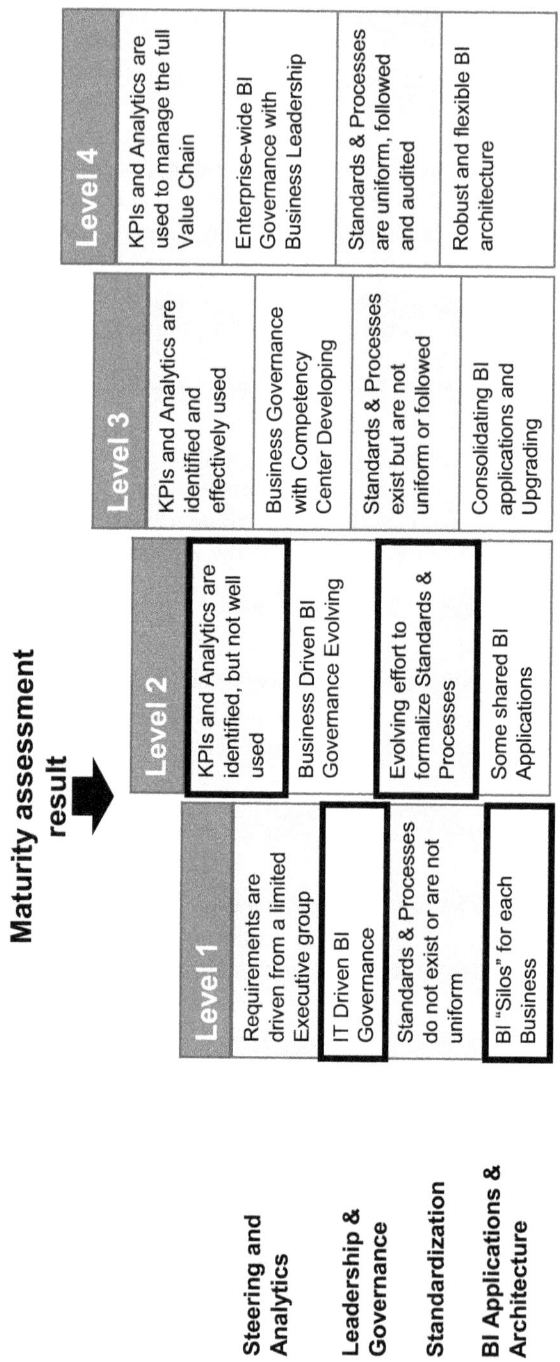

Fig. 3.17 BI Maturity model—Exemplary BI maturity assessment result (as-is)

In general, there is "no magic formula" to build such kind of a roadmap, but usually the approach is to move from left to right within the maturity model.

Key considerations for developing a BI strategy

- A maturity model provides additional guidance to stabilize processes, which can enable BI practitioners to sustain or to continuously improve the way of working.
- Due to the large variety of available maturity models to choose from it can be cumbersome to identify the most suitable one for a business intelligence roadmap.
- In any case, climbing up the maturity ladder should not be confused with producing tangible value add to BI customers. A higher maturity level should rather be valued as improving the predictability of processes and process results.

From Vision to BI Strategy

4

Without a clear process, a BI strategy simply cannot be developed. This process consists of multiple activities in a defined sequence and is typically iterated in defined cycles. To be able to direct these activities to a common and sustainable goal, it is additionally valuable to agree on a north star/vision upfront.

First, we will explore how to develop an attractive vision statement and which characteristics should be considered for further calibration.

Second, we will discuss the development of a BI strategy as such. However, how does a process for developing a BI strategy look like in detail? How to balance all the related strategic requirements toward BI while at the same time providing a sustainable and robust foundation for BI strategy development and enhancements. These and some more questions will be answered in this chapter.

4.1 BI Vision and Characteristics of a Good Vision Statement

Developing a meaningful and attractive BI vision is by no means a pure academic task. It provides guidance toward a specific direction of the BI journey, which is underpinned by a BI strategy, which we will discuss later. The BI vision statement helps to understand what this visionary ultimate long-term goal is. Thus, it helps to eliminate unintended other possible options. By describing the BI vision by a statement, it will help us to focus.

R. Exner, A. Zunic, *The Path to an Intelligent Enterprise*, Future of Business and Finance, https://doi.org/10.1007/978-3-031-69914-6_4

In this chapter, we will first introduce the basic understanding of developing a BI vision in terms of time horizon and sequence of typical activities. Based on this, we afterwards discuss key characteristics of a good BI vision statement and finally, we will explain benefits for BI managers.

A vision statement is explaining your future state, so what is the organization heading toward. As such, a BI vision outlines the most attractive future state scenario for Business Intelligence. This future state is typically associated with a long-term horizon. In a highly innovative environment such as business intelligence, a 5-year or even a 3-year horizon might be perceived as far outside of a reasonable range. There is no common rule, but typically it should be at least 3 years. This approach avoids likely conflicts with the current year and the next year which might be touched by the upcoming or already ongoing budgeting process. Furthermore, stakeholders are challenged to avoid a trap of linearity and confirmation bias by simply extrapolating already agreed upon operative objectives as, for example, by cutting costs here and improving service delivery there.

However, the vision itself does not describe any means by which this future state will be achieved. Instead, it should clearly explain attributes of the future state scenario that are admirable and attractive to all stakeholders and people concerned. The reason is that there are likely many obstacles, barriers, and organizational resistance along the road, such as conflicting targets, budget constraints, and key people leaving the company. We will only get closer to our vision if we are motivated to overcome these obstacles.

One guiding example is outlined by Tom Wright in his article "How to Write a Good Vision Statement" (Wright, 2022). He states: "A vision statement is the anchor point of any strategic plan. It outlines what an organization would like to ultimately achieve and gives purpose to the existence of the organization."

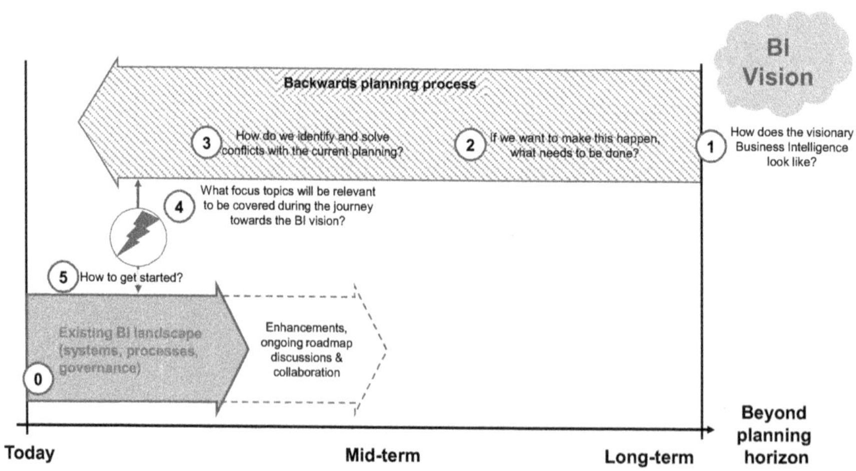

Fig. 4.1 BI vision in a time horizon context—The big picture

Translated to our scope of Business Intelligence, and assuming the "organization" is the BI organization, this makes perfect sense. Referring to our previous Sect. 1.2, where we discussed the key characteristics of an Intelligent Enterprise, this visionary view could serve as an exemplary desirable vision.

Based on the approach illustrated in Fig. 4.1 above, the typical steps are as follows:

0. The number 0 describes the current situation and starting point today.
1. The number 1 in above Fig. 4.1 is the development of a BI vision (we will explain later in this chapter). Currently, this can be imagined as a "future commitment," such as "exploring the world sites during retirement" in your personal life.
2. Assuming we have developed this BI vision, we start backward planning by asking ourselves "What do we need to do to get close to the vision, knowing that it will not be achieved in its entirety?"
3. Most likely plans already exist, either short term, medium term or even long term. Therefore, when we compare backward planning with other existing plans, we need to ask ourselves the third question: "How do we identify and resolve conflicts between the plans? Such conflicts could be, for example, that the underlying assumptions about resource availability are fundamentally different.
4. In practice, we will face many unanswered questions. Especially in larger organizations, it is like throwing a "visionary needle" into a haystack and then starting to search. Therefore, we need to focus our activities: "What are the most important issues to address during the journey?" Is it resource availability, like number of experts, or is it funding? Is it access to innovation?
5. "How do we get started?" is the fifth question. There are usually many ways to move forward and many questions to answer, but often, there is not much time to complete this exercise of connecting a vision to our current planning. Again, the key is focus–focus–focus.

Let us now begin to develop a BI vision. To ensure a stable and robust BI vision, a thorough reflection of the most attractive future state is needed. This means that input from various stakeholders is highly valuable and should be actively sought. This helps to establish a strategic dialog with the stakeholders. Furthermore, it helps to gain transparency on potentially divergent views on the desired target state and consequently provides early opportunities for visionary alignment. This strategic dialog should be seen as a platform for consensus building. It should be kept in mind that this process may require several iterations.

Who should own this vision alignment process? If there is a clearly assigned BI owner, he or she would be the ideal candidate to drive these activities. However, in the absence of such a role, or in the absence of organizational visibility or hierarchical power, this becomes a difficult exercise. In such cases, one possible approach could be to identify the stakeholders who are most dissatisfied with the current situation and who strongly miss alignment. This can be done through a stakeholder analysis. These stakeholders can be perceived as potential partners and allies.

The following sequence of activities is described in Fig. 4.2 below:

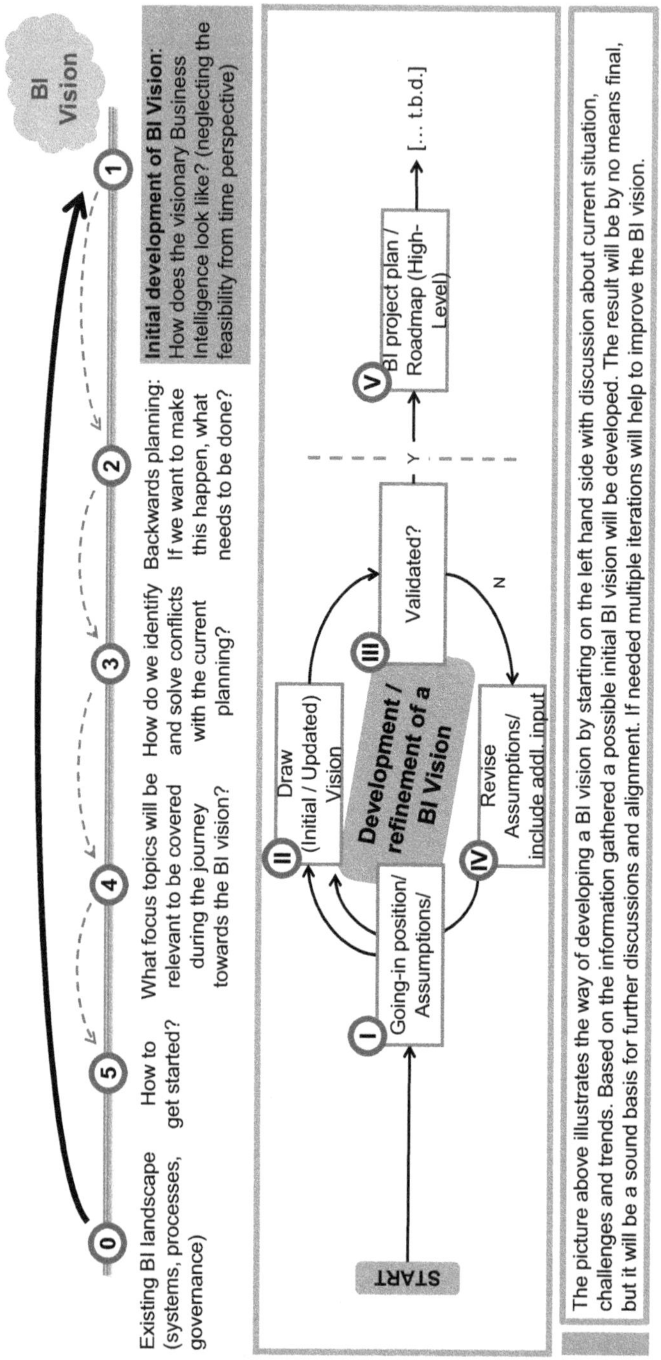

Fig. 4.2 How to develop a BI vision (© Exner/Zunic 2024. All Rights Reserved)

I. First, we start describing a going-in position and assumptions that come to our minds. Especially for people who are not experienced with writing a BI vision statement this might sound unfamiliar, but the key is to start with a creative technique such as brain-writing. The benefit of brain-writing compared to brainstorming is that you can share your initial ideas easily with others and ask for opinions to consider further. With brainstorming in a narrow sense, it is difficult to share thoughts because they are not captured in writing. Of course, the very first ideas will not be final, but they are a starting point. Therefore, let us be patient.
II. Based on step I, we started writing an initial BI vision statement. In the case of an iteration, the current BI vision will be updated.
III. Based on this initial BI vision statement, we validate this statement against the characteristics of a good vision statement, which we explain later in this chapter.
IV. If we are not satisfied with our current BI vision statement, we will revise it. In addition, we review and revise the assumptions, incorporate additional input, and begin the cycle of vision statement development again. We continue with these iterations until we are satisfied with the outcome.
V. Based on the finalized vision statement, we should now be able to use this for further activities such as alignment with a BI project plan and roadmap (if one already exists) or as a reference point for drafting a new BI strategy.

In Fig. 4.2 below, we combined the key content of the previous Fig. 4.1 with the main sequence 0 to 4 (planning horizon including backward planning from final vision to the current situation) and with the more detailed sequence of activities I to V (iterative processing of defining a final vision).

There are several characteristics of a good vision statement such as the following:

- Guiding
- Digestible
- Simple
- Inspirational
- Sustainable
- Specific
- Realistic
- Time based
- Consistent

Let us start with the characteristic of **guiding**.

A vision is a selected future scenario, which radiates the highest attractiveness and thus attraction. The greater the perceived power of attraction is, the more willing people are to move in this direction, and this from their own inner drive. The lower the perceived power of attraction is, for example, due to a low level of attractiveness or even a lack of understanding, the lower is usually the person's own drive. Consequently, in cases where a less attractive future scenario is sought, a greater external drive is needed, for example through incentives, rewards, or possibly also sanctions and disadvantages.

A BI vision, thus, strives to paint an attractive and equally understandable picture of the future, making the many other imaginable pictures of the future pale into insignificance. It is through this focus that a vision becomes a guide.

Digestible

Any BI vision statement should be digestible and easily consumable by a broad audience, including those outside the BI organization. Think from your employees' perspective. Who are the internal customers of your vision? What would they consider meaningful? Is the BI vision easy to consume, or is it so high level ("close to orbit") that no one can capture the essence of your vision statement? Do you need many additional explanations to reach the core of your vision? This may be a sign that the vision is difficult to understand.

Simple

Keep the BI vision statement simple enough for people inside and outside the BI organization to understand the essentials. Avoid extensive use of technical terms, generic or academic statements, or business buzzwords. Communication is the key. This includes a language that is free of buzzwords and jargon. The language must be easy to understand and consume. It is crucial to avoid content that has no apparent connection to business practice or strategy. Keep it short and to the point—no more than two sentences. It is okay to elaborate on a vision statement, but the key is to have a version that is powerful and easy to remember.

Inspirational

Why should the audience remember a vision tomorrow and the day after? Consider possible misinterpretations caused by emphasizing one area or topic over another. By overemphasizing one thing, you may unintentionally devalue others. By simply mentioning one area or topic and not including others, you may accidentally leave them out, which could lead to negative perceptions.

Sustainable

Imagine putting a lot of energy into your BI vision statement, only to have no one remember it a few weeks later. Therefore, strive for a vision statement that is catchy and will be remembered for a long time. Aim for a BI vision statement that is stable and robust enough to remain relevant despite ever-changing environmental factors and innovations.

Specific

Avoid interpreting the BI vision statement too broadly. "Optimized insight to action" sounds good. However, is this statement specific enough to describe other activities that contribute to achieving the vision? Or is it specific enough to exclude other activities that should be neglected? As mentioned earlier, a vision is a selected future scenario that is most appealing. When making this choice, you must exclude many other conceivable images.

Realistic
A BI vision statement that describes a scenario that goes far beyond a realistically achievable target state has limited appeal because no one is truly enthusiastic about it. It may be considered as utopia, that is, an impossible goal. Thus, this approach provides neither a realistic direction nor inspiration. It should be ambitious enough to be exciting but not so ambitious or beyond imagination that it seems unattainable.

Time Based
The time horizon of your BI vision will most likely depend on your organization and industry. However, certainly, any time horizon beyond 3 to 5 years for a BI vision statement should be questioned as to whether it is appropriate. In addition, the time horizon of a BI vision should not be confused with an operational mid- or long-term planning horizon but rather should describe the end of such a time horizon.

Consistent
It needs to align with the company culture and values that you want your workforce to accept as they perform their work. If there are inconsistencies, for example, between vision statements and strategies, people may be confused.

Considering beforementioned characteristics provides a sound starting point for creating a good vision statement. Let us finish off with a look at how a vision statement could look like for Business Intelligence. This vision statement is by no means final, thus, we invite our readers to validate against the above discussed characteristics.

BI Vision

"We design and deliver cross-regional, tailored BI services that are fact-based, decision supporting, and satisfying that every internal customer, who uses our services, does so with a smile."

If we decompose this statement into different elements according to Wright (2022), we can see each at work as follows:

- "We design and deliver cross-regional tailored BI services (1) that are fact-based, decision supporting, and satisfying (2), that every internal customer (3), who uses our services, does so with a smile (4)."
  Step 1—The output (2)—achievable/realistic
  Step 2—The twist (1)—guiding by a clear USP (unique selling point)
  Step 3—The quantification (3)—specific
  Step 4—The human connection (4)—inspirational

Certainly, there are different approaches to writing a vision statement. Choosing the right approach and the most relevant features that reflect a company's individual context will make a BI vision statement unique. However, the above characteristics can help to challenge and improve the maturity of BI vision statements.

Key Considerations for Developing a BI Strategy

- Clearly, consider the corporate culture, values, strategies, and long-term views of the future state of business intelligence by interviewing key stakeholders.
- Address the commitment the BI organization has to its key stakeholders, including BI customers, employees and BI communities.
- Ensure that the BI vision statement is clear and concise.
- Communicate the BI vision in clear, simple, and concise language. Avoid buzzwords, which sometimes tend to mask oversimplified or even meaningless messages.
- Build buy-in and support of all relevant stakeholders across the entire organization.

4.2 Process Model for Developing a BI Strategy

Based on a detailed understanding of the business strategies, which we explored in Chap. 2, and a BI vision, that we explored in Sect. 4.1, we will now introduce a process model for developing the BI strategy itself.

First, we will discuss the key characteristics of a sustainable and robust BI strategy. Based on this, we will introduce a process model for developing a BI strategy. We will explore the different activities and their sequence to support a BI strategy development from scratch. Furthermore, this process model will allow us to revise a possible existing BI strategy as well.

Before we are going to develop a BI strategy in detail, we should be clear about our motivation. We identified three main questions that should be thought through prior to start detailed BI strategy development activities:

1. Why should we develop a BI strategy as such?
2. How does a BI strategy framework look like?
3. How do we organize BI strategy development in an efficient way?

First, the reason for developing a BI strategy is that in many organizations a large number of different reporting and analytical applications are in place, starting from simple spreadsheets up to mature BI solutions, which are either run by business departments themselves or by IT or by a combination of both.

Legacy BI solutions result in significant licensing, maintenance, and operational costs. In addition, poorly aligned initiatives, unclear accountabilities, and

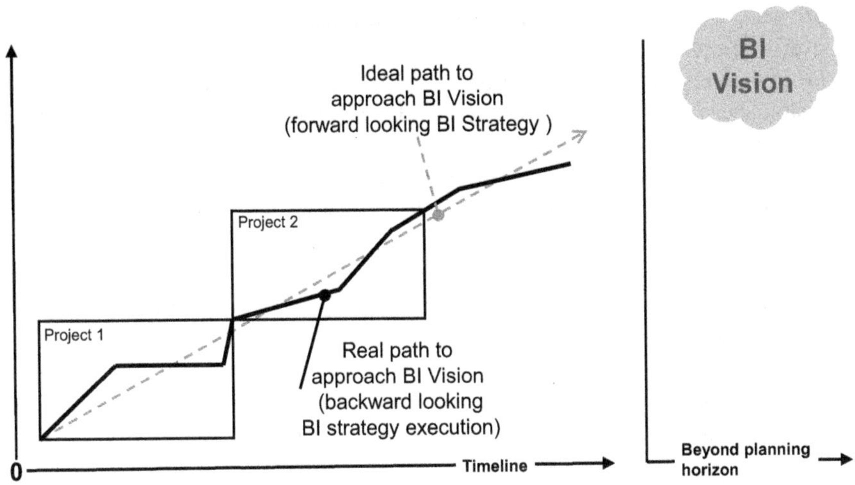

Fig. 4.3 Relationship between BI vision and BI strategy (© Exner/Zunic 2024. All Rights Reserved)

redundancies and overlaps in common work also lead to inefficiencies. A BI strategy framework can provide better direction and levers to reduce operational costs.

The BI strategy can be seen as a means to achieve efficiency. Organizational units and setups are constantly changing to better meet emerging needs. Therefore, BI organizations also need to justify their current setup to stay ahead of the discussion. This requires proving state-of-the-art delivery capabilities at a competitive cost for the entire organization.

As a quick summary, we can say that a BI strategy essentially formalizes the existence of business intelligence in an organization by providing answers to the questions above.

We now want to describe at a high level a process model, including its key activities, that will ultimately provide us a BI strategy. However, before we explore the process model for developing a BI strategy, let us briefly summarize our thinking based on Fig. 4.3 below:

- Starting from our current situation (0), we want to actively shape a future state. Therefore, we are thinking of something like a plan (see Sect. 1.1)
- We describe this future state by a BI vision, knowing that this vision provides us with guidance analog to that of a North Star. With the BI vision, we neglect the feasibility from a time perspective, thus, we assume this future state beyond our long-term planning horizon as illustrated in Fig. 4.3.

- The goal of developing a BI strategy is to have a transparent and aligned view of the required projects, initiatives, key activities, and their sequence and priorities in order to achieve an interim target state, that is closer to the BI vision. In Fig. 4.3, we illustrated them with project 1 and project 2. In addition to these

projects, there might be some other activities that we do not illustrate to avoid overly complex visualization.
- From the perspective of our starting point, we have the entire journey to the BI vision ahead of us. Ideally, we want to take the most effective and efficient path to the BI vision, which is shown as a dotted line in Fig. 4.3.
- Unfortunately, reality will be a different story, so in practice we will face deviations between the intended and the realized journey. The realized journey is in Fig. 4.3 visualized as a bold black line.

In addition, we can think of several other drivers that may additionally or independently trigger the creation or modification of a BI strategy:

- New information requirements driven by potentially emerging or existing new business models, which are not properly supported today.
- The existing information requirements are not sufficiently supported.
- Significant efficiency gains, which could be leveraged through a mature BI process model.
- The unclear and questioned Target Operating Model (TOM) including consistent target setting principles.
- Continuous screening of BI innovations and trends in the wider environment.

Developing a BI strategy first requires that we be clear about some underlying principles, the foundation or basic requirements that a BI strategy should meet. Typically, the following principles are key:

Adequate Consideration of Dynamics
Even if it sounds strange in the first place, the primary goal is not to realize a business-driven static(!) BI target scenario. Instead, it is key to create an agile process of continuous development and usage of emerging and new opportunities. Proven approaches to optimization in stable environments and differentiated methodologies and flexible organizational and technological platforms are needed to address unpredicted changes.

Continuous Adaptation While Protecting a Stable Core
A BI strategy needs to be robust against unpredictable change. The response strategy for dealing with these changes "sense and respond" to achieve continuous adaptation of a BI strategy, which remains stable toward its foundation: a stable core.

Complete Coverage of Areas of Activities
A state-of-the-art BI strategy needs to be comprehensive. Apart from comprehensible objectives, technologies, and built projects or programs, a BI strategy should also cover organizations, business capabilities, communication and BI marketing and above all, BI governance.

Continuous Improvement of BI Strategy Maturity
This is achieved by avoiding standstill, including loss of agility, as well as aimless activism that leads to waste or exhaustion of resources. Instead, we strive for

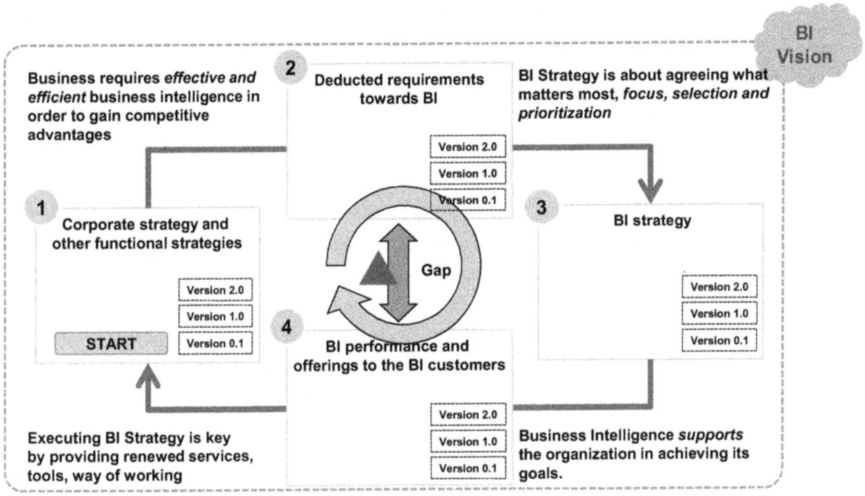

Fig. 4.4 BI strategy development lifecycle (© Exner/Zunic 2024)

continuous improvement based on systematic inspection and correction of malfunctions or the implementation of improvements.

Reduction of Complexity
We should, where reasonable, aim for economies of scale by enforcing standardization. Moreover, we need to (re-)balance customer requirements, flexibility, and speed of adaptation.

Now, we want to explore the process model itself. The process model for developing a BI strategy basically consists of four interrelated building blocks, as shown in Fig. 4.4 below. The numbers 1 to 4 refer to these building blocks:

- Corporate strategy and other functional strategies (1)
- Deducted requirements toward BI (2)
- BI strategy itself (3) and
- BI performance and offerings to the BI customers (4)

In practice, the starting point of the iteration is sometimes not the business strategy (1), but the BI requirements (2). As a result, multiple BI requirements need to be addressed. These may be structured in some way, resulting in a somewhat updated BI offering. However, these results will hardly be linked to business strategies. This, in turn, leads to a situation where updated BI offerings and resulting investments are not transparently linked to strategic requirements, and therefore the strategic value contribution of BI cannot be determined. For this reason, it is advisable to start with the strategy first (1).

This is the order in which we present the process model for developing a BI strategy: (1) → (2) → (3) → (4) → (1) → (…) in Fig. 4.4.

Let us assume that we enter the loop the very first time with an understanding of corporate and functional strategies. As we are further assuming that we are not yet familiar with the approach and the required activities, we call this initial release of our BI strategy "version 0.1," which indicates with a leading "0" that we are still in draft mode. Within this first building block, we aim to understand corporate and functional strategies as described in previous Chap. 2.

In the second building block, we compile all known BI requirements into an overall requirements backlog. Based on this, we group and consolidate these requirements for BI by referring to our learnings from Sects. 3.3 and 3.4. We analyze the requirements and identify what strategically matters most in terms of BI value contribution, hence we focus, select, and prioritize these requirements based on our objectives, knowledge, expertise, resources, and constraints.

The above will provide us with relevant input to develop an initial portfolio of new BI solutions, processes, services, and governance that will help us realize our BI strategy by serving the known BI requirements. Remember, this is still our initial loop from version 0.1. We have now closed the loop.

Now the reality check takes place. This is visualized in Fig. 4.4 by the centered cycle with the arrow, indicating that this should be seen as a continuous iteration. Based on BI customer feedback, we compare what BI has delivered (supply) to what is required (demand). In practice, it is likely that not all of our BI service and solution offerings will fully meet the expectations of BI customers. As a result, we identify gaps and, to improve our insights, we begin a root-cause analysis of why we failed and, more importantly, how we can do better. The knowledge of "how to do better" will be an additional input for our next release 1.0 of our BI strategy.

In practice, the reality check will not be a single point in time, but rather a continuous flow of information, feedback, and comments, which should be treated as valuable assets for further improvement of BI. This, in turn, will also serve our next BI strategy release, described in Fig. 4.4 as version 1.0. We have now completed the first iteration and developed a first version of our BI strategy. Realistically, however, we may already be aware of certain weaknesses and activities where we could improve.

In beforementioned process model for developing a BI strategy, we implicitly focused on activities, discussions, and alignment within our own company. In practice, there is much valuable information outside the corporate boundaries, which could additionally help us to further improve such as considering external trends, comparing, and benchmarking information with peers, discussing information with partners, and many more. This additional information provides us opportunities to improve our corporate and functional strategies, and in addition the chance to learn from others regarding their approach on developing a BI strategy. As illustrated in Fig. 4.5 below, all of the beforementioned four building blocks might be impacted and enriched by the environment. For some companies, the additional information from the outside may be perceived as a threat pressuring the organization to change. For other companies, it might be recognized rather as an opportunity to improve and adapt. Regardless of the organizational attitude to change, it is advisable to incorporate external expertise and learnings into the corporate business intelligence strategy process to stay aligned with the BI eco-system and related trends and good practices

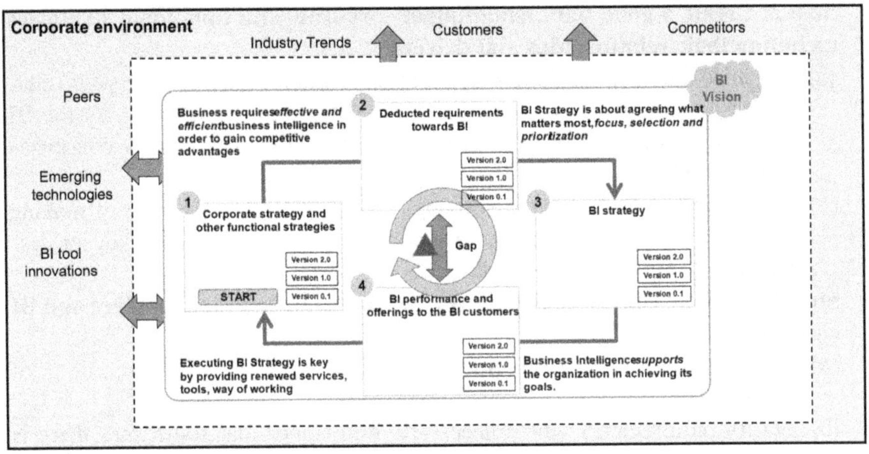

Fig. 4.5 BI strategy lifecycle embedded in wider corporate environment (© Exner/Zunic 2024. All Rights Reserved)

Let us discuss Fig. 4.5 using a more concrete example of technologies such as cloud computing. We can assume a likely impact on (1) functional strategies, as cloud computing provides the business with greater flexibility to cope with changing customer requirements. In addition, it provides more scalability when needed, due to growing business volumes. If these market trends are incorporated into business strategies, we can certainly expect to see similar requirements for BI (2), that pick up on these trends and ask the BI organization for flexibility in deploying BI tools, scalability to align BI service delivery and internal billing with actual demand. It is not advisable to ignore these trends and changing BI requirements. Consequently, these changes require a thorough assessment and further a fundamental redesign of the BI strategy (3). In addition, the BI roadmap will also be impacted to avoid one-off solutions. Once the BI strategy and decision is made, new BI offerings and solutions can be delivered to BI users (4).

In the next step, we will summarize our process model for developing a BI strategy in a more condensed way.

BI Strategy Process at a Glance

- **Step 1: Identify your relevant environment in a structured way (in the sense of strategies, key stakeholders, etc.).**
  (a) Identify the most relevant stakeholder groups and lines of business to partner with. Keep in mind, that the next BI strategy release will give you further opportunities to adjust where needed.
  (b) Set up meetings to share your ideas, start marketing the new or revised BI strategy and ask for input to make your internal customers even more successful.

- **Step 2: Create a good understanding of corporate and functional strategies including their relationships and drivers.**
  (a) Organize meetings to share your ideas and ask for input to make your internal customers aware of your goals of developing a BI strategy. As the BI strategy aims to be closely aligned with other strategies, aim for consensus and buy-in to join forces.
  (b) Begin a discussion about the strategic value of BI and the idea of making your key stakeholders even more successful. Aim to capture the key success factors on which you reach consensus.
- **Step 3: Compile the requirements for BI from your key stakeholders and BI customers.**
  (a) Gain visibility into requirements through the systematic recording of requirements.
  (b) Clarify requirements where necessary. Remember that sometimes there is business language, terminology, and implicit assumptions that you may not be aware of. Also, sometimes terminologies look the same but differ in detail.
  (c) Once the requirements are understood, prioritize them based on your current understanding. This may not be consensus in all cases, but it provides a reasonable starting point for further discussion and subsequent alignment.
- **Step 4: Development of a new/or revise the existing BI strategy.**
  (a) Develop an initial BI vision or, in case a BI vision exist already, validate if the vision is still meaningful and adhering to the criteria mentioned in the previous chapter.
  (b) Develop a set of new, customized action items to implement the intended (new) BI strategy (For further details, please refer to the next chapter).
  (c) Review and verify cause-and-effect relationships. Are the key planned actions capable of moving you toward your BI vision? Are you effectively addressing the key action areas, or are subordinate issues dominating?
  (d) Verify that existing problem areas are adequately addressed.
  (e) Create a BI strategy map to visualize the essentials. Include intentionally highlighted cause-and-effect relationships of the BI strategy. This can be considered optional, but such a BI strategy map can be a really powerful tool for promoting the essentials of the BI strategy.
  (f) Create a BI strategy document as a textual summary of the most important change and opportunity items in the BI strategy. In this context, "textual" should not be confused with listing bullet points. Instead, investing in easy-to-understand and meaningful descriptions will pay off later by helping others understand and buy in.
  (g) Present the BI strategy to the key stakeholders and explain why certain topics have been prioritized, while others have not. Key is to sell the BI strategy as a "Service" to help the BI customers to become even more successful.
  (h) Execute and deploy your BI strategy. Turn your BI strategy into concrete actions and make your BI customers aware of these changes. It sounds simple, but communication and change management are very important for everyone who will be affected by reports that no longer exist as a result of

report portfolio streamlining or newly implemented BI tools that users have not had a chance to get used to. For example, imagine the reaction of an executive when the report does not look like it used to. It is better to prepare your BI customers and be ready for their reaction.

(i) Finally, think about how to monitor the BI strategy operationalization. Simply said, either you decide to monitor, or you decide for "management by hope." Monitoring must not be misunderstood with micro-management. As we learned in Sect. 2.1, we can understand strategy as a promise to others to realize the most viable set of activities aiming to achieve the published goals. In other words, with communication of the BI strategy, we have made a commitment to our BI customers. It is a good advice to validate regularly, if we are on track or not. In the latter case, we have the opportunity to adjust.

In this chapter, we want to get more tangible and show you how to implement a BI strategy.

- **Step 5: Development of a (new) service catalog of BI based on the strategy as a (new) offer to the business.**
  (a) Create a new/revise the existing catalog of BI services and offerings. This activity helps you shape your offering, make it transparent, and make your BI USP (Unique Selling Proposition) understandable and digestible to the readers of the BI strategy. The process of creation or revision is a good opportunity for pre-testing. If you find that your BI service catalog is too broad, consider this finding in your next BI strategy release and ask yourself how you can improve, how you can focus.

Finally, let us discuss the main success factors for turning the BI process model into practice. What is required to make this happen?

Key Considerations for Developing a BI Strategy

- Clearly assign ownership (accountability and responsibility) of the BI strategy process along with the required competencies.
- Document roles, goals expected deliverables, and competences and clarify a collaboration model between the different roles.
- To gain routine in process execution, develop and implement guidelines and standards and train the workforce in the intended way of working.
- Monitor the BI strategy process against defined goals (Plan-Do-Check-Act).
- In case of any deviations set up activities to come back on track.
- Report based on an agreed meeting cadence to your key stakeholders/top management/sponsor and stay compliant with given guidelines and standards.
- Use best practices wherever suitable, but as long as they are not available continue with good practices.

4.3 Implementing a BI Strategy

In Chap. 3, we got familiar with our tool kit for strategy-aligned BI. In the previous sub-chapters of the current Chap. 4, we learned about BI vision, characteristics of a good BI vision statement and the process model for developing a BI strategy.

To do this, we will first discuss the difference between BI strategy and BI strategy process. Next, we will explore the concept of a "strategic impulse"that deliberately makes our environment look different than before. Finally, we will execute the strategic impulse concept using several examples to explain its essence and how it works in different use cases.

Distinction Between the BI Strategy and the BI Strategy Process

A BI strategy is usually expressed by the existence of a document. This approach makes the BI strategy somehow "tangible" in a sense of "touchable." Based on such a document, a BI strategy can be assessed regarding comprehensiveness and BI strategy readers can share their views with a clear and traceable reference. Furthermore, "tangible" requires that a BI strategy execution can be precisely identified or experienced.

Key Considerations for Developing a BI Strategy

- The creation of a BI strategy requires processes and activities that, when executed, lead to the desired outcome of the existence or revision of a BI strategy document.
- A clear structure of these processes and activities provides guidance on the sequence and describes what the first steps are, what comes next, etc.
- A minimum level of maturity should be the baseline for performing these activities effectively and efficiently.
- It is essential that a nominated "someone" takes ownership and ensures that all the activities required to produce the intended BI strategy are carried out ("BI strategy owner").

Without a BI strategy process owner, a BI strategy remains an abstract theoretical model. It will never find its way into reality, so it will never become "tangible." Furthermore, without processes and activities, there is and will be no initial BI strategy, because no activities will be performed, and without processes, an existing (possibly initial) BI strategy cannot evolve.

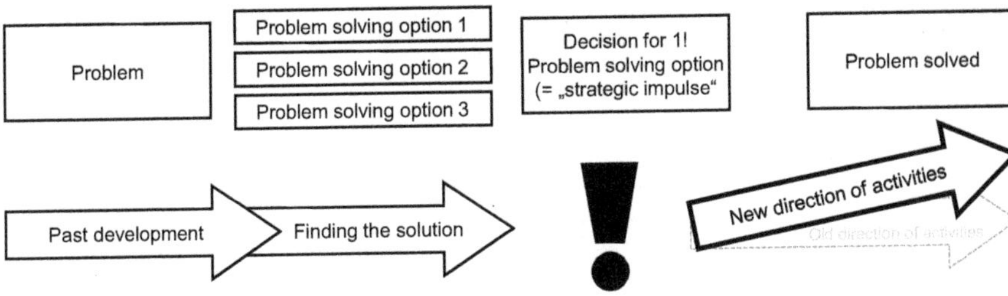

Fig. 4.6 Strategic impulse—trigger for change (© Exner/Zunic 2024. All Rights Reserved)

But even if all of the elements above are in place, it is still of utmost importance to implement a BI strategy. As we discussed earlier, all strategy is about change, and so is BI strategy. But what really triggers change?

To understand the change trigger, it is important to understand the concept of what we call the "strategic impulse." The strategic impulse can be understood as a clear, focused decision, including a resulting action, to overcome existing problems. As shown in Fig. 4.6, the trigger for change, or the strategic impulse, is the key element between the past problem, several options for solving this problem and a future state in which the problem is solved. If nothing changes, thus there are several options for solving the problem, but nobody decides on at least one particular option and, in addition, this chosen option is not executed, there will be no impact and no new direction, hence everything remains as it is.

The following examples may give a first impression of such an impulse:

- Accelerate standardization of BI by removal of less frequent requested services
- Increase customer/user satisfaction by
  - Shortening response times
  - Shortening and stabilizing response times
  - Improving data quality.
- Improve the quality and speed of BI processes.
- Make BI value contribution more transparent.
- Reduce costs per BI system and overall BI costs.
- ...

Action will make the desired change happen. Decision without action will not change anything, so the situation will most likely remain unchanged. Let us imagine that our BI customers provide us with their requirements. The customer's request that we evaluate these requirements, record them properly, and handle them in the customer's interest is a basic requirement, a matter of course. The core of this self-evidence is that it is not necessary to ask explicitly whether the customer is particularly happy about this self-evidence. Only the translation of the BI requirement into a new solution or a tangible improved BI service, which can be experienced by the BI users, is concrete and satisfies the original requirements.

In a next step, we will apply the described principle on the BI structure (Fig. 4.7), which we introduced in Sect. 3.3:

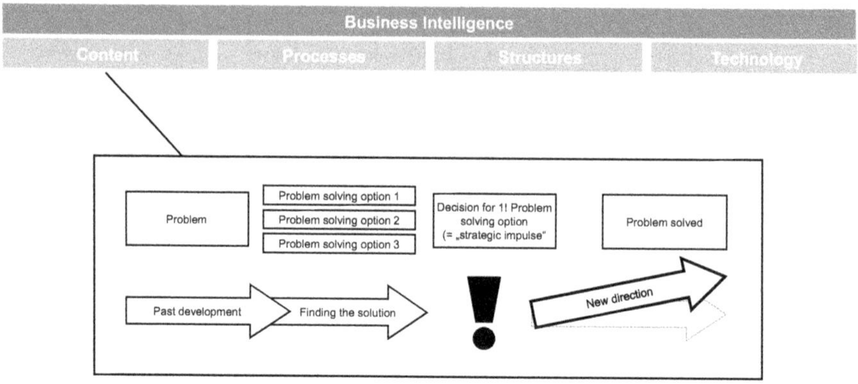

Fig. 4.7 Strategic impulse—working approach based on BI framework (© Exner/Zunic 2024. All Rights Reserved)

- New BI content (KPI's, master data, analytical dimensions, hiearchies, etc.)
- New BI processes (capturing requirements, service delivery, monitoring, etc.)
- New BI structure (organization, goverance, way of working, etc.)
- New BI tools & architecture (analytical tools, integrations, backend, technology, etc.)

The sequence of operations is as follows:

1. The first step is to reframe the problem or pain-point: Often we are used to talking about problems, so we use a negative wording. It is much more motivating to change this to a description of an attractive goal or opportunity or potential as a positive expression. This emphasizes the combination of achieving a goal with gaining a benefit. And this is usually more attractive than talking about solving problems.
2. Exam and validate the underlying goals. If necessary, reformulate the goal so that the requirements are still covered, and all participants have the same understanding.
3. Discuss the objectives and identify the essentials and key strategic impulses that must be made to achieve the objectives described before. These impulses may consist of modifying existing procedures, sanctioning unintended procedures in the future, or even positively reinforcing them.
4. Describe the necessary prerequisites for the realization of the strategic impulses. In other words, what needs to be done or avoided to make the strategic impulse happen.

Figure 4.8 below describes an example of the above working principle. This figure can easily be produced as presentation to support a direct communication, for example, in a meeting. The core element is our target, so let us put this into the center of our visualization (1). To achieve this target, we learned previously, that we need a strategic impulse. Let us put this left to the center to highlight, that this needs

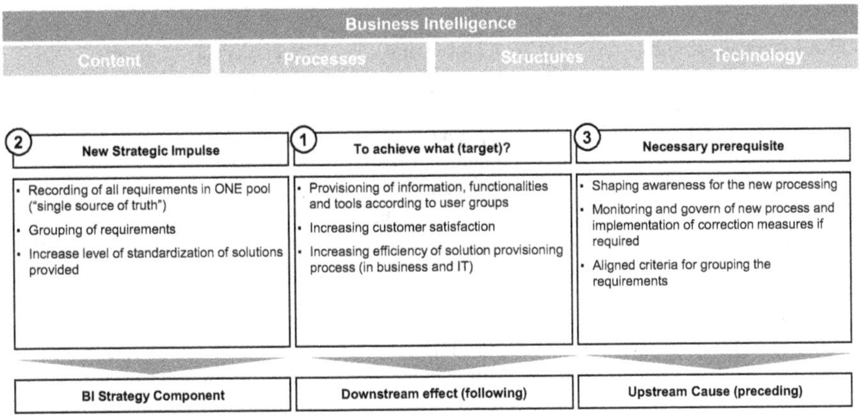

Fig. 4.8 Implementing a BI strategy—basic example (© Exner/Zunic 2024. All Rights Reserved)

Table 4.1 Implementing a BI strategy—basic example and working sequence

2) New strategic impulse	**1) To achieve what (Target)**	**3) Necessary prerequisite**
• Capture all requirements in a tool • Grouping of requirements • Increasing the standardization level of solution offers	• Demand-oriented provision of information, functionality, and tools • Increasing customer satisfaction • Increasing the efficiency of the deployment process (Bus. & IT operations)	• Strengthening the awareness of the need for a structured requirement recording in the entire organization • Monitoring of process compliance and, if necessary, corrective action • Coordinated grouping criteria
BI strategy component	**Downstream effect (following)**	**Upstream cause (preceding)**

to be in place to "get things in motion" (2). But what are the prerequisites for the strategic impulse? It will not be there automatically and we need to record them as well (3).

In the following examples, we will use the same content as above, but in a tabular format (Table 4.1). This enables us to record multiple use cases in a spreadsheet, which is particularly useful in the case of a large number of BI requirements and strategic impulses. However, the working principle and structure will remain the same, regardless of the tool used.

On the next pages, we will describe some examples of the working principles in more detail. In these examples, we will cover the following areas:

- BI information delivery
- BI organization
- BI business operations and
- BI information technology enablement

Let us start first with an example of BI information delivery. We develop a three-column table and headline it as illustrated in Table 4.2. Next, we start to fill in the

Table 4.2 Implementing a BI strategy—example on BI information delivery

2) New strategic impulse	1) To achieve what (target)	3) Necessary prerequisite
• Develop a comprehensive KPI catalog incl. taxonomy • Harmonize the logics for calculating KPIs across different countries and different source systems (use a uniform interface to BI) • Define and create a portfolio of standard reports that are documented and known to users • Implement a uniform access (1! Front-end; Single point of entry) per user group (back-end systems do not matter to the end user) • Implement new analytical dimensions along the value chain	• Clear and transparent definitions of KPIs • For the same KPIs the content of the reporting has to be harmonized across systems • It is important to create a transparent transition logic between the departments • The quality of data and KPI's is to be improved • Reports and analyzes must be defined on a company-wide basis	• Preparation of a decision proposal between Quality-at-Source (ERP) vs. Quality-at-Target (BI) • Preparation of a decision proposal between 1! Global BI vs. System hybrid model Global BI with the support of decentralized BI systems • Harmonization of master data (start with finance master data, but further future expansion) • Define clear responsibilities (tasks, responsibilities, competencies) • Clear sponsorship for the activities • Sufficient resources to carry out the activities
BI Strategy omponent	**Downstream effect**	**Upstream cause**

middle column with the exemplary BI requirements, such as "clear and transparent definitions of KPIs," "For the same KPIs the content of the reporting has to be harmonized across systems," "It is important to create a transparent transition logic between the departments," etc.

In the next step, we ask ourselves what needs to be changed or what needs to be triggered to meet these requirements? In our example, we conclude that the following responses are appropriate: "Develop a comprehensive KPI catalog incl. a corporate taxonomy with business definitions" "Harmonize the logic for calculating KPIs across different countries and different source systems (use a uniform interface to BI)," etc. It is advisable to formulate these strategic impulses in an actionable way and connect them with concrete tasks. So, instead of just stating a general intent as for example "Development of a comprehensive KPI catalog incl. taxonomy" you should aim for devising a specific action, like "Develop a comprehensive KPI catalog incl. a corporate taxonomy with business definitions in the next 3 months."

Before we move on to the third column "3) Necessary Prerequisites," we might ask ourselves that the results so far are not "rocket science," so why do we face the current situation of not having the beforementioned already in place. There are several possible reasons, of course, so let us pragmatically start with the ones that come to mind first. From a practitioner's point of view, it is advisable to avoid over-engineering. Often the first results are worth recording.

Let us now look at the next example on BI organization. As shown in Table 4.3, we use again our three-column table including the same headlines as before. Again, we start to fill in BI requirements on BI organization, such as "The BI strategy must

Table 4.3 Implementing a BI strategy—example on BI organization

2) New strategic impulse	1) To achieve what (target)?	3) Necessary prerequisite
• Establishment/ intensification of a controlled and regular dialogue between "representatives BI" and "representatives of top management" • Matching goals and plans • Increase the transparency of the fundamental and long-term value contribution of BI for the strategic business success • Introduction of a "translator function" as a mediator between business and IT	• The BI strategy must support the corporate strategy • Strengthen the mutual knowledge of technical requirements and technical solution options • Create / Strengthen the "Awareness" for BI strategy within the organization	• Organizational anchoring of Business Intelligence in the organization • Closing the ownership "vacancy," i.e. clarification of the central personal accountability (as clear as possible) • Definition of the task spectrum of the BI organization • Development and expansion of the necessary and task-relevant know-how on both the business and the IT side (e.g., concept BI introduction training for new employees) • Create a consolidated overview of the current goals and planning in the BI environment
BI strategy component	**Downstream effect**	**Upstream cause**

support the corporate strategy," "Strengthen the mutual knowledge of technical requirements and technical solution options," "Create / Strengthen the 'Awareness' for BI strategy within the organization."

As in the previous example, in our next step we ask ourselves the same questions, i.e. "what needs to be changed/what needs to be triggered to meet the requirements?" In our example, we conclude the following impulses as appropriate "Establishment / intensification of a controlled and regular dialogue between 'representatives BI' and 'representatives of top management'," "Matching goals and plans," "Increase the transparency of the fundamental and long-term value contribution of BI for the strategic business success," etc.

In the third column "3) Necessary prerequisite," we may find the following prerequisites as essential to make the strategic impulses come true: "Organizational anchoring of Business Intelligence in the organization," "Closing the ownership 'vacancy,' i.e. clarification of the central personal accountability (as clear as possible)," etc.

In our third example illustrated in Table 4.4, we will focus on BI business operations. The working principle remains, and we start to fill in BI requirements on BI business operations, such as "Establishment of clearly defined processes to accommodate and implement new information needs," "Establishment of defined service level agreements for throughput-time for the realization of reporting requirements," etc.

Like in the previous example, we now describe the suitable strategic impulses like "Establish single point of contact to avoid redundancy, reduce complexity," "Formalize the SLAs," "Establish a common platform in which the various projects and dependencies are made transparent," etc.

Table 4.4 Implementing a BI strategy–example on BI business operations

2) New strategic impulse	1) To achieve what (target)?	3) Necessary prerequisite
• Establish single point of contact to avoid redundancy, reduce complexity • Formalize the SLAs • Establish a common platform in which the various projects and dependencies are made transparent (technology, products, content)	• Establishment of clearly defined processes to accommodate and implement new information needs • Establishment of defined service level agreements for throughput-time for the realization of reporting requirements • Clear overall planning of the implementation (roadmap) of requirements together with responsibilities (standard reports (contents), tools) and dependencies	• Definition of "new information needs" • Differentiation of requirement types in order to be able to control different processes if necessary. • Who / How are the requirements directed to the different channels? • Conceptual description of "SPOC" (Single Point of Contact) • Definition of "Service Level Agreement" • Development of a storyline to be able to market the topic internally • Competence to establish a platform
BI strategy component	**Downstream effect**	**Upstream cause**

In the third column "3) Necessary prerequisite," we may find the following prerequisites as key: "Definition of "new information needs'," "Differentiation of requirement types in order to be able to control different processes if necessary," "Who / How are the requirements directed to the different channels?", etc.

In our final example, we will detail BI information technology enablement. We start again to fill in BI requirements on BI information technology enablement, such as "A clear, harmonized, evolving overall portfolio of BI Tools (frontend and backend, including planning, reporting, and consolidation)," "Optimal, i. e. uniform operational BI infrastructure," and "Using a State-of-the-Art BI Landscape."

Next, we describe the suitable strategic impulses like "Develop a visionary target BI tool and solution landscape," "Create a flexible, open landscape around a stable core," and "pro-actively examine new BI tools to handle new business models and new requirements" as shown in Table 4.5.

As most important prerequisites, we may record in the third column: "Create a willingness to re-think existing tools and solutions and to revise them where necessary," "Develop a 'storyline' for the internal marketing of the BI benefits to be expected by the new BI landscape," "Further detailing of the entire technology stack," and finally "Examine the existing documentation of the current BI landscape."

In the above examples, we have implemented the working principle in different BI domains. Based on these examples, it is now possible to consolidate each of the above columns. The consolidation of the first column will provide us with the core of our BI strategy document as intended (in a narrow sense), the consolidation of the second column is the summary of the BI requirements, serving as a reference to the

Table 4.5 Implementing a BI strategy—example on BI information technology enablement

2) New strategic impulse	1) To achieve what (target)?	3) Necessary prerequisite
• Develop a visionary target BI tool and solution landscape • Creating a flexible, open landscape around a stable core • Pro-actively examine new BI tools to handle new business models and new requirements	• A clear, harmonized, evolving overall portfolio of BI Tools (frontend and backend, including planning, reporting and consolidation) • Optimal, i. e. uniform operational infrastructure • Using a state-of-the-art BI landscape	• Create a willingness to re-think existing tools and solutions and to revise them where necessary • Develop a "storyline" for the internal marketing of the BI benefits to be expected by the new BI landscape • Further detailing of the entire technology stack • Examine the existing documentation of the current BI landscape
BI strategy component	**Downstream effect**	**Upstream cause**

origin, and finally, the consolidation of the third column will help us to understand the activities that support and drive our strategic impulses, hence our BI strategy. Overall, this three-column approach provides transparency and traceability of BI's value contribution.

We now want to summarize our learnings and the benefits of our approach.

Key Considerations for Developing a BI Strategy

- Familiarize yourself with the essential processes and their importance in developing or revising a BI strategy.
- Develop a motivating and understandable BI vision and consider the key characteristics to achieve a powerful tool for alignment within our organization.
- Start practicing the BI strategy development process model on your own. If you identify an even better process as you work through the various activities, be flexible and consider it as the new process.
- Start thinking in iterations. The first may not be perfect, but it is better than nothing. The second iteration will show improvements through experience and feedback. Trust yourself to become more routined as you repeat your BI strategy development processes.
- Aim to close the loops. Do not take it for granted that everyone knows about your idea of improving BI strategy maturity through iterations. Invite feedback, be transparent about the feedback provided, and be transparent about how you will use it for improvement.
- Consider your own growing experience, but do not neglect your own possible open questions and uncertainties. Try to use them as opportunities for change and refinement.
- Start practicing the three-pillar approach and strive for transparency and traceability of your tailored BI value contributions.

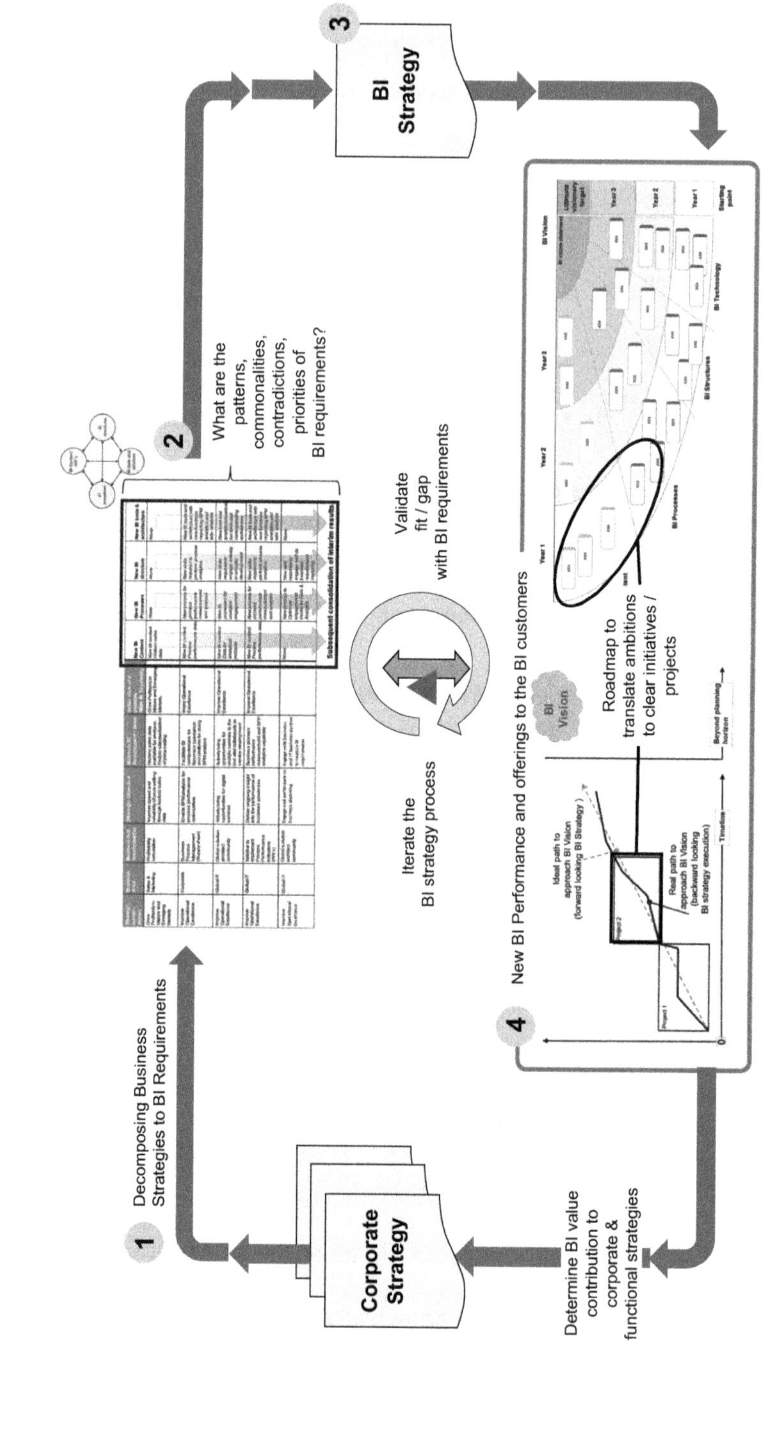

Fig. 4.9 Key elements of BI strategy development at a glance (© Exner/Zunic 2024. All Rights Reserved)

In Fig. 4.9 above, we describe the key elements of BI strategy development at a glance. The more generic descriptions from previous Chap. 3 are now replaced by more tangible visualizations, which we introduced in this Chap. 4.

Organizing BI Strategy

5

Expectations toward business intelligence and data-driven decision-making are continuously growing. At the same time new practices and technologies emerge to address these needs—hence a key obvious question arises:

> "How can we most effectively setup our organization around data, content and architecture and which approaches are most effective to use for which purpose?"

This is where BI governance plays a key role. In the past, we could observe two prominent patterns of BI governance. Either the governance of business intelligence artifacts was supported only tactically based on ad hoc requests and issue management, or it was centrally enforced to a degree that made an agile approach to BI almost impossible. Both approaches are not viable any longer.

In addition, BI governance needs to increasingly address ethical and data protection concerns resulting, for example, from AI and big data usage. It needs to establish guidelines and principles for responsible use of data, including addressing issues like bias, fairness, and transparency.

Hence in a nutshell, to be effective BI governance needs to organize collaboration among different stakeholders involved in data, AI, and big data initiatives. It should define and establish governance bodies and processes that bring together business leaders, data scientists, IT professionals, legal experts, and other relevant parties to shape an overall approach to corporate BI governance. This collaboration ensures alignment between strategic objectives, data management practices, and technological capabilities.

This chapter will explore the general principles and dimensions of BI governance and discuss alternative ways of setting up BI governance in organizations.

R. Exner, A. Zunic, *The Path to an Intelligent Enterprise*, Future of Business and Finance, https://doi.org/10.1007/978-3-031-69914-6_5

A BI strategy can be an effective enabler for promoting the importance of, and making a case for, an enterprise-wide BI governance setup with appropriate funding. It should also frame the boundaries of BI and corresponding governance layers to ensure the right balance between control and noncontrol.

5.1 Governance: Key Enabler for BI Strategy

There is no doubt that BI governance is one of *the* key enablers of BI strategy and can make the crucial difference between success and failure of enterprise-wide business intelligence. Governance essentially establishes the basic rules and guidelines for BI strategy execution. It ensures that BI-related activities in the organization are transparent, coordinated, and supported by a tailored organizational structure. Without a formal structure of control, decisions and processes will likely not be aligned with BI strategy and hence the overall value contribution of business intelligence is limited. However, there are many different flavors of a formal control structure for BI. A key decision that needs to be made is how and where to anchor BI governance in the organization and to define which domains of business intelligence require which levels of control both centrally and locally.In this chapter, we will discuss possible anchor points for setting up a BI governance structure.

BI governance is comprised of principles, procedures, and organizational structures. Ultimate objective is to ensure that the information and decision-making demands are supported by a tailored organizational setup. Tailored organizational setup means that the organizational design needs to support organization-specific effectiveness and efficiency goals. It ensures that the required resources and responsibilities are clearly defined, and risks are adequately identified and monitored.

Whereas a BI strategy is focused more on identifying, defining, and organizing the content and related information and data structures (data architecture), BI governance defines the processes how a BI strategy will be operationalized (planning, creation, revision, control). The BI strategy ensures the alignment of business intelligence with organizational goals based on corporate strategy (as outlined before). Therefore, BI governance needs to ensure a strategy-compliant design of the BI organization. This includes the coordination of its transformation into a desired target state as well.

A BI governance framework should describe first and foremost which aspects of BI require formal alignment and approval by an official governance body. In addition, it should describe who in the organization is responsible for making and owning these decisions. This is important, because not every decision requires a formal governance process.

For example, there might be a regular steering board to identify, prioritize, and approve new strategic requirements in a formal process. This typically involves representatives from different lines of business, board areas, and communities of practice. On lower levels of the organization there might be topic owners or community leads that make local, less formal decisions. This kind of setup serves meeting the needs of the local business community in a more autonomous and agile way.

Overall, it is important that the decision-making processes are transparent and interlinked. This ensures that important top-level decisions are cascaded down the hierarchy coherently ("one voice") via transparent, but still formal or less formally defined roles and responsibilities.

To deliver on BI commitments and decisions on an operational level, it is important that requirements are clear and transparent. This is a prerequisite for a translation to effective data and solution designs. It requires not only BI developers, but particularly BI architects, BI designers and data owners and increasingly data scientitsts to collaborate on requirement analysis and impact analysis. This helps answer questions like What needs to be changed to meet a requirement? What is impacted? What data is required? In addition, it is increasingly important to cover aspects of compelling consumption experiences. This is where architecture boards and/or designer communities can be valuable to provide guidance and best practice (as a form of community regulated governance).

Finally, governance around scheduling of changes and management of dependencies is very important due to the interconnected nature of BI. This is typically handled through architect or release boards who are making the main decisions on the delivery schedule. In addition, BI governance should consider the whole life-cycle of BI products, applications and BI services in order to be able to direct investments into growth areas instead of over-investing in outdated, oversaturated solutions or services with a declining adoption trend. This obviously requires defining a monitoring framework of metrics regarding the life-cycle stage. Consequently this needs to include decommissioning of outdated or increasingly less frequently demanded products and services as well.

All of this shows that BI governance needs to be managed and orchestrated on different levels while at the same time ensuring that the levels are aligned with each other. Without the alignment, there is a clear risk of unplanned double work (same requirements addressed multiple times), re-work due to misunderstandings, inconsistent user experiences and most notably data that cannot be trusted resulting in side-reporting and potentially shadow IT.

The positioning of BI within the organizational hierarchy is key. This positioning is expressed by reporting lines and defined areas of responsibility within a company.

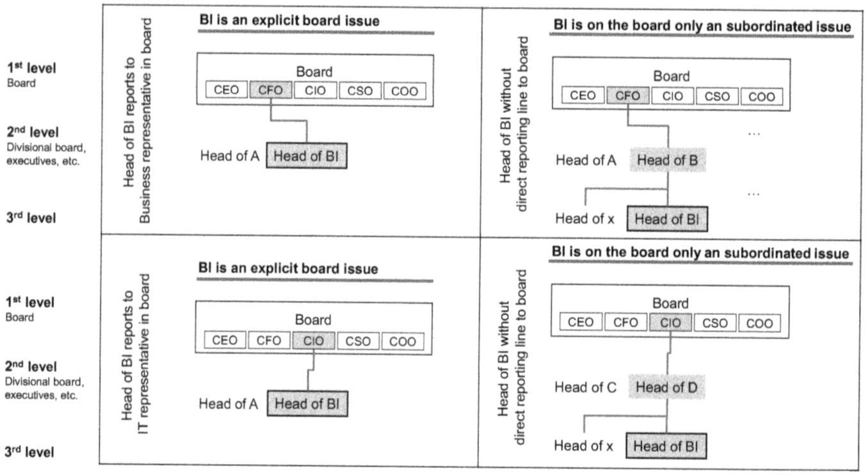

Fig. 5.1 Positioning of BI in the organization (© Exner/Zunic 2024. All Rights Reserved)

> The positioning of BI documents the board commitment or non-commitment to the strategic significance and value expectation on BI in a company.

The strengths and organizational empowerment of business intelligence and its "mandate" toward the entire organization depend on the organizational positioning as illustrated in Fig. 5.1. The advantage of a clear mandate would be that business intelligence has a clear and strong say with regard to cross-functional issues harming a data-driven decision-making like data quality deficits, data inconsistencies but also support a continuous improvement of BI maturity in the entire organization.

The matrix in Fig. 5.1 above consists of four quadrants, which we now will explain.

On the x-axis, we distinguish if BI is either an explicit board issue or perceived as a subordinated issue. This means, that the head of BI either has a clear reporting line to a dedicated board member, or an indirect reporting line via intermediate management levels to the board.

On the y-axis, we distinguish if the head of BI is reporting to a business or IT representative in the organization.

The basic assumption is that a BI organization with a designated head of BI exists. If a dedicated BI organization including a dedicated head of BI does not exist yet, the relevance of positioning BI nevertheless remains a key decision to be made by executives.

The positioning of BI as part of an organizational design has a significant influence on the BI governance.

As such BI governance can be designed very differently in organizations. One dimension is to agree on the level of proximity to either IT or business.

- An IT-dominated BI governance
- A business-dominated BI governance
- A balanced BI governance between business and IT

An IT-dominated BI governance sees responsibility for the subject of BI governance as a specialization of IT. The advantage of this flavor of BI governance lies in the reuse of existing structures, as many governance aspects around data, systems, architectures are typically already defined for other IT domains.

A business-dominated BI governance sees responsibility for BI governance as a specialization of a (dedicated) line of business, like finance or operations. The assignment of BI governance to a dedicated business function is typically driven by the ability to provide cross-functional guidance in a neutral and unbiased way.

5.2 Dimensions of BI Governance

Governance can be described as the act or process of overseeing the control and giving direction. It means exercising continuous formal authority. Therefore, the concept is often uniquely associated with formal rules and a top-down command chain. But this is only one aspect of governance. In the context of BI, governance plays an important role because it not only defines the structure of control but also formally establishes and authorizes the BI strategy process itself. Without BI governance the necessary corporate alignment and consensus needed to make BI a true value enabler in the entire organization is almost impossible.

But what does BI governance actually mean in practice?The following chapter will break down different dimensions of BI governance that can help to manage and control the BI product and service landscape and hence support the BI strategy and its realization.

It is useful to structure BI governance around the core value dimensions of business intelligence and establish a control framework that actively seeks to improve the overall value contribution of BI. We can distinguish several core dimensions of BI governance, which are ideally managed in a cross-company organization or continuous corporate activity. They also apply to smaller organizations, even though the scope and layers of complexity can vary very much from organization to organization:

- Oversight
- BI lifecycle value
- End-user adoption and support
- Continuous improvement

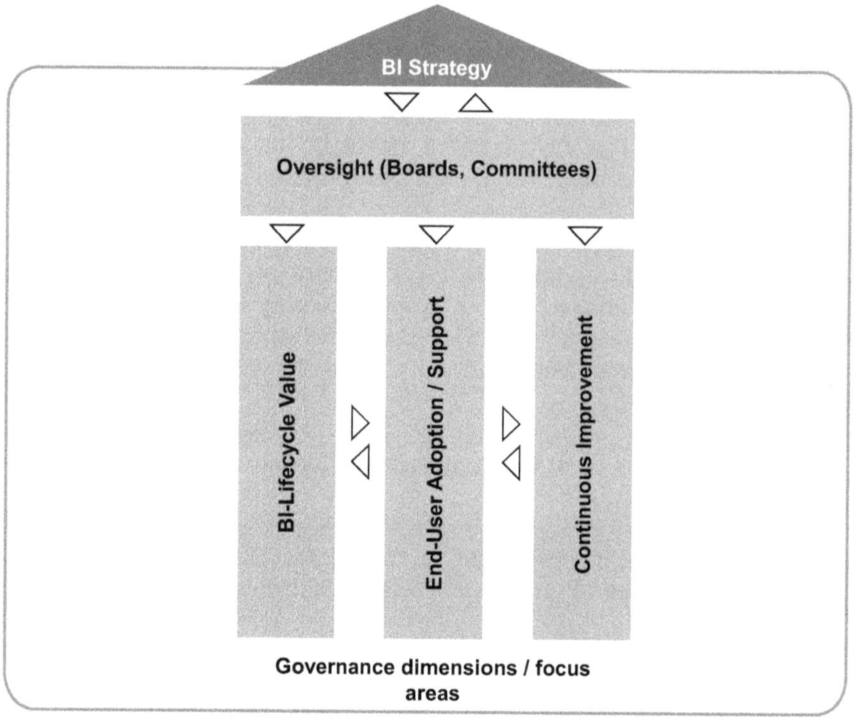

Fig. 5.2 Governance framework—key dimensions (© Exner/Zunic 2024. All Rights Reserved)

The **Oversight** dimension coordinates the company-wide BI activities and priorities. This ranges from aligning strategic business requirements, setting corporate BI and data standards to making decisions on the future BI roadmap and portfolio. Cross-organizational decisions are made via dedicated boards, committees, or a competence center. Furthermore, the Oversight dimension ensures that the BI strategy is up-to-date and reflects a common view on business intelligence aligned with corporate and business strategies.

The value contribution of BI largely depends on the degree to which BI products and services are adopted and used across the entire lifecycle (**BI lifecycle value**).

The decisions made in the Oversight dimension provide the basis for managing these individual BI products and services. Each product and service has its own lifecycle and user adoption and support requirements (**end-user adoption and support**). For enterprise-wide business intelligence to be successful, it is critical that BI products and services are aligned with the overall BI strategy and conscious decisions are made on which products and services to invest in, exploit, and phase-out based on a **continuous improvement** mindset.

The resulting governance dimensions are illustrated in Fig. 5.2.

Let us now examine each dimension in detail.

Oversight Dimension

This dimension is most commonly associated with BI governance in its traditional sense. Its key purpose is to ensure that corporate BI is managed holistically across organizational boundaries with clear accountability and ownership. It recognizes that BI is fundamentally a cross-organizational management challenge. This is particularly relevant for enterprise-wide BI ambitions, not so much for local or very confined BI initiatives with a limited organizational footprint.

The key objective of this dimension is to bridge the BI strategy with execution on an enterprise-wide scale.

This includes the formulation, update, and communication of the BI strategy, ensuring that the BI priorities are clearly defined, transparent, and accessible to all relevant business units and stakeholders.

Furthermore, it involves designing a BI target operating model. Among others this involves identification and segmentation of BI customers, BI end-to-end processes and solutions to service them and clear guidelines on organizational responsibilities. Any kind of BI organization requires clear official communication and escalation paths both within the core BI organization as well as to adjacent business and IT units.

It is not uncommon that the oversight dimension is not formally defined. It tends to evolve over time from an informal network of loosely coupled teams or individuals who interact on an ad hoc basis without any formally defined responsibilities. This may work in small organizations in which BI is not viewed as a strategic differentiator and is managed as an implicit part of the overall IT function. However, as the scale of BI grows and the importance of data-driven decision-making rises, this approach will not suffice.

Key resulting question is how a tailored BI organization setup could look like to even better support the enterprise-wide decision-making demands.

This can start with the initiation of a BI program or steering board in which representatives of business and IT mutually agree on the way forward.

Common topics that are addressed in this context include:

- Strategic (re-)positioning of BI
- Shaping of the BI product and service portfolio
- Definition of BI support processes and release management
- Strategic BI landscape decisions/roadmap (e.g., application strategy)
- Sharing and communication of good practices from successful projects and programs
- Ethics around use and access to data

In larger organizations who recognize BI as a core enabler of business strategy, the oversight dimension can be bundled in a BI Competence Center (BI-CC) or can be organized as part of a center of excellence.

A Business Intelligence Competence Center is a cross-functional organizational team that has defined tasks, responsibilities, roles, and skills for supporting and promoting the effective use of Business Intelligence across an organization. The concept of a BI-CC will be further detailed later in this chapter.

The value of a competence center is that it is a permanent organization in which dedicated roles can focus over a longer period of time on continuously improving and executing on the overall BI strategy and roadmap. Regardless of the IT or business flavor of a BI-CC its visibility in the organization and ownership help avoid misalignment, which is a key barrier of BI success.

However, a BI-CC organization requires investment. It effectively needs C-level commitment and funding over a longer period of time—which is one of the reasons why these organizations are often struggling to survive over a longer period of time.

In addition, experts argue that the traditional BI-CC is not the ideal governance model anymore in a drastically changed world of business intelligence. Especially the advent of big data and data science requires a new approach to managing enterprise business intelligence, including the support of a whole new set of analytical use cases, users, technologies, and developing new sets of skills. Often, the big data team, because of its different way of working, is not even part of the BI-CC. At the same time, all straightforward BI activities like dashboards, diagnostic analytics, etc., have gone "self-service." This puts the traditional, centralized BI-CC under pressure.

A well-managed Oversight dimension remains a key prerequisite for achieving strategy-aligned business intelligence especially in larger organizations. The need for cross-organizational business and IT alignment continues to be a key issue in spite of (or rather because of) the emergence of data science and self-service as defaults. But a centralized oversight function alone is not sufficient anymore. Additional decentralized dimensions of governance need to be taken into consideration as well.

One of these dimensions is the BI lifecycle and value dimension.

Lifecycle and Value Dimension

Let us think of BI as a set of internal corporate products and services. Just like any other marketable product, an organization produces BI products and services to meet demands of consumers.

BI products can be custom-built for a very specific purpose or built for self-service consumption without necessarily pre-defined use cases. Possible analogy for such kind of concepts of production can also be found particularly in discrete industries with similarities to "make-to-order" or "make-to-stock." Just like any other product BI products and services are usually priced based on usage or cost-to-serve. A difference is that BI products target a predominantly internal audience, and the production and marketing of BI assets is increasingly performed by decentralized communities in the lines of business, who are both creators and consumers.

However, as we learned in Sect. 2.7, just like any other physical asset or product, BI products "age" with time and have a product lifecycle. This implies that at some point in time the marginal return for every additional dollar spent decreases or even turns negative—a phenomenon known in economics as the "law of diminishing returns." In the fast-paced world of business intelligence this is particularly relevant, as a new alternative for an existing BI product or service is often just around the corner—sometimes even within the same organization. It is therefore critical to understand the lifecycle of a BI product in the context of overall BI strategy and business needs. For each phase of the BI product lifecycle, different governance aspects arise and need to be addressed.

To gain better control of the overall BI product landscape and align it with BI strategy and business demand, a comprehensive BI product and project portfolio

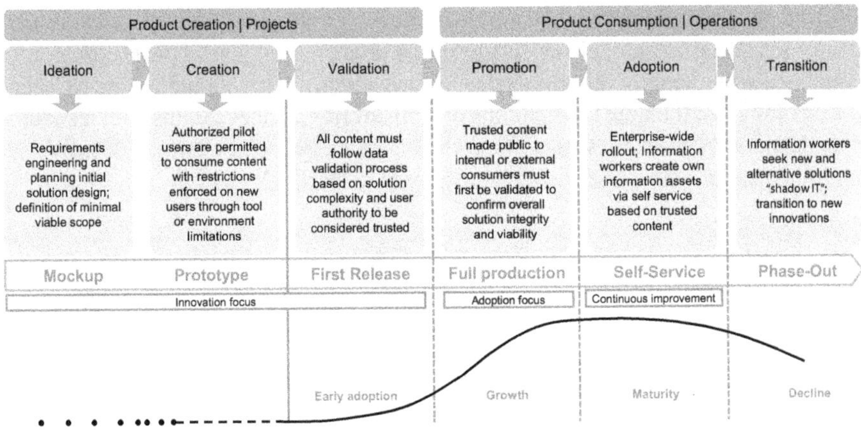

Fig. 5.3 The BI product lifecycle (© Exner/Zunic 2024. All Rights Reserved)

management is recommended. A BI portfolio structures the BI landscape into BI products and services with the objective to prioritize resources and investments and reduce uncontrolled redundancy and cost. This instrument addresses both the need for transparency ("which BI products do we have now, and which are in progress?") and strategy compliance ("what new BI products do we need in the future?", "which products don't we need anymore?")

A well-managed and balanced BI product portfolio is an effective governance and communication tool for aligning management and strategic priorities with BI capabilities and resulting BI products.

By additionally applying a stage model to the BI lifecycle, the relevant governance aspects of each lifecycle stage can be uniquely addressed, supporting and accelerating the creation and adoption of each individual BI product or service.

A typical BI product lifecycle consists of the following product stages (Figs. 5.3 and 5.5):

- Ideation (potentially including a prototype or mock-up)
- Creation (first release)
- Validation (pilot)
- Promotion (from early adoption to organizational scaling)
- Adoption (mass scaling)
- Transition (phase-out)

After product creation, validation, and initial release, a new BI product will typically attract a growing number of consumers over time. As the solution matures and a targeted mass of users is reached, the product lifecycle enters a "plateau of productivity" before moving into a phase of decline.

In recent years there has been a clear need for shortening the BI product and service introduction and delivery phase of the product life cycle. This is commonly associated with the term "time to value." However, this term should not be reduced to describing just the time length of the overall development cycle. Instead, it should be understood more in the sense of introducing shorter development iteration cycles to provide earlier and more frequent customer feedback.

However, we would like to issue a word of caution here. It must be noted that BI life-time value depends on one critical variable—the degree of trust in data and content. This is why we advise to make data governance, data validation, and data integration key priorities in every BI product across all stages of its lifecycle. Without getting the data part right, no BI product is viable for very long.

Trustfulness of data is a hygiene factor or a basic requirement, which needs to be fulfilled even without explicit request.

And this cannot only be in the ownership of one particular individual or team—it must be a continuous enterprise-wide effort. Therefore, across all stages of the design, creation, and operations phases, data governance around core data objects is absolutely key. Before rolling out enterprise-wide BI products, a limited set of users should be given a dedicated period of time to validate data in a (pre)production environment "on the job" during daily operation—this is the crucial litmus test.

But what exactly needs to be governed on which level? The following table outlines which governance aspects are relevant in which BI lifecycle phase:

Ideally, there is a continuous collaboration of local and central business and IT communities throughout all product lifecycle phases of a BI product. In the model illustrated in Table 5.1 above, central BI governance is reduced to the relevant minimum, ensuring that the key governance aspects of BI are defined and available, but leaving the concrete product ideation and product design to the local units.

However, experience shows that many organizations do not take a proactive lifecycle-driven approach to BI governance. One reason for this is that BI is often viewed as a mere reporting extension of transactional applications, and BI governance is therefore often managed as part of application governance. This viewpoint neither sufficiently reflects the nature of BI as a cross-domain and also does not consider the BI lifecycle which is detached from other applications. If there is no BI-CC or dedicated organization in place that aims to address the specific governance needs of BI throughout its lifecycle, there is a risk that non-fitting governance standards are applied, or projects will attempt to bypass them.

Another reason why a lifecycle approach is often a challenge is the absence of defined ownership in both central and local units. For example, if a BI product is not serviced by a dedicated "analytical owner" or "product owner" who actively promotes and supports the product over its entire lifecycle, it will likely not attract

Table 5.1 Relevant governance aspects in various BI lifecycle phases

<table>
<tr><th rowspan="2">BI life-cycle</th><th colspan="2">Governance aspects</th><th rowspan="2">Addresses…</th></tr>
<tr><th>Strategic (portfolio)</th><th>Operational (product)</th></tr>
<tr><td>Ideation</td><td rowspan="3">Central
• BI pipeline (strategic requirement inputs)
• Methodologies (e.g., design thinking)
• BI portfolio management (projects)
• Strategic vendors and platforms
• BI reference architecture
• BI capabilities
Central or local
• Data governance (creation, usage, quality)</td><td>Local
• Concretization of product- and service-related requirements
• Accelerators (templates)
• Tools for solution design</td><td>What do we miss?
What do we need?
What do we design?
How do we design?</td></tr>
<tr><td>Creation</td><td>Central
• BI tool selection guidance
• System environment and infrastructure
• Reference architecture and design conventions
• PM methodologies & tools</td><td>What do we build?
How do we build?
How do we plan?
Where is the data?
How to embed in given architecture?</td></tr>
<tr><td>Validation</td><td>• Testing strategy and tools</td><td>How do we test?
Definition of “ready for productive use?”</td></tr>
<tr><td>Promotion</td><td rowspan="3">Central
• BI portfolio management (products)
• BI services
• BI support organization and processes</td><td>Local
• Change management
• Content ownership
• Product ownership</td><td>How should we use?
Who should use?
Who educates?
Who owns?</td></tr>
<tr><td>Adoption</td><td>Central
• Release management
• End-user support model
• Service Level agreements</td><td>How do we support?
How do we run?
Who operates?
How do we measure adoption?</td></tr>
<tr><td>Transition</td><td>Local
• Phase out plan
• Replacement options</td><td>When do we end support?
How do we sunset?</td></tr>
</table>

enough critical mass to be considered successful. Usage rates of BI in many cases are still astonishingly low, in extreme cases an estimated 10% or less of employees have access to or use corporate BI products and services. As a consequence, a high percentage of BI investments are deemed failures and might never yield a return on investment or have long passed the maturity phase and are in decline.

Below table shows an illustrative example of how the BI product portfolio could be governed based on a product lifecycle model indicating product maturity, ownership, adoption, and tool support for each active BI product/application.

In Table 5.2, we highlighted items 4.1 and 4.2. While item 4.1 describes a report which is still in growth phase, item 4.2 is deemed to be phased out (removed) of the BI product and service portfolio.

Using a portfolio management approach helps ensure that the BI product landscape is both valuable and strategy aligned on a continuous basis. It also enables

Table 5.2 Illustrative example on how the BI product portfolio could be governed

No.	BI product/application	Product owner	Phase in product life cycle	Active users/ growth	Data Warehouse (DWH) & Extract, Transform, Load (ETL) services	Business planning	Dash-boarding and reporting	Analysis and self-service
1	Investments planning and reporting		New		Tools and releases (as-is/to-be)			
2	Real estate reporting		New					
3	Management Information cockpit		Growth					
4	Order-to-cash reporting		Growth					
4.1	**O2C—Open receivables**		**Growth**					
4.2	**O2C—local sales stats**		**Remove**					
5	Sales and pipeline reporting		Growth					
6	Financial reporting (BS, P&L, CF)		Maturity					
7	Cost accounting information system		Maturity					
8	Solvency controlling		Remove					

making strategic choices on the target portfolio and finding the right balance between growing and well-established BI products and services. Typical portfolio strategies in this context include:

- "Grow or die" (achieve targeted adoption or get removed from portfolio) and "Fail fast" (avoid keeping failed product innovations alive for too long)
- Exploit "quick wins" (reduce the time to value from introduction to early adoption)
- Stabilize and promote "rising stars" (ship incremental improvements of quickly growing BI products to stabilize them and retain/grow user community)
- Harvest the "cash cows" (extend the period of mass adoption by incrementally investing in minor enhancements, releases)
- Explore "moon shots" (keep a healthy pipeline of new product introductions to provide consumers with new innovations and keep the portfolio fresh, but nevertheless aligned with BI strategy)

There are different ways of how BI products and services can be categorized from a portfolio perspective which provide different insights regarding focus areas and priorities. Common examples of portfolio dimensions include:

- Lifecycle perspective: Growth (e.g., user adoption) vs. age of product
- Value perspective: Value potential vs. degree of feasibility
- Strategy perspective: Performance (value) vs. strategic importance
- Timing perspective: (operational, short-term) urgency vs. (strategic, long-term) importance

An example BI portfolio is illustrated below in Fig. 5.4 which plots products by their growth and age as well as importance (measured by total user numbers indicated by the bubble size). This can aid prioritizing investments.

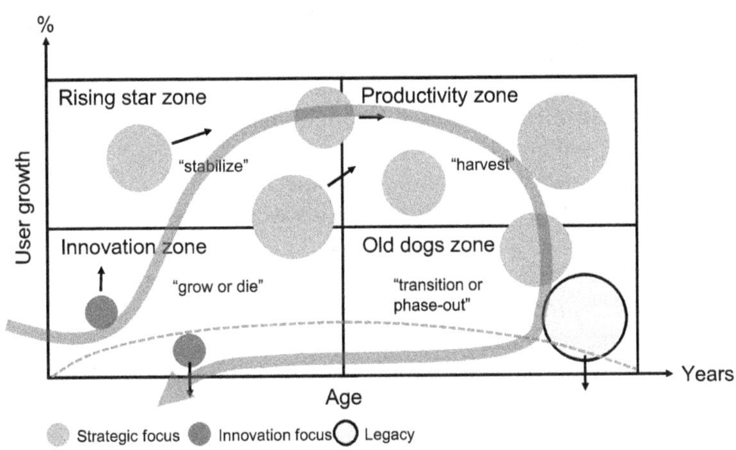

Fig. 5.4 BI portfolio management along life-cycle (© Exner/Zunic 2024. All Rights Reserved)

Regardless of the beforementioned models used, to capture the value dimension in the portfolio, the following KPIs can be considered:

- Productivity gains (process output related to process input)
- Return on investment (Dollar output per Dollar spent)
- TCO (CapEx/OpEx)
- End-user satisfaction (perceived user satisfaction score)
- Net promoter score
- BI landscape complexity (number of BI applications per user group or per function)
- Age of BI applications (age of BI application versus adoption)

The life cycle of BI products and services is typically governed on different levels of detail depending on the life-cycle stage.

New product ideation and planning will often be governed on a portfolio level to avoid an uncontrolled redundancy of BI products and services and to ensure that they are prioritized based on anticipated value contribution.

Once the product life cycle reaches the implementation and validation stage, BI products and services are typically governed on the level of individual projects or programs based on defined requirements. A specific governance aspect to be considered in BI projects is the cross-organizational nature of BI. This requires a close alignment between the project level and an overarching steering level (Oversight) including touchpoints to data and information owners, process owners, enterprise architects, and other cross-domain experts in the organization. Once BI products are delivered, they are typically governed by Ops or DevOps teams who manage maintenance, changes, issue resolution, and continuous monitoring. These different levels of governance along the product lifecycle enable the core governance pillars "BI lifecycle value," "End-user adoption," and "Continuous improvement" as shown in Fig. 5.5.

Let us now take a closer look at the core pillars of BI governance.

End-User Adoption Dimension

The overall value contribution of BI depends on both the business value potential and the attractiveness to BI users (user adoption). Ideally, we have both high business value potential and high BI user adoption.

Therefore, governance cannot afford anymore to stand in the way of making adoption easy due to, e.g., over-regulations. This would consequently lead to ineffective BI governance.

On the contrary, effective BI governance should ease information consumption as much as possible by removing any organizational, technological, and other usage barriers, of which there are many in practice.

Some potential examples of why BI products and services are not widely adopted include:

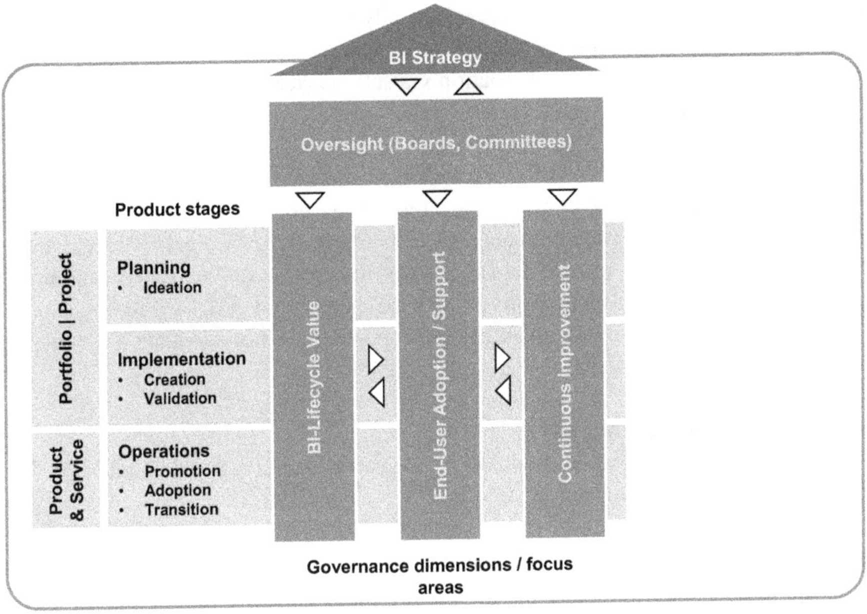

Fig. 5.5 BI governance framework—across product stages (© Exner/Zunic 2024. All Rights Reserved)

- Required data is not available or outdated
- Available data cannot be trusted (e.g., data reconciliation issues)
- Presentation of data is confusing
- User experience is nonintuitive
- User experience does not cover inclusion of the disabled
- Performance issue
- Lack of training
- Too restrictive access policy
- No improvement to legacy
- Too static to meet changing requirements

Most of these barriers have to do with governance that is either not in place, too restrictive, too unresponsive, or too little aware of the real BI user needs.

Additionally, some BI trends have emerged in recent years that challenge traditional BI governance even more such as:

- Data usage trends
- Tooling and deployment trends
- Data Integration trends

Data Usage Trends

The following data usage trends have emerged and need a consideration within BI governance:

- Shift from static pre-definable reporting to dynamic data-driven storytelling
- Increased demand for non-corporate data (big data)
- Increased local report content creation via self-service
- Mobile consumption as default

As report creation and report usage become more and more self-service, exclusive central governance of content (e.g., reports) is not viable anymore. Content ownership and content production need to be increasingly embedded on a local level in the respective lines of business. Flexible integration of governed and non-governed data sources also needs to be increasingly considered. Closed-shop solutions designed exclusively for management reporting are not adequate anymore as they limit data access, analytics use cases, and adoption.

Tooling and Deployment Trends

The following tooling and deployment trends can be observed and should be considered within BI governance:

- Shift from a formerly "best of breed" only approach to a more balanced approach also considering "best of suite" opportunities
- BI platforms instead of BI tools
- De-coupling of BI tools (e. g. reporting tools) from BI data foundation (e. g. data warehouse, data lakes)
- BI consumption in the cloud

As the BI vendor and tooling landscape gets more fragmented, it becomes increasingly challenging to centrally enforce a common enterprise-wide BI tooling strategy. Many organizations struggle with adequately responding to an ever-growing demand for new analytic features while at the same time administering, securing, and servicing the installed base. The emergence of locally installed BI tools ("shadow IT") in the lines of business is the logical consequence.

Typically, centrally enforced tools are less and less able to contain, let alone eliminate "shadow IT." Many organizations have therefore taken a different approach and decided to embrace local autonomy by decoupling ownership and governance of front-end/user experience tools from data foundation. More and more organizations are replacing on-premise BI tools with best-of-suite Cloud offerings. Cloud (Software-as-a-Service—SaaS) increasingly becomes the default deployment option. The typical related benefit expectations of SaaS are accelerated innovation adoption (no customer activities for upgrades or support packages anymore), open integration while at the same time reducing infrastructure and operations costs. The governance and operation of BI tools is hence essentially outsourced to the preferred BI vendor of choice, while local business units are free to use whichever front end they prefer.

Data Integration Trends

The following data integration trends should be evaluated regarding BI governance impact:

- From centrally governed data warehousing ("single source of truth") to approaches open to keep source data where it is including less strictly governed data (exploration of unprocessed data)
- From ETL (Extract Transform Load) to ELT (Extract Load Transform), which means load first, explore second. Data not necessarily pre-defined for a specific use case.

BI reference architectures need to increasingly be able to integrate larger and less structured data sets from more diverse sources (commonly known as "big data"). This requires rethinking architecture guidelines and practices in the BI architecture domain. Until recently it was still common practice to physically integrate (mostly) corporate data in data warehouses via extract, transform, and load (ETL) mechanisms. This resulted in high data redundancy, limited real-time integration, and no access to semi- or unstructured data. But it was technically the only way to provide a harmonized view on corporate performance. With the technology advances of the last decade, BI architectures are increasingly able to integrate large data sources without physically moving data. This also means that more ungoverned (external) data can be queried and hence finds its way into corporate reporting. The once holy concept of a "single source of truth" across all data domains is increasingly unrealistic up to the point that some voices have deemed BI "dead." While we fundamentally disagree with the latter, it is still true that new architecture concepts need to be considered and integrated in established BI reference architectures.

Continuous Improvement Dimension

As the adoption of enterprise-wide BI grows, governance and operations will be increasingly confronted with change. Over time new stakeholder groups will be involved, requirements are likely to change, new technologies emerge and at the same time the scale at which the solution needs to operate expands. All of these environmental forces place tensions on the BI organization and its governance structures, which means it cannot remain entirely static and resilient to change. On the other hand, if there is no governance at all or it is too fluid and adaptive, BI threatens to dissolve into "analytical chaos."

> Therefore, the challenge is to design BI governance structures and architectures for stability while at the same time allowing sufficient flexibility to introduce change and innovation to achieve continuous adoption and value.

A good strategy to achieve an "effective" level of BI governance is to embed a formal continuous improvement process from the start. In addition, it is good practice to establish an enterprise-wide BI community and/or focus groups in which product and service owners, analytical users, and BI mentors can collaborate and informally share and exchange experiences and practices. This helps create and strengthen a continuous learning culture, in which projects and users can benefit from others.

However, what is often lacking is a true commitment including funding to learning and continuous improvement providing employees sufficient space and training investment to achieve this. Let's take an example to illustrate the relevancy of funding. First, we assume an investment of 10% per employee based on the contractual agreed hours per week, which should be dedicated for knowledge-sharing with others, populating internal knowledge-databases, creating improvement ideas and others to foster innovations in our BI domain. If we further assume a contract with 40 hours per week, this results in an available time budget of 4 hours per week and employee. Let's further assume that our BI organization has 20 employees and out of 52 weeks per year we consider only 30 weeks relevant for our use case due to vacation, illness, other priorities and other constraints. The equation would look like follows: 20 employees * 30 weeks * 4 hours/week = 2,400 employee hours. If we assume 8 working hours per day/per employee, we end up with 300 person days per year which equals to 1,5 FTE. This example should emphasize the need to include the funding in the governance and adoption conversation. It is worth to mention, that this only reflects the cost aspect. The value contribution of the activities is likely exceeding the individual time investment by far, however it is hard to measure.

With the beforementioned we focused on commitment and funding. What is equally important is the factor of acknowledgment and appreciation throughout the entire organization.

We view this as probably one of the most challenging aspects of BI governance, because it depends on the organizational culture and degree of freedom which employees have to continuously explore, engage, and share learnings with others.

We recommend to at least make an effort to embed a continuous learning culture from the start in the BI governance setup. This means, for example, attracting self-motivated individuals who proactively engage in collecting project/program experiences and insights "from the field" across all BI initiatives and projects. This can serve as a knowledge management base to which the entire organization has access. Even if only a few employees are engaged, the benefits can be leveraged for the entire organization.

Regular meetings can be established in addition to providing a knowledge exchange forum as well as sounding board for BI project managers and product owners on improvement potential.

Key Elements to Be Governed

To overcome previously mentioned adoption barriers, an effective support and governance structure is required throughout the entire BI lifecycle. Such a support structure will need to include the following key elements as illustrated in Fig. 5.6 below:

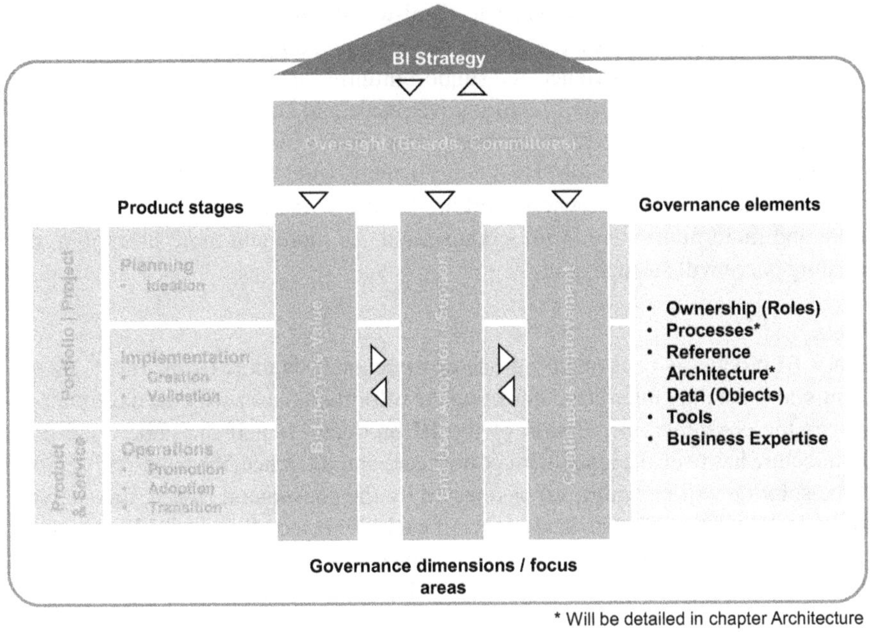

Fig. 5.6 BI governance framework—governance elements ()

- Ownership
- Data
- Tools
- Business expertise

Ownership

Successful user adoption starts with active ownership. The entire BI portfolio should be supported by dedicated product owners who are capable and incentivized to both promote and support the adoption of the BI product across the entire lifecycle. This includes, for example, building relationships to key users and multipliers in the organization, implementing feedback channels (e.g., via user focus groups, SME communities), active communication (e.g., via Wikis, Blogs, How-To's, FAQs) and acting as a single point of contact for issue identification and resolution.

Data

A further key success factor of enterprise-wide BI adoption is data literacy and data education. As new data is introduced into the BI environment, it becomes crucial to guide particularly casual BI consumers from the start in working with the data in a daily business context. This includes, for example, a clear understanding of data structures, data dependencies, filters, data sources, available analysis depths, and business logic and how they relate to "real-world" analysis and decision needs. Well-designed BI products have certain metadata and corporate taxonomies "built-in" to enrich the user experience and support intuitive data understanding. Yet, even the best designed product will require governance and support around content and information consumption. To support data education, a blended approach of official trainings and daily "on-the-job" shadowing usually works best. This can be achieved by key users and product owners working hand-in-hand to build a community of more and more multipliers in the organization. As more and more users join, the learning curve will steepen quickly.

Tools

Every BI product is consumed via one or more analysis tools (front ends). As the front-end is the only interface connecting the information user with the data, it alone shapes the consumers perception of the BI product. Even if the underlying data architecture has been designed with utmost care and diligence, the front-end decides if the solution will be embraced or rejected by the consumers. Hence, the analysis tool selection process is a critical aspect of each BI project. Successful BI organizations have realized this and aim at reducing the uncontrolled growth and diversity of the analytics portfolio, because this leads to higher complexity in support and operations while users are potentially confused about which solution to employ. It is good practice to develop a BI tool and vendor strategy (in collaboration with the vendor's product roadmap) on a corporate level (BI-CC or governance committee) and guide projects and initiatives from the start regarding recommendations for the best fit in a given BI project.

New BI tools will require introductory training, mentors or SMEs, and ongoing education (e.g., with upgrades). The BI lifecycle needs to include additional tool support activities—e.g. help the end-consumer choose the right tool; monitor data availability and quality; segment the user community to support each group appropriately; establish service level agreements for response times and issue resolution; and communicate a clear escalation path and contacts.

Business Expertise

The degree to which a BI solution is meaningful depends significantly on the ability of the information consumers to interact with and interpret data to generate new actionable insights from it. This requires both a business and analytical mindset as well as the business experience in how data-driven decision-making processes work effectively, i.e. thinking and acting in iterative closed-loop analysis and decision processes.

This involves, for example, the ability to define decision-making models, apply statistical concepts, and finally querying the data in the BI solution to derive the relevant output to prepare a decision.

As BI practitioners we believe that no BI tool can fully automate the decision-making process by preconceiving all potential analyses the business requires for decision support. This is why business expertise ultimately decides upon successful usage of any BI solution or product. BI solutions are mere facilitators that should be designed with an anticipative mindset to allow users to explore, experiment, simulate, test assumptions, and be aided by the system as much as possible, but they will not replace the business decision-maker!

Conversely, well-designed and structured decision-making processes can be extremely valuable inputs to designing BI solutions in the most effective way. It is good practice to trace the causal chain of analyses that led up to a sound business decision and use this as feedback to incrementally improve the BI system. For example, this could help to separate business-critical information that was actually used in decision-making processes from non-needed or even confusing information. This can result in leaner performance measurement systems and information supply chains.

The key challenge is how to bundle these often widely dispersed skill sets of business expertise, analytics expertise, and data/IT affinity and apply them effectively to business related questions.

One way of achieving this is BI mentorship. This involves super users—financial, marketing, or operational analysts who understand the data and the BI tool and have been successful in using it to provide value. Data stewards and architects could also assist here. The mentors can help end users understand key dimensions and metrics and how they need to be interpreted in a particular business context. BI mentors are business partners with a unique contribution to the BI strategy. Their contribution includes (but is not limited to) helping new users get started, identifying and developing data mining opportunities, pinpointing data trends, and staying focused on the business goals.

KPIs to measure user adoption success include:

- Number and growth of active users
- Key-user to end-user ratio
- User-to-employee ratio
- % of users trained

Governance Framework

Why is BI governance different? Let us now take a deeper look.

It is important to recognize that BI governance is different from other IT governance domains (especially compared with transactional applications) due to the following unique characteristics:

- Making sense of data is typically more difficult and context-dependent than running a transactional process, which is highly standardizable
- Data consumption by reports and data creation by transactional processing are separated, while data creation is embedded in the transactional process execution
- True insight requires exploration and experimentation with data, while repeatable business processes aim to adhere to given process standards

- Majority of requirements emerge during data usage, while majority of business process requirements are pre-defined by standard practices or harmonized upfront
- Data integration needs are changing over time, while process integration between standard applications and systems is more and more built-in
- Analytics is critical for data-driven decision-making, while transactional process execution is critical for business operations to run

This list is by no means exhaustive, but it shows that governance principles applying to transactional processing cannot be transferred one-to-one to business intelligence.

However, traditional BI governance models were often centered exclusively around standardization and centralization. The key imperatives were stability, consistency, and reliability to enable enterprise-wide BI across large, complex system landscapes.

This was typically achieved by establishing central corporate functions with the mandate to define and enforce corporate BI guidelines and a target operating model (roles, responsibilities, processes) aligned with strategic objectives. Hence, the predominant emphasis was placed on a centralized *Oversight* dimension.

While this paradigm still remains relevant, it does not fully meet the needs any longer. An effective governance framework should balance centralized and localized governance while keeping centralized governance oversight to a reasonable minimum. Aspects typically requiring a more local governance focus include, for example, user adoption, lifecycle value, and continuous improvement (ideation).

BI Governance in the BI Strategy Process

The BI governance model outlined above plays an important role in the BI strategy process. As illustrated in Fig. 5.7 below, it defines the responsibilities and "rules" in the BI strategy process as well as the ownership of the inputs (like requirements, strategic priorities) and outputs (like strategy document updates, decisions on product and service portfolio, funding needs). Additionally, BI governance supports the realization of BI strategy by providing guidance and best practices.

Centralized governance (Oversight dimension) "owns" the BI strategy and ensures that the BI products, services, and BI project portfolio are strategy compliant. This includes:

- Integrating strategic priorities, technology drivers, and operational drivers into a BI roadmap.
- Being mandated to make decisions and shape the fundamental building blocks of enterprise-wide BI (like ownership, processes, data, architecture, tools).
- Advising enterprise-wide BI initiatives on fundamental design decisions and also reviewing compliance.
- Defining roles and responsibilities as well as how these roles interact across the BI product and service lifecycle from delivery (project management) to operations (incident and release management).

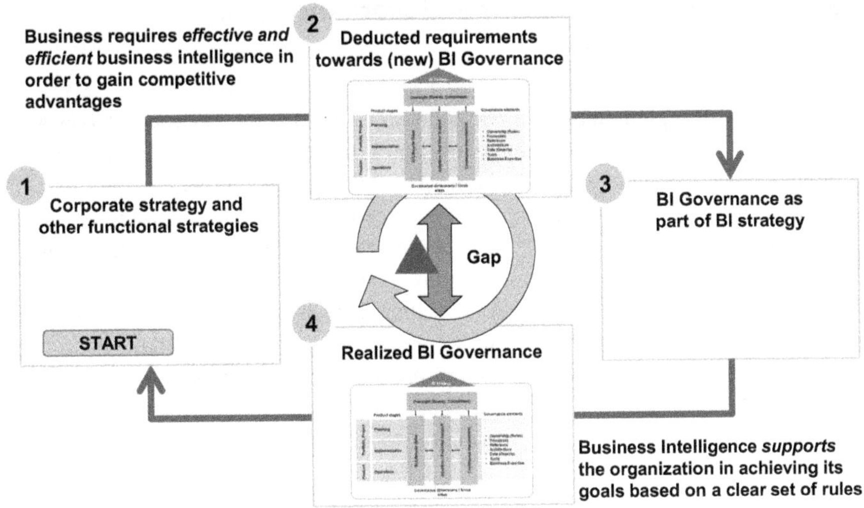

Fig. 5.7 BI governance provides a clear set of rules (© Exner/Zunic 2024. All Rights Reserved)

- Establishing the governance bodies and boards needed for formal cross-organizational alignment between BI and other IT domains and business communities (e.g., master data governance, transactional system governance, local system governance).
- Defining the operational processes and end-user support processes. It should be business-centric and co-owned with IT.
- Focusing on an enterprise-wide perspective and does not micro-manage local point solutions.

Localized governance "owns" the BI lifecycle and adoption on BI product and service level. This includes:

- Ensuring continuity of BI product and service ownership ("single face to the customer") throughout the BI lifecycle from ideation to adoption.
- Focus on removing adoption barriers from the start.
- Establishing a business and end-consumer mindset.
- Adopting central governance recommendations, but at the same time focuses on creating flexible solutions that allow information consumers sufficient autonomy to integrate, use, and consume data also from non-IT governed sources.
- Acting as the trusted advisor in the business and feeds back experiences and observations from the field to the centralized governance layer in a continuous loop.

5.3 Working Principles for BI Governance Design

The concrete implementation of BI governance in the organization involves a number of key management decisions. As outlined in previous chapters, this includes among others the positioning of BI in the organization, the definition of areas of responsibility, the split between centralized vs. local ownership as well as the scope and design of the product and service portfolio. Such fundamental decisions are ideally supported by a set of principles and practices that have worked in other organizations and can hence provide direction and guidance. In this chapter, we will outline some working principles that have proven to be effective in practice and are supported by large-scale research on digital initiatives.

Traditional business intelligence governance approaches placed a high priority on formal corporate control and authority usually supported by centralized teams of business and IT owners. The primary goal was to support senior management decision-makers with high-quality information from a single version of truth. While this approach safeguarded a high data quality standard, it at the same time limited access to and integration of relevant data, both from within and outside the organizational boundaries. This limited the overall value of BI for the entire organization and resulted in high efforts and project durations to implement and incorporate change. As more and more data becomes accessible and requested for data-driven decision-making on all levels of the organization, a rigid, entirely centralized governance approach increasingly becomes a major roadblock to successful business intelligence initiatives.

This is an example of how overregulated governance can limit value to the organization. In fact, many of the top challenges encountered by organizations in digital transformations surround governance related questions, including:

- Achieving closer alignment between business and IT
- Enabling continuous improvement of analytics and business processes
- Breaking down functional silos
- Setting up effective governance structures for managing major change efforts
- Governing common data structures across the entire enterprise

In the following, we will introduce some working principles that can be applied to business intelligence governance to address the abovementioned challenges. We will look at seven fundamental working principles:

- Centralize information about digital initiatives
- As the digital maturity grows move to more decentralized governance
- Decentralize ideation and centralize evaluation and prioritization

- Make sure KPIs are set to measure the real impact of the initiative
- Avoid standalone solution by ensuring data compatibility and continuous integration with existing systems
- Implement a methodology that values the potential for each initiative
- Evaluate different scenarios to steward initiatives to full-scale impact

We will now explore each working principle in more detail from a business intelligence perspective.

Centralize Information about digital Initiatives

It is often striking how few organizations have a truly holistic view of their digital initiatives, let alone BI and analytics related initiatives. This is often a result of decentralized organizational power structures that prevent sharing and alignment of local activity with a central unit. Local business units often fear of being controlled and losing autonomy the more they reveal. But without a corporate inventory of BI initiatives, it is impossible to manage a holistic BI portfolio—hence redundancies and unrealized synergies are likely.

Therefore, we recommend establishing a centralized repository of all initiatives for a centralized view and to develop a value-based communication strategy to collaborate with business units across the entire organization ("walk the talk").

As the Digital maturity Grows Move to Decentralized Governance

The more business intelligence matures and data-driven decision-making becomes pervasive, the less centralized governance is required or even helpful. As mentioned before, enterprise-wide analytics is hard to do—it requires a central body of oversight and alignment to make it work initially in the early stages of adoption. But once the organization has crossed the threshold of early adoption, local teams and communities of experts should be increasingly empowered to take the lead of the initiatives.

Some central oversight will always be required, but management intervention on a micro-level should be avoided.

Decentralize Ideation and Centralize Evaluation and Prioritization

Ideation is the creative process of generating, developing, and communicating new innovative ideas. It is one of the key catalysts for change and innovation within the organization. In a dynamically changing business landscape, embracing and fostering ideation is of existential importance. However, as ideation is by nature unpredictable, local, and dynamic it is difficult to be governed centrally. The challenge is to close the distance between the idea creators and the governance representatives (management) required to make it happen. Organizations use different approaches to do this. Successful organizations seek to empower and reward employees to make their ideas visible. This can be done, for example, by incubator or intrapreneurship programs in which employees are encouraged to bring an idea to market. Another common approach are innovation events such as hackathons to enable teams to collaborate on software projects. Many organizations also implement ideation platforms to encourage idea formulation and sharing. These are all ways of promoting idea generation and capturing these ideas, which would otherwise not be visible. Once captured, these ideas can be formally evaluated and prioritized in a centralized decision-making process. An innovation lead can funnel these ideas into the project portfolio where they have a chance to demonstrate their potential.

Make Sure KPIs Are Set to Measure the Real Impact of the Initiative
Enterprise-wide initiatives are expensive and difficult; they require stamina and tolerance of disruption on many layers of the organization. To be worth the effort, there needs to be a return that is measurable. However, expressing a return in financial terms is not always easy, especially if there is no direct, mono-causal impact on the bottom line.

Therefore, our advice is to link enterprise-wide initiatives as closely as possible to KPIs of corporate strategy and clearly demonstrate how they influence business outcome strategically. This goes beyond just measuring adoption rates and user satisfaction—it requires a value realization framework as part of the Oversight function.

Avoid Standalone Solution by Ensuring Data Compatibility and Continuous Integration with Existing Systems
An aspect which is often underestimated when planning enterprise-wide BI initiatives is the importance of a standardized, integrated data foundation and infrastructure. Although this might sound obvious, it is in practice a huge challenge. Not well-integrated or siloed legacy systems represent an enormous cost driver for enterprise-wide BI solutions and often lead to a siloed BI architecture which does not scale well. Sound design involves using a common reference architecture for modeling, standard integration technologies and techniques, re-using of corporate data, semantically aligning disparate sources. Integrated architectures need central oversight and enforcement, but they pay off in the long run.

Implement a System that Values the Potential for Each Initiative
As your BI portfolio grows, we recommend categorizing your BI initiatives along dimensions of value and adoption. To do this, it is advisable to establish a metadata repository for each of your initiatives and/or products which captures these dimensions. In its simplest form, this results in a 2x2 matrix visualization (see Fig. 5.4 in

Sect. 5.5.2), based on which you can attach different governance levels. For example, innovations in a very early adoption stage need entirely different roles and governance policies than large-scale transformation initiatives or enterprise ventures.

Evaluate Different Scenarios to Steward Initiatives to Full-Scale Impact
Scaling initiatives on an enterprise-wide level is challenging and there is no "blueprint" for success. Yet we can observe recurring behaviors and practices of successful digital leaders. A good practice is to concentrate all efforts on making the initial product/release/service a success. This involves a project management approach that embraces change and focuses on removing roadblocks, organizational obstacles, or communication barriers that limit product or service success.

Once the initial product is introduced, the transition period to full adoption needs to be carefully managed with a slightly different mindset. This is a critical moment for any initiative because the transition period will still require an extended period of tender care. At the same time, new aspects of governance are introduced which to some extent limit flexibility to change.

The transition phase is critical for creating the needed pull effect from the organization to allow the initiative to scale.

"Stable Core" as the Guardian of BI Governance
The conflicting interests described above in the area of BI management information often require careful balancing and trade-offs. To achieve this, it is advisable to identify and separate areas which should not be subject to regular change. These areas are sometimes difficult to isolate but can be referred to as "stable core" as illustrated in Fig. 5.9.

In practice, it is often challenging to clearly cut the boundaries of the stable core along different dimensions (e.g., content, functional, technological, architectural, organizational), which need to be protected from undesired changes by appropriate governance structures ("guardian of the stable core"). For this reason, below illustration in Fig. 5.8 should be seen as "food for thoughts."

5.4 BI Organization Design Options

In this chapter, we will take a closer look at the different flavors of BI organizations, their individual characteristics, and their value propositions. Depending on the company size, structural complexity, and last, but not least corporate culture and behavioral conditioning, certain types of BI organizations are better suited than others. From a practitioner's point of view, this leads to the obvious question of which organizational design options exist in principle and how they can be evaluated in a fact-based manner.

This chapter will illustrate different BI organizational design options and introduce a set of criteria to evaluate the best-fitting option for an organization. The underlying assumption is that the BI organization is a permanent entity with a defined mandate, ownership, clear and transparent working model, and defined governance processes, as opposed to a temporary project or program.

At the end of the chapter, we will also provide some practical examples illustrating alternative organizational designs and the mechanics of how they operate.

In the previous chapters, we outlined the general dimensions and principles of BI governance and its relation to BI strategy. We discussed the need for a blended approach of centralized and decentralized governance and why business intelligence requires a unique approach. We introduced concepts such as the BI lifecycle, BI portfolio management, and continuous improvement to aid the design of enterprise-wide BI governance.

The first thing to recognize is that there is no standard "best practice" organizational model that just needs to be rolled out. Each organization needs to evaluate which type of governance structure provides the best fit to the organization's size, complexity, and culture. We will therefore describe alternative organizational designs and evaluate them from a practitioner's point of view.

Secondly, organizations using business intelligence on an enterprise-wide scale and thinking about creating or redesigning new BI governance structures do not operate in a vacuum. They will need to embed BI-specific governance structures in

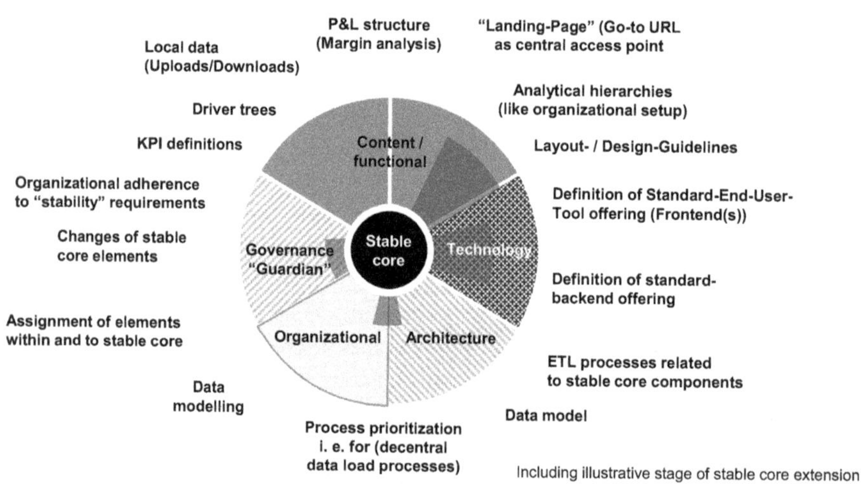

Fig. 5.8 Exemplary elements of a "Stable Core" (© Exner/Zunic 2024. All Rights Reserved)

Of the total of 7 optimization goals, the respective BI-CC options (=columns) ... are ... (row headers) by x targets (cells).	Virtual BI-CC	Virtual BI-CC with BI Mgmt and Central Build Teams	BI-CC without operations (BI-DC)	Full BI-CC for Ramp-up technologies	Full BI-CC
COMPLETELY SUPPORTED	0	3	5	1	7
PARTLY SUPPORTED	1	2	2	2	0
NOT SUPPORTED IN KEY AREAS	1	2	0	1	0
ENTIRELY NOT SUPPORTED	5	0	0	3	0
	7	7	7	7	7
			2nd recommendation		1st recommendation

Fig. 5.9 Approach for evaluation of best organizational BI-CC option (© Exner/Zunic 2024. All Rights Reserved)

an existing environment of IT and business governance frameworks. In case an IT governance model already exists, it can be the central reference point for designing a tailored BI-specific governance framework. In an ideal state, only BI-specific adaptations and enhancements are needed. We will also explore this aspect by illustrating the needed collaboration between different organizational units and roles.

As already mentioned previously, the typical organizational setup for orchestrating the various aspects of BI governance is known as BI-CC (BI Competence Center)/BI CoE (BI Center of Excellence) or BI-DC (BI Development Center). The term was first introduced around the turn of the millennium, recognizing the need for a coordinated cross-enterprise approach to business intelligence bundled in a dedicated organizational unit.

- *What is a BI-CC / BI-DC?*
  A BI-CC is a dedicated organizational unit which bundles the know-how, tasks, and responsibilities required to provide an effective management information supply throughout the entire enterprise.
  The scope and range of a BI-CC can vary. Some organizations decide to include BI management, BI consulting, and BI build activities in a "BI-DC" (Development Center) but exclude IT and business operations from their BI organization.

- *Why is this of particular importance for BI?*
  The BI domain is characterized by seemingly conflicting interests: standardization versus flexibility, centralization versus decentralization, single point of truth versus controlled redundancy, etc. A BI-CC can help establish effective mechanisms to balance these conflicting interests on a continuous basis.

- *What are the key duties of a BI-CC / BI-DC?*
  A BI-CC is typically associated with the following duties:
  - Guiding the users in self-service to meet their BI needs, primarily by training them on how to use the data, as well as on how to use BI tools as a mechanism to access the data and manipulate it. This allows the center to have some leverage, instead of having to create every report or query itself.
  - Performing ad hoc or complex analysis, in conjunction with the business units. After all, the center's personnel are analytic experts. In case the analysis becomes repetitive, it can be turned into a self-service task for the users, e.g. by extending BI functionalities or implementing BI applications.
  - Oversee the analytics approach across the enterprise to ensure consistency and scalability. The center connects different parts of the organization that have similar needs and problems.
  - Coordinating use and re-use of business metadata in the enterprise and helping to define and integrate definitions of the relevant business terms.
  - Set standards for BI tools used and supported across the enterprise.

Once the different available options, which we will explain in detail later in this chapter, are clear, the next logical question is how to prepare and finally drive a decision on the organizational setup. The decision should be properly grounded based on arguments which remain true even in retro-perspective. So, we need to be clear about decisive factors based on which we are going to make our decision.

From practical point of view, it makes sense not to confuse both activities of a) identifying and describing the options with its characteristics in a neutral way and b) the evaluation of the different options based on a set of decision criteria.

How could some exemplary criteria look like? Please keep in mind that these need to be tailored to specific organizational situation. We first will introduce exemplary objectives each of the options should ideally support.

In our example below, we assume to have seven most relevant objectives a BI organization should support. These are:

1. The BI organization supports **efficiency gains** by
   - Faster reaction to business requirements (measured, for example, by response time)
   - Shorter overall processing time (measured, for example, by process throughput time from request to solution)
   - Optimized process setup (processes, sub-processes, and activities)

2. The BI organization supports **quality gains** by
   - Detailed definition of accountability for the end-to-end process like (requirements gathering)
   - Reduction of error rates (measured, for example, based on number of incidents after go-live based on a structured "error tree")

- Establishing of a strong governance for the stable core and a more flexible governance for the remaining topics
- Standardized guidelines for up-skilling (people development plan, training on the job, and others)

3. The BI organization supports **grouping of requirements** to reporting, planning by

   - Centralizing the entry-point for all requirements
   - Transparently assigned responsibility within organizational setup of the company
   - Technical bundling of requirements (supporting a single-source-of-truth principle) by provisioning a suitable central tool for requirement collection

4. The BI organization supports improving the overall organizational integration by

   - Consistent and undivided responsibility for content, processes, organization, and technology in business intelligence
   - Dedicated counterparts for internal customer groups, provide support to these groups end-to-end, or establishing a key-account principle

5. The BI organization supports improving the overall perception of BI value contribution by

   - Consistent and overarching marketing of BI solutions and services
   - Transparency of achievements compared to known plans (for example shown on an intranet portal page)

6. The BI organization supports a better anchoring of innovations and BI strategy process by

   - Unique responsibility for BI strategy and BI strategy development
   - Suitable budget for innovations and systematically screening of relevant market trends in the BI domain
   - Synchronizing of innovation- and BI strategy processes

7. The BI organization supports **a better anchoring within the overall corporate organization** including a clear and unambiguous responsibility for BI strategy

Based on the beforementioned examples, the concrete available BI organizational options in the given context need to be developed. Based on this, we will have objectives and decision-making characteristics clear and documented, hence we are ready to conduct an evaluation. A simple and pragmatic approach could look as follows:

- The respective objective is **supported** by a particular governance design option **completely** (1 point in first row) or
- The respective objective is **supported** by a particular governance design option **partly** (1 point in second row) or

- The respective objective is **not supported in key areas** by a particular governance design option (1 point in third row) or
- The respective objective is **entirely not supported** by a particular governance design option (1 point in last row)

If we now evaluate each option with its characteristics based on the above objectives, we might be able to produce a result as shown in Fig. 5.9 below. Of course, there are many different and more advanced approaches to reaching a conclusion. However, the essential result of this exercise is that we have followed a transparent and traceable way to make a decision, or at least to develop a decision proposal.

The BI organization design options used in this example will be introduced subsequently.

5.4.1 Option 1: Virtual BI-CC

A virtual BI-CC preserves the existing organizational structure and is designed to align BI development and operations across all BI topic areas in a virtual team of experts and managers. All participating members of the virtual BI-CC have parallel day-to-day jobs in the line organization and are only dedicated to the BI-CC with partial capacity.

This is probably the most common type of BI-CC because the effort to set it up is very low and major organizational change is not required.

However, the main downside of this organization is that there is no formal commitment of and access to key resources. Thus, there is practically no overall process responsibility and due to multiple virtual dotted reporting lines, clear responsibilities are hard to be assigned to individual members.

A virtual BI-CC typically does not improve the end-to-end integration and quality of critical BI processes and tasks. There is often little or no ownership of processes and often not even a clear commitment from senior management to improve the BI domain overall. Hence, there is little room for BI innovation and BI strategy design because operational and tactical tasks fully occupy the limited resources.

In summary, this kind of organization is typically designed for "keeping the lights on" but it does not have the power to sustainably improve the effectiveness, efficiency, or quality of corporate BI. The absence of governance can in fact lead to fragmented departmental "shadow" BI solutions which contradict the concept of a "stable core" which we introduced earlier.

5.4.2 Option 2: Virtual BI-CC with BI Management and Central Build Teams

In this setup, a BI management office is established as a dedicated staff or line function on top of the Virtual BI-CC for centrally coordinating and driving all BI topics.

This will typically lead to higher awareness of the BI domain within the organization and can help establish a visible governance around the innovation and BI strategy process in addition to keeping the daily operations running. This includes, for example, a regular exchange with key stakeholders and decision-makers on the expected future BI capabilities and services which can serve as a foundation for the future BI portfolio. With the appointment and designation of a single point of accountability for BI, you can improve access to business stakeholders and decision makers. You can also improve the marketing of BI.

In addition to creating a BI management office, BI development and consulting activities are centralized in a single department as well. This enables efficiency gains by combining development capacities and know-how in one organizational unit. This also facilitates improved process standardization around a shared governance model for BI development.

BI operations however are not changed or affected by this type of organization and remain purely virtual. This usually implies that no significant improvement in process quality is possible, as BI operations have no direct access to BI development.

Multiple reporting lines of employees in the continued virtual setup complicates a strict governance function around the stable core, especially at the BI development/BI operation interface.

5.4.3 Option 3: BI-CC Without Operations (BI-DC)

This type of competence center bundles BI management, BI consulting, and BI build activities into one organization to ensure an integrated delivery process from demand management to project initiation and realization. With this option and its dedicated staff, we enter the space of non-virtual organizational setup.

A BI-DC further strengthens the organizational role of BI and enables a closer integration of the innovation and BI strategy process with the actual delivery process. This type of organization is typically funded by line of business budgets which give the BI-DC the ability to proactively drive the BI topic agenda. Hence, the BI organization has an official mandate to collaborate with the sponsoring business areas to improve overall BI maturity. This also improves the knowledge about available data, systems, and responsibilities in the overall BI environment—key information which is otherwise often unknown.

Often a BI-DC setup is chosen, when a large multi-year BI program on group- or headquarter-level ends and needs to transition to a line organization. Typically, such an organization is driven and sponsored by a board member like the CFO when traditional reporting approaches fail to provide the expected level of decision support or data quality. Hence, the original program objectives are now pursued in a dedicated organization on a continuous basis. These objectives typically include common data definitions, central data maintenance processes, common reporting formats, and BI tools.

To maintain a standardized BI process beyond the original BI program, a BI-DC can be ramped-up in parallel. Once the BI-DC is in operation it can achieve increased efficiency through faster response to business requirements, shorter total process time, and improved process organization.

Yet, BI operations remain unchanged. In this setup, the focus is on supporting the BI build activities, but there is no change of BI operations, which are still distributed. This can result in quality issues particularly at the interface between BI development and BI operation.

5.4.4 Option 4: Full BI-CC for Ramp-up Innovations

In this setup, a full-fledged BI competence center including BI management, BI consulting/build, and BI operations is installed—but with a predominant focus on the introduction of major new innovations during a ramp-up phase (e.g., big data applications, in-memory technologies, cloud delivery, artificial intelligence).

The goal is to introduce new innovations in a controlled and well-governed environment to ensure a smooth, non-disruptive transition. The new innovations accompany established technologies, services, and approaches via existing BI responsibilities.

Commonly, this type of setup is interesting when ground-breaking innovations affect the entire BI landscape. It is advisable that possible organizational impact is evaluated upfront, for example, in a BI lab. This might include the disappearance of entire roles and tasks or the opportunity of shifting organizational boundaries, e.g. from a completely separated Build and Run organization to a DevOps model in which development, operations, and administration collaborate in an agile model. The close connection between technological innovation and organizational innovation leads relatively easily to high management perception.

However, with a technology focused innovation mindset, scaling a ramp-up BI-CC across the entire organization could lead to substantial complexity. This complexity is mainly caused by isolated consideration of technology innovations without sufficient end-to-end process focus. Hence, an evolution from this scenario toward a full BI-CC is difficult to manage in terms of scaling and because BI is primarily viewed through technology innovation lenses, less from an integrated process point of view. Last but not least responsibilities are bound to change over time with the technological innovation lifecycles.

5.4.5 Option 5: Full BI-CC (Line of Business)

A full-fledged BI-CC is a permanent organization which coordinates all activities and resources across the entire BI domain to ensure that a fact-based approach to decision-making is systematically implemented throughout an organization. The BI-CC is responsible for both the governance structure of BI as well as the analytic applications, projects, practices, services, software, and architecture. Accordingly, the BI-CC provides strategies, plans, priorities, infrastructure, and competencies which the organization needs to derive maximum business value from the BI investment.

The aim of the BI-CC is to empower the whole organization to understand and effectively use BI across all departments. A centralized setup ensures that information and best practices are communicated and shared across the entire organization so that everyone benefits from success stories and lessons learned.

The BI-CC also plays an important organizational role in promoting the interaction between different units and their cultures within an organization. One of the central tasks is knowledge transfer, improvement of analytical skills, tutoring, and training.

The degree of influence a BI-CC has on the surrounding business areas strongly depends on the mandate and commitment from the board. If the value contribution of a BI-CC is fully understood, it can play an extremely important central role in the decision-making process and its continuous improvement within the organization.

By establishing a comprehensive organizational structure to control all BI activities, significant improvements are achievable in many relevant areas:

- Efficiency, effectiveness, quality
- Consolidated and sound understanding of requirements
- Improvement of the overall integration and perception of BI value contribution
- Improvement of the overall know-how about available data and information
- Organizational anchoring of innovation and the BI strategy process

Depending on the size and structure of the organization, multiple BI-CCs with different areas of responsibility and structures might need to coexist side-by-side. This is common in many larger organizations and is often the only practical way of balancing speed and governance.

5.5 BI Organization Examples

5.5.1 Virtual BI-CC

The virtual BI-CC is quite common in practice because it is easy and cost effective to set up and operate. As all members of the BI-CC remain in their line functions (rf. point 1, Fig. 5.10) and only align, for example, via jour-fixe meetings or BI steering boards there is no significant organizational change impact and overhead that needs to be managed. There is neither a dedicated department in place (rf. point 2), let alone board level representation (rf. point 3).

Such a model can be effective in smaller or decentral organizations that aim to empower local communities with a close proximity to the actual business decision-making. But it is difficult to scale because there is no organizational visibility and authority of the BI function in the organization. Hence, for larger organizations aiming for enterprise-wide BI, a virtual BI-CC is typically not sufficient. The lack of formal alignment can result in an uncontrolled spread of localized BI products, data redundancy, and inconsistencies.

In a virtual BI-CC the role of IT is reduced to "keeping the lights on." The IT department will typically not provide dedicated BI products or services and only assign a bare minimum of capacity to BI development and BI operations (rf. point 4, Fig. 5.10 above). Moreover, the capacity allocated to BI is typically shared among

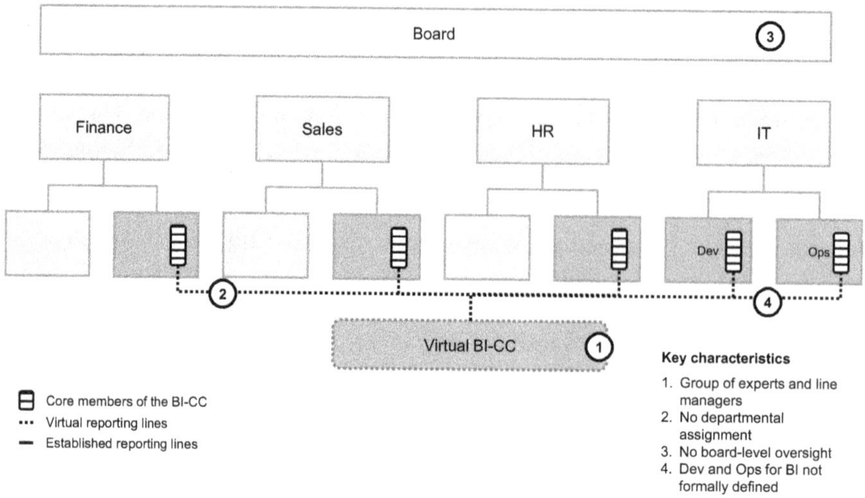

Fig. 5.10 Virtual BI-CC (© Exner/Zunic 2024. All Rights Reserved)

different IT domains and applications. Tactical and strategic alignment between business and IT on management level is entirely absent, because no dedicated leadership roles and responsibilities for BI have been established. On a daily basis, the business communicates BI requirements on an "as needed" basis via change requests and support tickets. Often this kind of "transactional" relationship between business and IT is not specific to business intelligence but reflective of a general perception of IT as a mere cost and hygiene factor.

However, regardless of the perception of IT, there is a growing demand in most organizations for innovative and state-of-the-art BI environments for data-driven decision-making. This includes, for example, business-focused, easily consumable, ready-to-use BI, and artificial intelligence products and services (typically cloud-based). This trend requires a strengthening of IT's role as a BI innovation driver and business enabler that a Virtual BI-CC most likely cannot adequately address.

5.5.2 Virtual BI-CC with Management

The virtual BI-CC with Management is typically an evolution of a virtual BI-CC that establishes a formal central responsibility for business intelligence in the organization. This is typically a dedicated full-time role in a line of business function (like Finance or IT) (rf. point 1, Fig. 5.11 below). The establishment of a BI management role gives BI first visibility in the organization. It aims to coordinate and foster closer alignment between business functions and IT regarding BI-related requirements such as long-term data and reporting strategies (rf. point 2). A Virtual BI-CC with management has the mandate to plan and develop relevant skills, can request the appropriation of needed staff (as members of the Virtual BI-CC), and can influence the needed future technical capabilities (owned by IT).

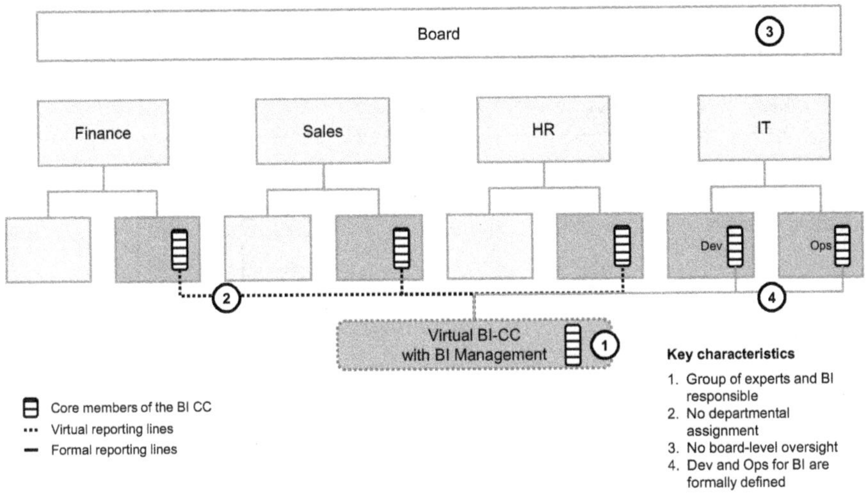

Fig. 5.11 BI-CC with management (© Exner/Zunic 2024. All Rights Reserved)

Often a virtual BI-CC with management is established as part of a larger business or IT transformation program. Typically, such programs recognize the need for more standardization, enhancing enterprise-wide data capabilities or re-engineering business processes and analytical capabilities on an enterprise-wide level. A virtual BI-CC with management could therefore be a temporary step toward a permanent BI organization after the transformation program has been implemented.

However, the BI-CC with management in principle faces the same challenges as the virtual BI-CC. It cannot act like a real business function with the authority to hire staff or define and execute an enterprise-wide BI strategy. It depends on funding and directive from other lines of businesses or programs (rf. point 3, Fig. 5.11 above). Its primary focus is typically the improvement and standardization of BI operations which are in the interest of all business functions who consume BI. There is less of a focus on re-defining and strategically enhancing the BI function, let alone innovating in this area because this requires senior management and C-level backing.

5.5.3 Full BI-CC

A Full BI-CC is not as common as one might assume because it requires a certain perseverance, enterprise readiness, and entrepreneurial spirit to build over a longer period of time. It needs to demonstrate business value like any other business function and at the same time "market" and "brand" itself as an effective business partner in the organization. Only if this can be proven consistently, the BI-CC will be able to secure long-term commitment on board level and funding from different lines of business. In practice, the establishment a full BI-CC requires a continuous, consistent, and multi-year engagement of key stakeholders—this is what we can summarize as "perseverance."

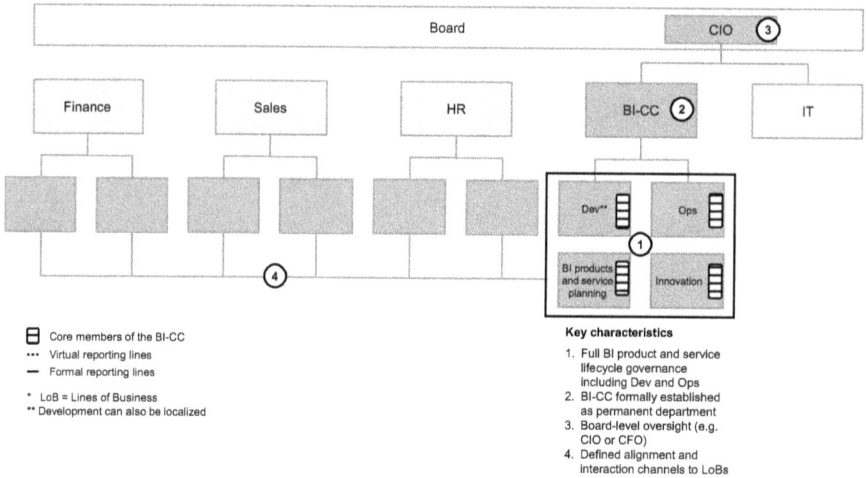

Fig. 5.12 Full BI-CC (© Exner/Zunic 2024. All Rights Reserved)

Therefore, it is no surprise that a full BI-CC is usually not the governance setup that companies establish from the start. It takes a learning curve and experimentation with different types of governance setups to truly understand the value of a full BI-CC and how it needs to be structured to operate most effectively. It is often established in a close context to a significant enterprise transformation. Organizations aiming for truly data-driven decision-making and monetizing data in their business model will typically benefit most from this type of governance setup.

A well-organized BI-CC organization can be characterized as follows:

- Organized as a permanent department which can hire employees and develop needed skills and competencies (point 2, Fig. 5.12)
- Represented on Board level or having a direct solid reporting line to a dedicated board member, for example via the CFO, CIO, CTO, or CDO (point 3, Fig. 5.12)
- Acts as a neutral ambassador for "democratizing" data access across the enterprise and establishes permanent interaction channels with LoBs (point 4, Fig. 5.12).
- Owns, defines, updates, and communicates the enterprise-wide BI strategy
- Organizes the adoption of new BI product and service innovations
- Provides sufficient autonomy to local teams to build and adopt
- Owns the entire BI portfolio and BI product and service life cycle (point 1, Fig. 5.12)
- Establishes permanent roles to guard the "stable core" (point 4, Fig. 5.12)
- Represents the ultimate organizational manifestation of BI value contribution.

Architecture Foundation of BI Strategy 6

Architecture essentially defines the structural design of a system that has to fulfill its purpose over a long period of time. Star architect Norman Foster once put it this way:

"Architects design for the present, conscious of the past, for a future that remains largely unknowable."

This describes a dilemma faced by business, IT, and corporate architects. On the one hand, architectural design is influenced and constrained by a legacy environment that has developed over many years. This includes aspects such as the organizational structure, a historically grown system and IT landscape, organizational skills as well as corporate culture. Awareness of these factors is important, and long-term architectural decisions and designs cannot neglect these boundary conditions. For this reason, large-scale architectural designs are usually not developed on a greenfield basis. On the other hand, while architecture is concerned with long-term stability, it must also be able to adapt to changing requirements and future needs. This applies in particular to business intelligence architecture. BI architectures need to be able to provide timely updates to new data and information requirements and furthermore extend the reach to new sources of data to meet unknown future requirements without major disruption, while at the same time meeting current business needs.

In the following chapter, we will explore architecture patterns and elaborate how a reference architecture for business intelligence can be designed using an enterprise architecture approach. In the context of this book, architecture is not the main focus, but we will provide some guidance on how archtitectural aspects of enterprise-wide business intelligence can be addressed as part of a BI strategy to be able to effectively deliver on the strategic vision and value contribution of business intelligence.

R. Exner, A. Zunic, *The Path to an Intelligent Enterprise*, Future of Business and Finance, https://doi.org/10.1007/978-3-031-69914-6_6

6.1 Why Is BI Architecture Important?

Although Business Intelligence has long been a high priority for both business and IT decision-makers, there are still many examples of failed BI strategies and programs. What is the reason for this? Before looking at concrete architectural concepts and a BI reference architecture, we will explore and review some of the key challenges organizations face and the role architecture can play in addressing them.

Business intelligence and analytics have been among the top priorities of the senior management agenda for more than a decade. And most likely, this will not change soon. This shows that there has been a continuous executive priority on effective use and management of enterprise data for a long time, regardless of the latest technology trends. But the continued relevance of this domain also shows that BI has in many cases still not been able to keep pace with evolving business expectations. Meanwhile most organizations have invested heavily in BI applications and analytical capabilities but still struggle to achieve the expected business value and required BI adoption rates.

Why is this? What makes business intelligence such a tough practice to master?

Some of the main BI-related challenges in organizations have to do with the failure to link business intelligence capabilities effectively to business and enterprise architecture. Common challenges include the following:

1. Business intelligence is not understood as an organizational/business competence
   Many organizations face challenges to systematically embed and develop the practices of business intelligence and data-driven management in their main business functions. One of the reasons for this is that BI is not sufficiently linked with business architecture (processes, business capabilities).
   As a consequence, critical skills to adopt a data-driven culture and respective behaviors (pragmatic vs. fact-based approaches) are often not sufficiently developed. This includes, for example, data literacy and effective usage and interpretation of data in a specific decision-making context. It extends further to behaviors and routines which contribute to high data quality when using or creating business data. And finally, it includes awareness of data privacy and ethical use of data.
   Building such capabilities on an enterprise-wide scale is critical for a data-driven enterprise.
   This situation is further aggravated by a shortage of BI skills in the labor market, sometimes referred to as the "analytical skill gap."

2. BI architecture ownership is undefined
   Due to its cross-domain nature, business intelligence does not naturally fit well to the traditional business function and process boundaries in which companies are used to think and operate.

Hence, companies often face the challenge to find a suitable anchor point within the organization for cross-functional ownership of enterprise-wide business intelligence (for further details, please refer to Chap. 5).
It is not uncommon that BI is managed as a set of disconnected projects or programs which address similar requirements using different approaches, tools, and data. Due to a lack of enterprise-wide architecture standards and transparency on BI activities, the resulting solutions and products are often redundant, or even worse inconsistent.

3. BI portfolio and architecture are inadequately defined
After years of investment in analytical tools and processes, organizations often struggle to master the resulting complexity of applications, products, and services. Typically, a multitude of solutions, often from different vendors, technology stacks, and architectures coexist side-by-side serving very similar purposes and use cases. BI products and services can come in many different flavors ranging from standardized enterprise reporting solutions to semi-automated spreadmarts, integrated planning solutions to sophisticated data science, or even AI-based predictive modeling tools. Organizations often encounter difficulties to manage such a wide range of applications as a cohesive portfolio. As a result, BI operations and maintenance costs can be significant, while adoption rates remain low.
These symptoms are not only caused by a lack of strategic oversight and governance as we explored previously. They also indicate a lack of architectural alignment on an enterprise level. An enterprise-wide business intelligence portfolio of products and services based on a centrally managed core architecture is an important prerequisite for business intelligence to be successful. This includes making sure that the technology and data foundation is guarded against arbitrary change and is incrementally extended toward one cohesive, shared data and analytics platform (principle of "stable core").
Enterprise-wide BI essentially requires a holistic "architectural" view on data management, governance and data consumption. This includes the coherent management of a wide range of interrelated disciplines, skills, and tools which require cross-organizational alignment to function properly. This includes for example:

   (a) Defining and aligning the enterprise-wide information needs, including aligning corporate semantics and taxonomies (information architecture)
   (b) Managing the process of enterprise data creation and required governance (data governance)
   (c) Designing the data architecture including integration, harmonization, and enrichment of data (data architecture)
   (d) Simplifying the solution architecture by avoiding architectural complexity and redundancy (application architecture)
   (e) Ensuring ease of consumption (usability and user experience)

All of these architectural aspects and many more must work together to ensure effective data-driven decision-making and high BI adoption rates. If BI is "mis"-interpreted as being simply a set of software solutions providing tools and features for analyzing and visualizing data, then the focus is clearly too narrow for an enterprise-wide BI and data management approach.

4. Architectural silos and barriers to data access
   A key reason why large-scale enterprise-wide BI initiatives fail is the inability to penetrate and integrate organizational silos. For instance, these can be business units or lines of business which have established a certain level of independence in the organization. The situation is further impaired if such business units are unwilling to share and contribute data or resources in an enterprise-wide context. Another example are architectural silos and resulting data access barriers. And most common of all might be cultural and geographical silos that can be the most difficult to address and overcome in a large-scale BI transformation.
   Hence, the success of an enterprise-wide business intelligence transformation depends on many non-IT related factors such as:

   (a) Willingness to share local data with the entire enterprise (transparency)
   (b) Willingness to accept and adopt common data definitions and taxonomies
   (c) Willingness to agree on a common product strategy
   (d) Willingness to agree on and adopt a common architecture and design

   The more fragmented an organization, and the more independently local units operate, the more likely an enterprise-wide approach to BI will face resistance. Common issues that need to be tackled include:

   - Overlapping responsibilities between business functions
   - Unclear ownership for master data, data structures, and processes
   - Business unit silos
   - Weak connections between departments that each claim to be independently mandated to structure the business architecture

5. Agile BI delivery is burdened by technical debt
   The IT of a typical organization that evolved over many years tends to accumulate more and more complexity in terms of the number applications, interfaces, databases making changes increasingly difficult. This phenomenon is often referred to as "technical debt."
   This is a key reason why current application landscapes are often not agile enough for adding new innovations as quickly and seamlessly as required by the business. Yet typically no or too little budget is made available for systematically reducing the technical debt which accumulated over many years. And this is not an IT problem as we have seen above.

What do all of these challenges have in common?

They all show that BI is much more than just a technical challenge and that a key for effective BI is an alignment between different levels and domains of the organization.

Driven by the demand for more data and new exploratory BI use cases, communities around agile and design thinking are growing rapidly. While these ideas focus on speed and innovation, they do not answer the question of how to ensure that the solutions created fit together and into the bigger picture of the business. They also do not answer the question of how to deal with the enormous "technical debt" that has been created over the years by insufficient integration of new digital solutions with legacy or with each other. Calling for a greenfield approach is no replacement for a solid architecture roadmap, which includes systematic steps to decommission legacy solutions in a governed way.

Organizations need to find the right balance between agility and sustainability across their different BI use cases. We will illustrate some ideas in this chapter on how this can be achieved in an enterprise-wide context using architectural concepts.

6.2 Relevance of BI Architecture in a BI Strategy

Architectures describe the structural elements of systems that are typically used as stable reference points for business and IT designs. In the context of business intelligence, architecture plays a key role in connecting organizational data, processes, and technologies for the purpose of data-driven decision-making. This chapter explores the role of BI architectures as key enablers for the effective and consistent implementation of BI strategies across the organization.

Architecture can in general be described as the "fundamental organization of a system, embodied in its components, their relationships to each other and the environment and the principles governing its design and evolution" (The Open Group®, 2001).

In a business and IT context, architecture is not a new concept. We will explore some of the related architecture frameworks in this chapter.

The purpose of enterprise architecture is to achieve cross-enterprise alignment between business strategy and technology by establishing a common model of the enterprise. It describes the individual business and IT entities as well their interactions and relationships. Enterprise architectures facilitate cross-organizational dialogue and communication between business stakeholders regarding both the status quo and the planned future state. They establish a traceable link between the business-focused structure of the enterprise and the IT and technology-oriented perspective. It is important to emphasize that the design of an enterprise architecture is an ongoing, multi-stakeholder activity with a long-term focus. Enterprise architects play a key role in connecting the different architecture perspectives and needs based on an enterprise-wide framework.

Solution architectures, on the other hand, typically apply to a project or release and focus on the design and architecture of technical systems that support specific business needs. The time horizon is thus shorter, typically short to mid-term. The solution architecture typically describes high-level functional and technical solution specifications and can include implementation plans and work packages. Key purpose is to define the scope and blueprint for a technical realization. Typically, solution architectures address process design, data model design, user interface design as well as data integration aspects and security. Solution architecture is all about implementation and delivery of concrete IT products based on a defined set of business requirements.

Let us now apply these notions of architecture to business intelligence.

Business intelligence is by nature an enterprise-wide concept and hence requires a matching architectural approach. Apart from adopting a cross-organizational mindset, BI architectures should aim as much as possible to:

- Be business-oriented
- Be concise and clear (especially regarding semantics and terminologies)
- Remove organizational complexity (instead of adding to it) and
- Provide a common understanding of the main structural components of the organization, the interfaces between them
- Describe the relevant data to operate

In the end, the goal is to build effective and maintainable solution architectures that are based on an overarching reference architecture defining consistent and proven standards in order to keep the development and maintenance efforts predictable across the lifecycle of the applications. Thoroughly applied architecture principles usually pay off very quickly, especially as complexity and business requirements increase. Linear or even exponentially increasing costs per shipment cycle or release usually indicate a bad underlying architecture design. Typically, architectures which are not designed based on proven practices make it extremely difficult to introduce change at later stages in the product life cycle. Such changes often require updates to already existing parts of the solution with knock-on effects on testing, delivery timelines, and user acceptance. Often these architectures evolve if long-term sustainability is sacrificed for delivery speed.

Even though the effects of bad architecture design are obvious and can be extremely costly, it is often striking how rarely a consistent approach to architecture is being applied. This is especially true for the BI domain in which few dedicated architecture frameworks have appeared as "best practices."

> The absence of a holistic BI architecture framework is one of the reasons why companies fail at BI projects and as a result fail at making their BI strategies a success.

Architectural skills and a business-driven mindset are often undervalued in BI solution implementations. The focus is often very technology-centric without consideration for the bigger picture. Yet, both are critical, because without understanding of how analytical data is actually being used and embedded in decision-making processes, a sound data and technology architecture will suffer.

Hence, the role of architects is critical to support sound designs, especially in a cross-domain context such as BI. Architectural principles should be embedded in the design and implementation phase of every BI project from the start and trade-offs with respect to project speed should be made with care.

So, let us summarize.

Enterprise architectures describe the interaction of business activities with the enabling information technology within the enterprise. It differs from isolated architecture concepts such as information architecture or solution architecture by taking a more strategic and holistic view of the enterprise. The Enterprise architecture is intended to ensure the alignment of enterprise IT with business goals. An architectural description is usually structured into one or more views or layers. Each view addresses one or more of the considerations of the system stakeholders. An enterprise architecture initiative should be supported and, ideally, sponsored by the C-level, and it should be aligned with the overall BI strategy.

But where exactly is the connection to BI strategy?

A BI strategy does not need to operationalize an enterprise architecture, but it should provide clear answers to the following key questions:

- Who is the owner of the BI architecture (who is sitting in the driver seat)?
- Which architecture framework is used for BI?
- What are the key architecture layers and design principles?
- What does the as-is and target architecture look like?
- How does the roadmap including transition scenarios toward target look like during the next 3 years?
- How is the architecture governed on a continuous basis? (e.g., architecture board)
- How are architecture decisions made, executed and the process monitored?

Overall, a well-defined architecture strategy will make BI more effective. In addition, IT investments will be more valued and unnecessary investments avoided. Furthermore, the corporate BI architecture can be used to train and educate employees.

In summary, the main purpose of a BI architecture is the attainment of the following goals:

- Alignment and close synchronization of BI needs with solutions
- Consistency of solution design and data semantics across time
- Transparency of systems, solutions, dependencies, and changes

What tends to happen if architecture is not actively managed? Typical symptoms are:

- We see fragmented, incomplete, and inconsistent views of performance across the company. This typically leads to a lack of consistency as multiple versions of "the truth" exist.

- The high BI investments will not necessarily align with end-user expectations. Thus, end-users do not receive what they requested and expected. A lack of alignment often causes such situations.
- If data marts grow uncontrolled, this may also lead to an increase in costs. If there is no agreed way to balance both sides, this may indicate a lack of transparency.
- Lack of confidence in numbers has many faces but often originates from reports on the same indicators showing different numbers. Thus, either the definitions or the implementation of indicators is not consistent.
- Many reports are generated by employees, but not the right ones to steer the business. This situation may indicate a lack of alignment between those who manage the business and those who struggle to translate partially understood requirements into meaningful information.
- The BI application landscape shows BI software from many different vendors with overlapping functionality. It is difficult to clearly assign use cases to specific BI applications because the functionalities are somewhat blurry, and there is little to no transparency about which BI application should be used for which purpose.

6.3 BI Architecture Goals

To fully understand the value contribution of architectural thinking and design in the context of business intelligence it is useful to review the overall architecture goals. As might be expected there can be different drivers and objectives for BI in the organization that may conflict with each other.

This chapter discusses these goals and how goal conflicts can be mitigated through a systematic approach to architecture.

To be effective, business intelligence architectures need to balance seemingly conflicting goals:

- Lower TCO (total cost of ownership)
- Higher agility
- Higher quality

These goals are usually key business priorities and therefore cannot be ignored in BI architectures. Figure 6.1 below shows the key business drivers and architectural enablers which influence the effectiveness of the business intelligence architecture.

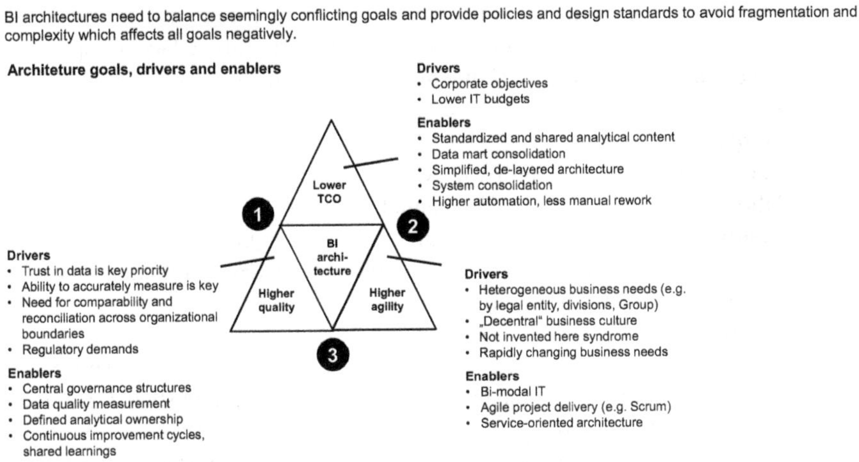

Fig. 6.1 BI architecture—balancing areas of conflict (Westenberger, 2018)

Let us discuss the individual goals first.

TCO:

The total cost of ownership includes the cost of implementing, enhancing, and operating the architecture.

Agility:

Agility is the degree and speed at which an architecture can adapt and respond to new requirements (for example, by organizational change, new business priorities). It can be measured by time to value, i.e. the length of time necessary to finish a project or phase and realize the benefits of the solution.

Information Quality:

The quality of information is typically described with attributes such as correct, complete, consistent, and up-to-date. All of these attributes determine if information is trusted within the organization which is the key value promise of any BI solution and strongly determines acceptance and solution adoption.

We will now investigate the goal conflicts and areas of mutual benefit in more detail:

- Information quality ↔ Agility
- Agility ↔ TCO
- Information quality ↔ TCO

1. ***Information Quality ↔ Agility***

   Area of conflict

   To achieve a high level of information quality in a complex corporate business environment, a formal BI and data governance process is typically required. This includes, for example, the definition and enforcement of rules around data architecture, data creation, data usage, data lifecycle management, regulatory data storage requirements …etc. of these beforementioned. All of these aspects require a continuous, long-term effort in terms of both time and resources to maintain a stable architectural foundation. This may initially reduce the speed of delivery because data and architecture readiness need to be ensured before delivery of new feature increments.

Area of mutual benefit

In the long run however, agility depends on a stable and quality-proven data foundation—otherwise trust in data cannot be established. So, investments in data quality improvement will also be an enabler for higher agility as more and more data assets can be re-used and at the same time data reconciliation time and error correction time can be saved.

Conclusion

Data quality is a key prerequisite for successful BI. But not all analytical use cases require the same level of data quality scrutiny. A BI architecture should therefore provide the flexibility to support both explorative ad hoc needs based on (new) data sources with little or no data governance as well as traditional standard reporting requirements around an established governance model ("stable core"). This requires clustering the inventory of analytic assets and assigning appropriate data governance levels. The architecture must be built to support these different flavors and decide whether different application and technological architectures are needed.

2. ***Agility ↔ TCO***

   Area of conflict

   Agile BI delivery requires a continuous investment in a common architecture foundation (concept of "stable core") and the adoption of agile practices in design, development, and delivery. The changes required to become agile, especially on an enterprise-wide scale, will require time and sufficient funding. However, without laying a solid foundation, an agile approach risks to increase the amount of "technical debt." "Technical debt" typically arises when highly customized or workaround solutions are implemented without sufficient reflection of long-term implications. Such solutions often result in cleanup, consolidation, and harmonization efforts down the line, in particular when relevant contacts or know-how are not available anymore.

   Already back in 2004, Eckerson estimated that "the time to consolidate complex analytic structures (data warehouses, data marts, data stores or spread marts) can range from 4 to 10 months, and the required consolidation projects can last for years" (Eckerson, 2004), easily resulting in hundreds of thousands of dollars of project spend. Analytic silos can increase operating costs by 30–50% due to redundant systems maintenance, redundant data storage, reconciliation issues, side reporting …etc.

   Area of mutual benefit

   The incremental cost and time to value of a new analytic requirement can be lower in an agile project environment. By responding more quickly to evolving business needs through a series of shorter project cycles (Sprints), solutions can be incrementally improved, while delivering business value sooner. This typically translates into lower overall projects costs, as extensive design and specification phases are avoided.

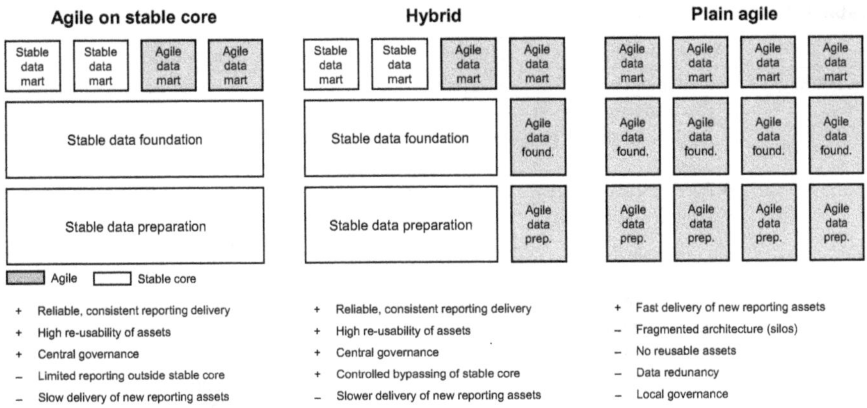

Fig. 6.2 BI architecture—the three modes of agile (© Exner/Zunic 2024. All Rights Reserved)

Conclusion

Agile delivery of BI solutions has almost become a default—because there is hardly an area in IT in which requirements change as frequently as in BI. Key driving factors contributing to this development are increasingly shorter innovation cycles, new and volatile customer demands, higher pressure for faster decision-making on management levels and increasing levels of volatility, uncertainty, complexity, and ambiguity ("VUCA"). However, agility does come with a cost, if agile projects are not embedded in a well-governed architecture foundation. Once a foundation has been established and different speeds of innovation are supported, both agile and TCO requirements can be balanced (see Fig. 6.2 below).

As shown in Fig. 6.2, agile practices can be applied to BI on different layers of the architecture (data preparation/sourcing–data foundation–reporting and analytics) and to varying degrees. Agile means producing incremental output in defined time boxes (for example, Sprints) and hence tends to achieve an earlier time to market for new BI products and services.

While agile can work on every layer when done right, it needs to be used with caution, especially when "output" is measured exclusively by the number of individual BI products or artifacts that have been shipped or released in a defined increment. Without enforcing architectural alignment and governance, this tends to create a backlog of "technical debt" that takes more time and effort to clean up later than if designed properly from the start.

We observe three main modes of agile BI in practice:

- Agile on stable core
  This mode is based on an "architected" BI environment with a stable and well-governed "core" data warehouse that is extended in an agile manner only on the data mart layer for specific business purposes. This mode has long been considered a best practice, for example using the Layered Scalable Architecture approach.

Table 6.1 Comparison of different modes of agile

	Agile on stable core	Hybrid	Plain agile
Advantages	• Reliable, consistent reporting foundation • High re-usability of assets • Formal governance around stable core	• Reliable, consistent reporting foundation • High re-usability of assets • Formal governance around stable core • Controlled bypassing of stable core for new requirements	• Faster delivery of new business requirements • Flexible architecture enhancements • Governance around products • Data-as-a-product concept
Limitations and risks	• Limited reporting outside stable core • Enhancement of data foundation is time-consuming	• Risk of eroding the stable core	• Fragmented, siloed architecture • No shared governance framework • Data redundancy and inconsistency

- Hybrid
  The hybrid mode preserves the "stable core" principle based on the core data warehouse. In addition, this approach is enriched by a controlled bypassing of the core data warehouse for selected new data and analytics requirements. This can be accomplished by data lake house or data mesh architectures that we will discuss later in Sect. 6.6.
- Plain agile
  The plain agile mode means that no rigid, formally governed data foundation (core data warehouse) exists, and the data warehouse architecture evolves continuously with the changing needs of the business ("agile data warehousing"). Hence, the resulting BI products and services are typically loosely coupled and tend not to share a common data foundation. Cloud BI and low-code/no-code technologies are a key enabler for this kind of approach. Low-code/no-code allows scaling across a larger "citizen" developer base to flexibly enhance a data warehouse in shorter increments.

Each mode has advantages and limitations which are outlined in Table 6.1 below. The best fit depends on the organization's BI strategy and governance model.

3. ***Information quality ↔ TCO***

   Area of conflict

   Achieving accurate and reliable information quality requires a continuous process with active, ongoing management of data quality involving cross-business and IT teams and responsible owners. Hence, this requires funding both for focused project initiatives (e.g., data cleansing) and ongoing data quality management.

   Main cost factors include:

   - Permanent roles and responsibilities for data governance and ownership

- Training in processes and policies to influence behaviors and resolve potential goal conflicts between transactional processing (data creation) and decision support (data use)
- Investment in software solutions to track and resolve data issues

Area of mutual benefit

The avoided cost of misinformed decisions, inability to react to business events due to unavailable or inaccurate information, efforts to track down and resolve data quality issues are a huge benefit. However, the benefits are very difficult to measure. In contrast, the data quality efforts in data generation processes (e.g., transactional customer-related processes in sales) are typically easier to measure and hence weighted higher than the expected benefit increase in decision-making processes.

Conclusion

The question is not if you can afford high information quality—it is a must have. However, it is worth to focus data quality efforts on the main corporate analytic dimensions which are particularly relevant for strategic decision-making. This will typically include master data around customers, vendors, employees, products but also external data related, for example, to competitors and markets. The BI architecture guidelines should clearly define these key data assets, define their structure, and apply governance along the entire reporting chain from recording to reporting. For other less-critical areas, other data quality standards can apply. So, which key requirements can we derive for BI strategy?

Key considerations for developing a BI Strategy

Stable core

Decide on the areas of architecture which must be stable and well-governed long term, create policies and guidelines around this foundation, and define ownership.

Think broad

Build the architecture with a broad "anticipative" mindset—avoid thinking in narrow silos on a request-by-request basis; invest strategically in a shared, common BI platform.

Business oriented

Ensure that your target architecture vision and roadmap is derived from the business strategy roadmap. Embed your architecture know-how and best practices into a shared architect community within the BI-CC which has regular touchpoints to business representatives. Avoid technology-driven architectures.

Support different innovation speeds

Maximize re-use of your high value reporting and data assets; promote agile project delivery based on top of the stable core as default (agile data marts). Allow bypassing of stable core for explorative new requirements (e.g., agile data preparation), but clearly identify the boundaries of governance (e.g., certain reporting assets are governed from data source to report—for other reporting assets governance is only provided for source systems)

6.4 BI Architecture Expectations

While the role of business intelligence as a key enabler of data-driven decision-making has remained relatively constant, the surrounding data landscape and business expectations have changed significantly. BI architectures need to be able to respond to these new demands, while at the same time avoiding excessive complexity.

Business intelligence and data warehouse architectures are pressured by the growing demand for data in all dimensions (see Fig. 6.3 below). Whereas companies could in the past enforce centrally governed monolithic data warehouses for decision-making based on corporate data only, this has become an inacceptable restriction today. If you think about the increasing relevance of predictive analytics and data science on large data sets in data-driven decision-making, it is clear that BI architectures cannot ignore this going forward.

The heterogeneity of analytical systems in large corporations today can be enormous. They can range from classic management support systems, including paper-based reports from legacy systems in mainframe technology, to highly sophisticated, state-of-the-art data analysis and simulation systems. Local reporting solutions based on PC databases and spread marts, often owned by individual employees or teams are still quite common. This diversity creates one of the main obstacles for a common business intelligence architecture approach.

It is primarily caused by two factors. On the one hand, the evolution of information technology has resulted in numerous innovations and technology shifts

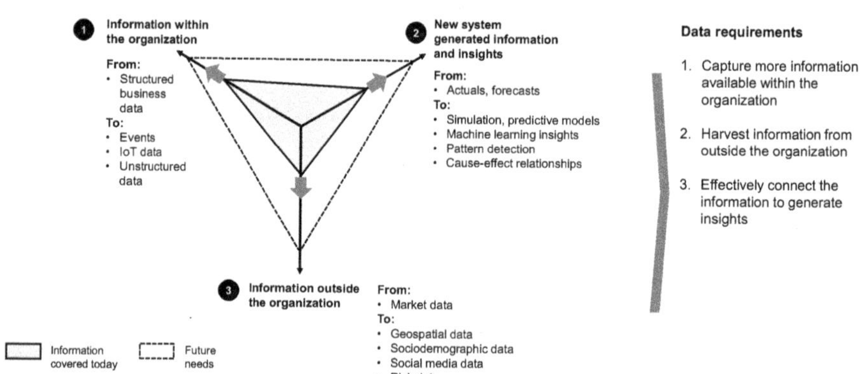

Fig. 6.3 BI architecture—moving the boundaries of information capture & insight (© Exner/Zunic 2024. All Rights Reserved)

which have been incorporated in the IT landscape of companies over years and decades (for example, solutions based on mainframes, medium-sized data technology, client-server computing, desktop computing, Internet, cloud exist side-by-side). The introduction of new IT systems and technology is often driven by short-term considerations ignoring the impact on complexity and maintainability. Projects to decommission legacy systems and remove technical debt in the landscape are often postponed or denied approval. As a result, the IT landscapes in some companies mirror the IT development of the past 30 years, and this also applies to BI systems.On the other hand, companies themselves have typically undergone massive organizational change in recent decades. They have either grown organically, restructured operations, or merged with or acquired other companies. As these change dynamics accelerate, companies increasingly struggle to keep pace and adequately re-align their information technology with the new business environment. Hence, staying in control of complexity and heterogeneity is a real challenge.

This raises the critical question of how BI architectures can expand their scope and their value contribution without running the risk of losing control and being overwhelmed by complexity.

6.5 What Can We Learn from Enterprise Architecture?

To systematically establish and sustain a consistent architectural design, an enterprise-wide BI architecture approach is advisable. The domain of Enterprise Architecture is a useful reference point to start from, because it was invented to address the cross-organizational alignment challenge in architecture development. This chapter will explore different Enterprise Architecture approaches and illustrate how they can be applied in a business intelligence context.

Enterprise Architecture (EA) is not an emerging field. In fact, enterprise architecture frameworks have been in use for more than a decade and are still evolving. They share the common goal of aligning and integrating all components of the enterprise from business strategy to technology.

Over the years, enterprise architecture frameworks have been developed. Next, we will discuss the following five representative frameworks commonly used:

- Zachman Framework™
- The Open Group Architecture Framework (TOGAF®)
- Federal Enterprise Architecture Framework (FEA)

	Why	How	What	Who	Where	When
Contextual	Goal List	Process List	Material List	Organizational Unit & Role List	Geographical Locations List	Event List
Conceptual	Goal Relationship	Process Model	Entity Relationship Model	Organizational Unit & Role Relationship Model	Locations Model	Event Model
Logical	Rules Diagram	Process Diagram	Data Model Diagram	Role Relationship Diagram	Locations Diagram	Event Diagram
Physical	Rules Specification	Process Function Specification	Data Entity Specification	Role Specification	Locations Specification	Event Specification
Detailed	Rules Details	Process Details	Data Details	Role Details	Locations Details	Even Detail

Fig. 6.4 Zachman framework™ (Zachman, 2008)

- Business Process Reference Models (APQC's Process Classification Framework®)

Zachman Framework™ (Zachman, 2008)

The Zachman Framework™ is a popular enterprise architecture metamodel used by architects to organize and describe an organizational structure and information landscape. The framework does not define a procedure how to develop an enterprise architecture. Instead, the model provides a fundamental classification schema based on six interrogative categories (What, How, Where, Who, When, and Why) and six perspectives as illustrated in Fig. 6.4 below (Executive, Business Management, Architect, Engineer, Technician, and Enterprise).

Each intersection of a category and perspective defines a different independent representation of the organization with a different level of abstraction.

Typically, business architects will be using concepts and artifacts associated with the first two perspectives: Executive and Business Management whereas data and solution architects will be addressing the Architect and Engineer perspectives. The role of the enterprise architect is to integrate the different categories and perspectives in one common model.

The Open Group Architecture Framework (TOGAF®)

The Open Group Architecture Framework (TOGAF®) was developed by The Open Group® in 1995. Like other enterprise architecture frameworks, the TOGAF® standard helps companies to align business and IT goals across departments and business units.

It helps companies define requirements and set the organizational course before starting implementation programs and projects, ensuring that processes are implemented in a consistent and efficient manner.

When using the TOGAF® standard, the enterprise architecture is usually modeled in four architectural layers: business architecture, data architecture, application architecture, and technology architecture.

The business architecture considers the strategy, the organizational setup, the business processes, and the business capabilities of the organization. The data architecture identifies and describes the data and its relationships that are required to run and operate the business processes. This is done via a data model that is stable, complete, consistent, and understandable for all parties involved. The applications required for the execution of business processes are managed within the application architecture. In addition to creating an inventory of all applications, also the relationships and interfaces between the applications are considered. The technology architecture describes the architectural elements and capabilities for setting up and operating the IT infrastructure.

The main objectives of the TOGAF® standard are to:

- Enable a holistic view of the enterprise landscape
- Ensure that everyone speaks the same language
- Enable organizations of all sizes and industries to work from the same enterprise architecture standard
- Avoid lock-in to proprietary solutions by standardizing open methods for enterprise architecture
- Save time and money and utilize resources more effectively
- Achieve a demonstrable return on investment (RoI)
- Act as a modular, scalable framework that enables organizational transformation

Federal Enterprise Architecture (FEA) Framework

FEA is the Federal Enterprise Architecture Framework used by the United States government. It was developed by the American CIO Council in 1999 to address the issue of duplicated processes, IT systems, and data across independently developed services and programs within government agencies. The framework consists of a set of interrelated reference models designed to identify duplicative investments and opportunities for collaboration across agencies. Describing organizations, IT systems, data, and infrastructure in a common language helps uncover and eliminate waste, improve service quality, and reduce cost.

The Federal Enterprise Architecture Framework (FEAF) consists of five architectural domains represented by reference models: performance, business, data, applications, and infrastructure/technology (see Fig. 6.5).

FEA can effectively be combined with the Zachman framework™ as it addresses the top rows of the What, How, and Where columns of the Zachman Framework™ taxonomy.

Additionally, FEA provides a process model for developing and updating an architecture description. The process is defined in four steps: consider stakeholders,

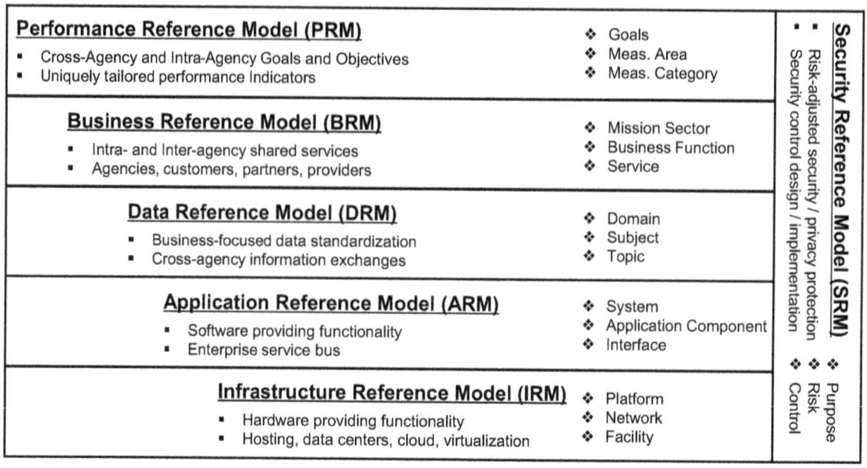

Fig. 6.5 Federal Enterprise Architecture (FEA) Framework (Zachman, 2008)

define strategy, describe current architecture status, and describe future architecture status.

Process Models (APQC Process Classification Framework®)

Business Process and Industry reference models are frameworks that provide a best practice set of structures, processes, activities, knowledge and skills to conceptually model and design an organization, its activity flows and the process outputs measured by key performance indicators.

The APQC Process Classification Framework® (PCF) is a well-known business process reference model that allows organizations to both track their process performance internally and also benchmark it with other organizations from any industry.

Organizations can use the PCF common process taxonomy to name, organize, and map their processes. It helps explaining a business in terms of horizontal end-to-end processes rather than vertical functions. The framework also provides performance metrics for measuring and tracking the performance of each process.

It is designed as an accelerator to be tailored for use in any particular organization. The PCF does not necessarily list all processes within a specific organization, and not every process listed in the framework exists in all organizations, but it provides a standard way of documenting an organization's business processes.

These reference models work well as a basis for an analytics business architecture, if an organization has already established (or plans to establish) a business process model and utilizes a predominantly process-oriented performance management approach.

Below Fig. 6.6 illustrates on a high-level the main structural commonalities and differences between the above enterprise architecture frameworks:

Without discussing each approach in detail, all enterprise architecture frameworks have three characteristics in common:

1. They aim to integrate the perspectives of the business and IT.

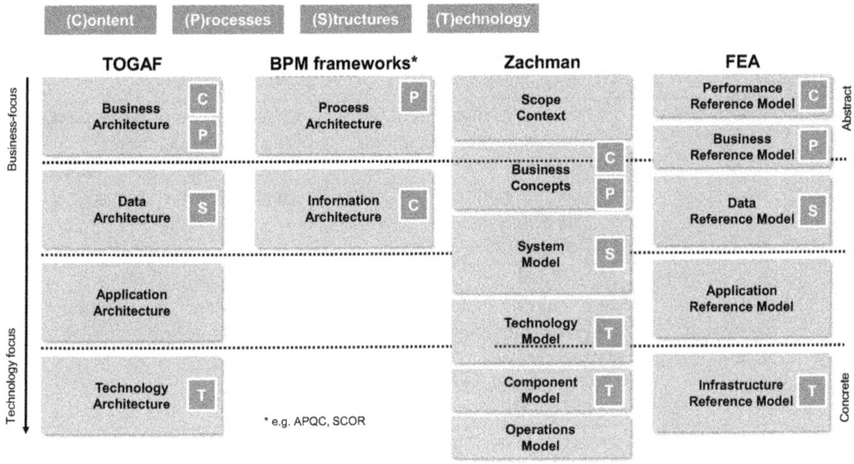

Fig. 6.6 High-level comparison of Enterprise Architecture Frameworks (© Exner/Zunic 2024. All Rights Reserved)

2. They set different levels of abstraction to manage complexity, as not every aspect of architecture requires the same level of detail and concretion—otherwise, complexity would be unmanageable.
3. They all incorporate a dedicated data perspective.

Experience from several enterprise architecture initiatives indicates that making a lasting value through Enterprise Architecture Management (EAM) requires a firm and long-term commitment and business buy-in. Without this buy-in, EAM risks to be perceived as a practice exclusively for IT architects, which in consequence discourages non-architects in IT and business to contribute.

How Can We Apply These Learnings to BI Strategy Development?

As we have already noted in Sect. 6.2, the absence of a holistic BI architecture framework is one of the reasons why companies fail at BI projects.

Although there are many well-established enterprise architecture frameworks available, only few have an explicit enterprise BI focus, which is surprising given the growing demand for fact-based decision-making and data-oriented performance management. This can make agreeing on a suitable architectural approach for BI challenging and occasionally lead to conflicting views in BI strategy development.

To compound the issue, enterprise BI architecture best practices such as enterprise data warehousing (developed primarily in the 1990s and early 2000s) have been questioned in recent years. Changed user expectations accompanied by disruptive innovations as big data and generative AI challenge traditional approaches and practices.

However, traditional enterprise architecture approaches could easily contribute more to enterprise BI architecture by:

Table 6.2 Suitable aspects of available Enterprise Architecture frameworks for BI architectures

Framework	Usability for enterprise BI architectures	
	+ Strengths	– Weaknesses
TOGAF®	• Process-oriented approach • Data architecture layer is integrated • One of the most established and widely used frameworks • Holistic and complete • Detailed	• Complex in administration • No explicit business intelligence or performance management reference
Business process management models (e.g., APQC's Process Classification Framework®)	• Capability-centric approach • Process templates and KPI content • Benchmark content • Short time to value	• Incomplete (missing the application and technology aspects)
Zachman Framework™	• Perspective-centric approach • Well-established and accepted • Holistic and complete	• No practical data or analytics guidance • Lack of concrete architecture methodology and process
FEA	• Standardization-centric approach (common vocabulary) • Explicit performance management reference model	• Not widely used outside the United States • Public sector and government focus

- Enriching the predominant business process and capabilities perspectives in business architecture with a sufficient connection to data and analytical decision-making processes.
- Providing guidance on designing cross-enterprise semantic information and data architectures.
- Integrating a strategic, cross-process perspective with focus on performance management.
- Simplifying usability and application of EA Frameworks also in an agile environment.

It is critical that enterprise BI architecture programs are not implemented as isolated efforts, but instead are connected to or even embedded within the enterprise architecture of the organization. The architectural framework for business intelligence should integrate the perspectives of various stakeholders who rely on, interact with, and provision BI. This includes decision-makers, data consumers, data owners, data and content creators as well as technical architects and operations teams. Hence, a distinction of different architectural layers/components, their respective artifacts and interrelations need to be defined.

So, what works best in a BI strategy context?

Each of the discussed Enterprise Architecture frameworks can add valuable inputs to a business intelligence centric enterprise architecture as shown below in Table 6.2:

Our recommended approach is to implement an enterprise BI architecture on top of EA framework that has been established in your organization or industry and enrich it with BI-specific architecture requirements and artifacts.

You can also consider mixing aspects of different frameworks to concretize or emphasize BI-specific aspects while persevering the principles and structure of the selected framework.

In the following chapter, we will provide guidance on how BI-specific architecture aspects can be integrated with a TOGAF®-based enterprise architecture, as the TOGAF® standard is one of the most commonly used and complete enterprise architecture frameworks well known to architects across industries and domains.

Key Considerations for BI Strategy development

- Relevance and re-use of enterprise architecture practices for enterprise-wide business intelligence is affirmed.
- None of the discussed EA frameworks provides sufficient guidance for a BI-specific adaptation.
- This calls for a dedicated cross-industry EA-based approach for BI and analytics—especially as the domain remains a key business and IT priority on board-level.
- Until such a framework becomes available, BI architecture development should be aligned with existing corporate EA frameworks and emphasize BI-specific aspects.

6.6 Enterprise BI Architecture Framework

In the following chapter, we will introduce an architecture framework for enterprise-wide business intelligence which served us as a useful mental structure in practice. The framework consists of several architecture layers which we will explore from a strategic perspective. For each layer, we will summarize good practices, as well as methodologies and tools that can be applied to support an enterprise-wide BI architecture design. This chapter aims to motivate the reader to think about the different dimensions of business intelligence in an architectural, structured, and interconnected way. However, this book is not primarily about architecture. We therefore do not attempt to deep-dive into specific aspects of architecture like data warehouse design or Bi application design. Nevertheless, as BI architecture is the concrete manifestation of business intelligence in the organization it strongly impacts the effectiveness and efficiency of BI. Therefore, it cannot be ignored in a BI strategy. Our main aim is to equip our readers, especially those without an architect background, with the business intelligence architecture basics using a pre-defined architecture model and illustrate on each layer the key architectural considerations and decision needs that require alignment on a strategic level.

We propose to divide an enterprise BI architecture into the following five architectural views:

- Business Architecture
- Information Architecture
- Data Architecture
- Application Architecture
- Technology Architecture

By Enterprise BI, we mean an architectural approach that can be used to design BI and analytics solutions that address the information needs of the entire organization. The approach aims to integrate both repeatable and standardizable information needs as well as exploratory, less predictable data needs.

As indicated in the previous chapter, we will illustrate a BI architecture framework in the following chapters based on the TOGAF® standard, as this is the most widely adopted enterprise architecture framework and structurally aligned to many other frameworks. In addition, we strongly advise to add (or highlight) "Information Architecture" as an additional layer to emphasize the important role of actionable "information" (semantics) as the connection between the business and data architecture.

The architectural layers can be viewed as a hierarchy in which the output of each layer provides the primary input to the next layer, and vice versa, receives input back in the form of a more concrete artifact or representation of the target solution.

The layers are ordered by level of abstraction (from highly abstract and generic) to very concrete and detailed. A holistic view of the architecture is illustrated in Fig. 6.7 below:

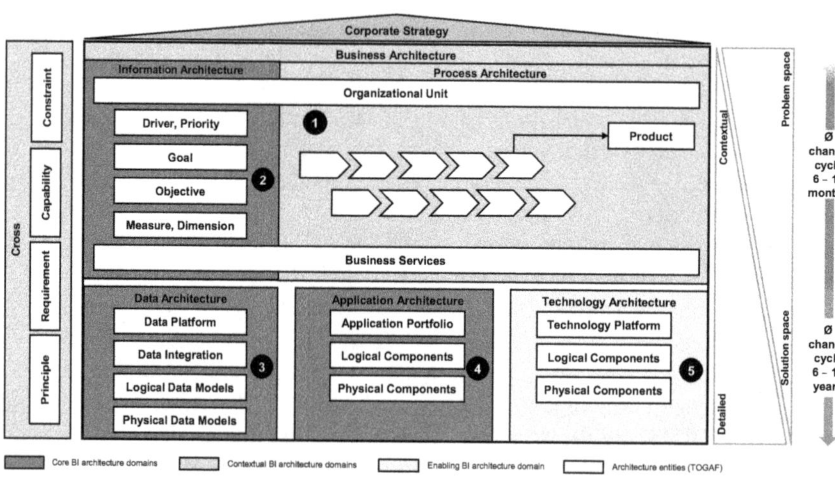

Fig. 6.7 Enterprise BI architecture framework (adapted from TOGAF® Content Metamodel) (The Open Group®, 2018)

1. The business architecture is the key starting point for the BI architecture design. It generally defines the main business entities and how they interact to create measurable outputs of value (products, services, revenue, …etc.), based on the business priorities defined by corporate strategy.
2. Whereas the focus of business architecture is on business processes and the overall value creation process, the information architecture captures the related value and performance measurement framework by defining the business-relevant information models.
3. Derived from (1) and (2) the data architecture is responsible for creating the logical and physical representation of data models; it collects, governs, integrates, and transforms all kinds of raw data into meaningful information.
4. The application architecture defines and governs the required analytics application portfolio to support the business, information, and data architecture.
5. The technology architecture governs the physical technical deployment of the IT solutions supporting enterprise BI; it also governs the technology platform.

Typically, the business and information architecture layers are undergoing frequent change—these can be caused by re-organizations, strategy updates, acquisitions and often occur in 6–12 month intervals.

By contrast, the data, application, and technology architecture layers providing the foundation of enterprise BI are more stable and long-enduring ("stable core"). This requires a different level of governance and design effort in these architecture layers.

The individual architecture levels are described in detail in the following chapters.

6.6.1 Business Architecture

The business architecture is a prerequisite for architecture work in any other domain such as Information, Data, Applications, and Technology. For this reason, it typically is the first architecture activity that needs to be undertaken. Business Architecture can be described as a blueprint of the enterprise that provides a common understanding of the organization and how strategic business objectives are aligned to tactical demands and operations on a business level. It is often developed by an interdisciplinary practice area of business architects, analysts, or strategy professionals focused on defining and analyzing holistically what the business does (or intends to do), how it does it (or intends to do it), how it is organized, and how it realizes value.

The business architecture can be viewed as a model or metamodel of the organization's value creation process and provides a business perspective on how strategy is supported by the organizational design (Target Operating Model). It provides a reference model for understanding and aligning an organizations internal business structure, scope of activities, and value flow. It de-composes the organization into capabilities and value streams describing how activities, functions, and processes interact to produce results and outputs of value (products and business services) by and for internal/external stakeholders.

It is important to realize that business architecture might be subject to regular change depending on the industry. Strategy shifts, business model adjustments, mergers & acquisitions, internal re-organizations all introduce significant transformational change throughout the organization. Take, for example, an IT service provider that spins off its entire after-market and spare parts business into a new business entity and decides that this is not a core competence any longer. This introduces a major shift in how the business operates and creates value. Or consider a bank which decides to expand its business into blockchain based payment services—suddenly competing with a completely different set of players requiring new technological capabilities and business processes.

To avoid overloading the business architecture with the complexities of day-to-day business operations, it is advisable to keep the business architecture concise and high-level reflecting change only if it is significant and strategic. To achieve this, business architects often employ one of the following methods and tools as illustrated in Fig. 6.8.

- Business model canvas
- The business model canvas has become a wide-spread methodology for holistically describing the main elements of an organization's value generation model (business model). According to Osterwalder "a business model describes the rationale of how an organization creates, delivers, and captures value." It can be described by the following key characteristics in the so-called business model canvas (Osterwalder & Pigneur, 2010):
  - *Key partners*
    Who are our key partners? Who are our key suppliers? Which key resources are we acquiring from partners? Which key activities do partners perform?
  - *Key activities*
    What key activities do our value propositions require?
  - *Key resources*
    What key resources do our value propositions require?
  - *Value propositions*
    What value do we deliver to the customer? Which one of our customer's problems are we helping to solve? What bundles of products and services are we offering to each customer segment? Which customer needs are we satisfying?
  - *Customer relationships*
    What type of relationship does each of our customer segments expect us to establish and maintain with them? Which ones have we established? How are they integrated with the rest of our business model? How costly are they?
  - *Channels*
    Through which channels do our customer segments want to be reached? How are we reaching them now? How are our channels integrated? Which ones work best? Which ones are most cost-efficient? How are we integrating them with customer routines?
  - *Customer segments*
    For whom are we creating value? Who are our most important customers?

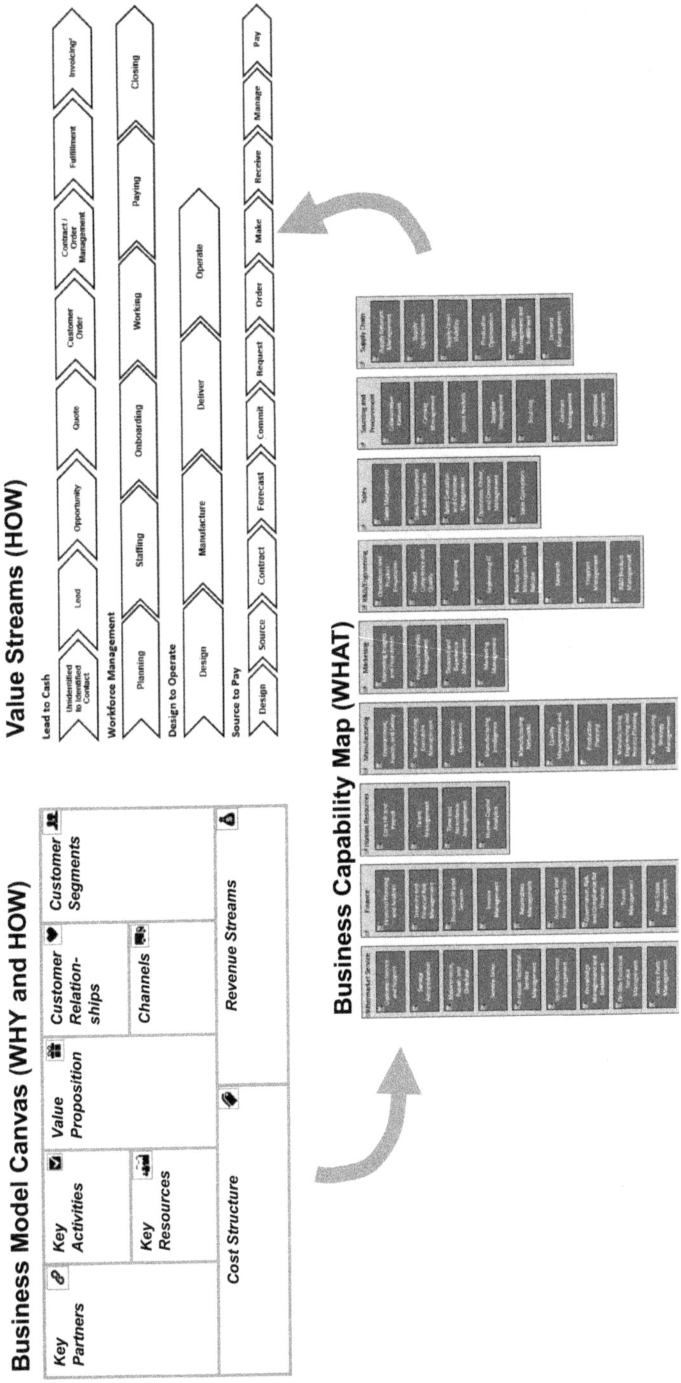

Fig. 6.8 Business architecture–key artifacts (adapted from Osterwalder & Pigneur, 2010)

- *Cost structure*
  What are the most important costs inherent in our business model? Which key resources are most expensive? Which key activities are most expensive?
- *Revenue stream*
  For what value are customers really willing to pay? For what do they currently pay? How are they currently paying? How would they prefer to pay? How much does each revenue stream contribute to overall revenue?

- This fundamental and simple description of a business model can provide an effective framework for describing and visualizing the essential business drivers, resulting decision and controlling dimensions and required data points.
- Business capability models
- Business capability models describe the activities and capabilities an organization performs to create value. They are often organized hierarchically to illustrate business capabilities on different levels of detail. They are used by business owners and business architects to identify and describe the most critical capability areas for long-term success, especially when fundamental change requires a revision of business strategy.
- Each strategic business capability needs to be supported by relevant information and data for decision-making providing important strategic inputs to a BI strategy.
- Value stream and business process models (example: APQC's Process Classification Framework®)
- Business process models or value chains define *how* the processes of the company create customer value. They describe the end-to-end sequence of interactions between organizational entities to produce valuable results for the customer.

In our view, a well-described business architecture is an important starting point for any IT initiative/project because it establishes clarity on business structure, operating model, key priorities, and organizational value sources.

However, with the shift from business process automation to digital transformation and more recently to the Intelligent Enterprise, a pure efficiency and transactions driven view on business architecture is not enough anymore. The increased demand for understanding business performance on all levels of the organization quickly and reliably places an even higher importance on the information and data perspectives. In recent years, new business models have emerged that are grounded on data provisioning and monetarization that cannot be ignored anymore on business-architecture level.

We suggest therefore to carefully evaluate the business architecture and enhance it or at least tightly link or integrate it to performance and value aspects.

Modeling the organization around value drivers, key performance indicators, and process performance indicators is well supported by performance management concepts, such as balanced scorecard and business process reference models. Both concepts help ensure that the information requirements are understood and linked up vertically (from strategy to execution) as well as horizontally (end-to-end business processes).

This means, for example, that strategic statements and calls for action are consistently communicated and cascaded throughout the corporate hierarchies down to the operational workforce. At the same time, the value flows should be measured throughout the end-to-end business processes and aligned with the given strategies on various levels. Hence, a key prerequisite of business architecture is a common understanding of business semantics and business performance metrics. It cannot be overstated how important this is—as incorrect or misinterpreted performance data can lead to wrong management decisions with severe consequences.

Key considerations for developing a BI Strategy

- A BI strategy must support the current operating model described by business architecture.
- In case the current operating model and underlying business architecture is intended to be changed, business intelligence needs to be involved right from the start. This aims to respond to foreseeable new and changed information demands in a timely manner. This should be integral part of the BI strategy process, for example it might trigger a new or revised BI strategy increment (see Sect. 4.2).
- Key success factor is a close collaboration between the head of business architecture and head of business intelligence. Ultimately, this results in the need for alignment between the head of business intelligence and the C-level.

6.6.2 Information Architecture

Information is data that has first been translated into a meaningful purpose and enriched with context. Only then can information be used to answer questions or make decisions. Turning data into information is a process that requires understanding and expertise, in other words, knowledge. To benefit from a knowledgeable workforce, organizations require a combination of skills, experience, and processes that enable developing experts to extract meaning from an exponentially growing pool of data. And knowledge, by definition, is specialized, dependent on individual personal development, and takes time to develop, both individually and within a collective.

Obviously, the problem is not a lack of data. The majority of this data is unstructured and not generated by humans (for example, Internet of Things (IoT) or sensor data, streaming data, generative AI), making it challenging to capture and use in a decision-making situation. But collecting raw data alone without context and structure means nothing and thus has no inherent value per se. Only through an integrative and contextual understanding of how data can be used to enable actionable insights, the beforementioned business architecture can be effectively enabled.

We therefore consider information architecture to be the most important "alignment" layer of a holistic BI architecture, as it links the business architecture (which is primarily owned by the business) to the data architecture, which is typically assigned to IT. In practice, ownership of business processes is naturally accepted by the business, while ownership of the underlying data is often neglected by the business and assigned to IT. In contrast, IT does not naturally accept ownership of data because data is an inherent part of business processes. As a result, data ownership is in a state of limbo. The existence of an information architecture layer could be an opportunity to resolve this situation. The information architecture layer separates the business-oriented content question from the physical data design. This layer should be owned by the business as it covers the business-related content.

In practice, the information architecture focuses on creating, organizing, structuring, and labeling all information assets within the organization. An information asset or "BI product" can be defined as an information package or set of data that provides contextual business meaning to a defined target audience. The information architecture does not define the physical representation of the information asset. For example, the information architecture does not decide if an information asset is provided via an operational system of record, or via an analytical data store or via a spreadsheet. It simply defines the data components including contextual meta-information necessary to communicate an intended meaning (i.e., business semantics).

The information architecture mainly serves the following four purposes:

1. Information architecture owns enterprise-wide data definitions and information standards.
2. It translates business priorities and requirements (derived from business architecture) into conceptual and consistent semantic models and user experiences based on enterprise-wide information design guidelines and semantics (for example, business dimensions, hierarchies, labeling, definitions, notations, user interfaces). It consults projects in structuring and framing the problem space from a business perspective and describe an enterprise-wide solution design to support the business needs.
3. Information architecture aligns information designs with business architecture to ensure common understanding and usage of information assets. Additionally, information architecture identifies and communicates prerequisites to business architecture such as, for example, required new or enhanced business capabilities.
4. Information architecture aligns information design with data architecture to ensure that logical and physical data designs can be derived and relevant prerequisites, for example, regarding data availability and data quality are met.

As shown in Fig. 6.9 below, information architecture uses semantic models based on business language to connect goals, priorities, and KPIs from the business architecture to contextualized and consumable information assets. They are sometimes

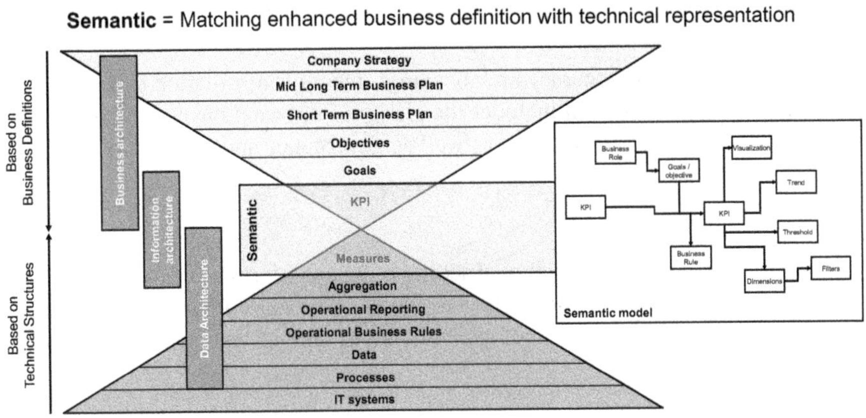

Fig. 6.9 Information architecture—semantic modeling (© Exner/Zunic 2024. All Rights Reserved)

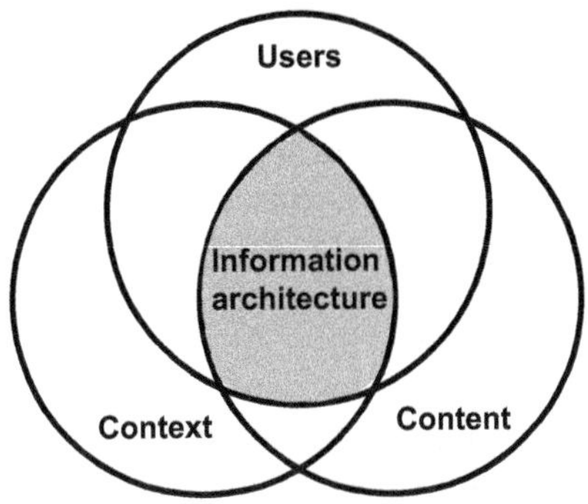

Fig. 6.10 The three pillars of information architecture (adapted from Rosenfeld & Morville, 2002)

also described as conceptual data models but are not to be confused with logical or physical data modeling which have a more technical focus.

Information architecture has particularly been studied and researched in the context of web site design. The research suggests that in order to create an information architecture, you need to understand the interdependent nature of users, content, and context. Rosenfeld and Morville referred to this as the "information ecology" and visualized it as a Venn diagram in Fig. 6.10 (Rosenfeld & Morville, 2002).

Users:

- Refers to the target audience (target users) who are consuming the information, their tasks, needs, information-seeking behavior, and experience.

Content:

- Content refers to the accuracy and meaningfulness of information in the context in which it is consumed. It includes the clarity of information, ease of consumption, accessibility of information as well as governance and ownership.

Context:

- Context refers to the organizational setting in which information is created, used, and distributed—this includes business goals, political climate, corporate culture, technology affinity, technology constraints, and the level within the organizational hierarchy.

Information architecture aims to connect these pillars and provide relevant business information in a consistent and actionable way. This can be done via the following artifacts:

- Catalogs (e.g., inventory of key measures and dimensions)
- Tagging (e.g., labeling of information assets and purposes)
- Documents (e.g., description of information design standards)
- Taxonomies (e.g., classifying and structuring information assets)
- Templates (e.g., corporate notations, style templates)
- Terminologies (e.g., business glossary, definitions)

Examples of information assets:

- Sales forecast and pipeline (opportunities and leads)—Key Account manager
  Measures: Leads, opportunities, opportunities lost, order conversion
  Analysis: YoY (Year over Year)/YTD (year to date)/daily/monthly trend—breakdown by product, brand, country
- Sales backlog and new order entry (bookings)—Head of sales, Account managers
  Measures: Order backlog, order entry, revenue
  Analysis: YTD/YoY/BUD (Budget)/FC (forecast)/deltas—breakdown by market, region, product group
- Propensity-to-buy model (based on past buying behavior)—Marketing
  Measures: Customer propensity score (from data science model), purchase volumes
  Analysis: YTD/Month/day—breakdown by time, store, products, correlation analysis

An information asset like other assets has business value and runs through a lifecycle. The value of an information asset varies over its lifecycle and is dependent on the relevance of the underlying data, as well as characteristics of the system that manages it (for example, system responsiveness or accessibility). In addition, the value of an information asset depends on the contextual relevance, as for example IoT data of a machine, which is going to be sold, might become less valuable. The discipline of information management is centered around how the information asset lifecycle is managed.

Be sure to clearly distinguish information from data. "Raw" data (without context) is not information, and therefore data architecture cannot be the same as information architecture. Unfortunately, the two terms are often being used interchangeably. The situation is not helped by architecture frameworks which only talk about data architecture and practically ignore information architecture.

Table 6.3 illustrates how information assets can be inventoried, cataloged, and tagged to understand the business use and purpose of the information available.

Information architectures are typically designed as part of IT implementation projects and not as part of a more permanent architecture discipline (like other architecture layers). This is a valid approach, because information architectures and assets can change rather quickly based on new business requirements and/or changes in business architecture. And these changes will trigger projects to create a changed information architecture. However, to ensure that the information architecture remains consistent and up-to-date over time, it is advisable to establish a suitable form of governance (see Chap. 5).

As the information architecture should always be driven from a strategy and business-perspective, a corresponding information architect role in larger BI implementation projects is therefore highly advisable. This role ensures that a holistic understanding not only of the specific business requirements of a project are considered but also the business context in which the project is delivered.

The delivery of an information architecture is well compatible with concepts like Design Thinking and agile, because this typically requires interdisciplinary collaboration and discussion in an explorative manner.

Moreover, it should take behavioral aspects into consideration as well such as:

- How do users interact with data?
- How do they search?
- What do they need to see?
- What is less important ...etc.

Specific information architectures can be defined, for example, as "Product Visions" or "User Stories" and then be delivered in incremental time boxes (sprints).

The maturity of an information architecture can be assessed by criteria such as:

1. Findable: Is information located easily? Is it required to search by (unknown) key words of an unknown taxonomy or is it possible to retrieve meaningful results supported by a fuzzy search
2. Consistency: Is the information asset consistently classified/labeled across all platforms?

Table 6.3 Inventory of information assets (© Exner/Zunic 2024. All Rights Reserved)

ID	Information asset	Description	Purpose	Category	Prio	Freq.	Owner	Pers. data?	Type
IA1.02	Churn-rate	Detailed churn-rate analysis by product, industry, and customer classifications	Supports key accounts to understand and avoid lost sales	Sales	High	Weekly	Key account management	No	OLAP
IA1.03	Customer profile	Segments customers by any attribute and provides 360° view	Central point of access for all customer data	CRM	High	Weekly	Key account management	Yes	OLAP
IA1.04	Claims rate	Detailed claims analysis by reason code	Revelation of quality issues	Quality management	High	Weekly	Service management	No	OLAP
IA1.05	Product contribution margin	Detailed profit center report by product	Optimized sales controlling	Controlling	High	Weekly	Controlling	No	OLAP
IA1.06	Customer segmentation	Segmentation model based on purchase patterns	Targeted marketing campaigns	Marketing	Medium	Weekly	Marketing	No	Predictive model
IA1.07	Balance sheet	Group balance sheet	Fast close	Finance	High	Monthly	Group accounting	No	Standard report
IA1.09	Profit and loss statement	Group P&L	Fast close	Finance	High	Monthly	Group accounting	No	Standard report

3. Clear: Is the information asset easy to understand? Is the key message close to business language?
4. Communicative: Is it informative and does it help a user to complete tasks?
5. Usable: Is the user able to derive targeted actions from the information asset?
6. Credible: Is it worthy of confidence and reliable?
7. Controllable: Is the user able to tailor and personalize information within their context?
8. Valuable: Is the information asset desirable and improve customer satisfaction?
9. Learnable: Can the information asset be easily understood and used?
10. Delightful: Are user expectations exceeded?

A remaining question is about what methodologies exist to support the development of a mature and effective information architecture. Based on the previously introduced concepts, user, content, context, below methodologies have proven to be effective.

- User focus—Design Thinking
  Design thinking is an iterative process in which a designer or architect seeks to understand the user, challenge assumptions, redefine problem statements, and create innovative solutions which can be prototyped and tested. In the context of Information architecture, Design Thinking can be a useful approach for understanding the structure and nature of a data-related business problem or requirement.
- Content focus—Semantic Modeling
  Semantic modeling is essentially used to describe data entities and their relationships to structure, define, and label data meaningfully and consistently. It utilizes generalized entity descriptions to simplify complex information and make it understandable. In this sense, "Semantic data modelling" can be defined as the development of descriptions and representations of data in such a way that the latter's meaning is explicit, accurate, and commonly understood by both humans and computer systems. This definition encompasses "a wide range of data artifacts, including metadata schemas, taxonomies, knowledge graphs, entity-relationship models and others" (Alexopoulos, 2020).
- Communication Design focus
  For almost a decade, we have seen a growing interest in standardizing the design of business reports and presentations through guidelines and best practices aimed at better structuring and expressing key messages in a comparable way. This includes recommendations on how to use appropriate visual representations and

semantic rules that enable consistent descriptions, analyses, and indicators to simplify a common understanding of business data.

Key considerations for developing a BI Strategy

- The creation of an inventory of information assets across the entire organization is a prerequisite to gain efficiency and remove redundancies. Additionally, it concretizes the connection (or disconnection) and integration with business architecture.
- Understanding user groups and users with their needs and usage behaviors is critical for achieving the intended BI value contribution.
- The identification of (major) information and/or analytical capability gaps is key to derive mitigation activities.
- The existence and communication of a standardized glossary of business terminology and notations helps to avoid misinterpretation and wasting time and effort for subsequent resolution of potential errors.
- A clearly defined ownership is necessary to guard and protect the information architecture against unintended changes.

6.6.3 Data Architecture

Data architecture refers to all the processes and methodologies that govern and define the different types of data collected within an organization. This includes aspects such as how data is used, stored, managed, and integrated. In this regard, data architecture provides a formal approach to creating and managing the flow of data and its processing through enterprise IT systems and applications.

In contrast to information architecture, data architecture is focusing on the logical and physical design of data structures. In addition, data architecture covers processes involved in collecting, enriching, and transforming raw data into usable information. Data architectures address both data in storage and data in motion. This requires a description of end-to-end data flows including data sources, data stores, and relevant data transformations. In addition, it describes the structure of data, such groupings, hierarchies as well as meta data, such data qualities, applications, locations, etc.

Once the data architecture has been physically implemented, it provides a foundation for information architecture which converts data into actionable business insights.

As both information and data architecture deal with data modeling, they are often used interchangeably or sometimes the information architecture is seen as part of data architecture.

It is strongly advisable to not confuse information architecture with data architecture because they serve different purposes and require different skill sets and experience.

Typically, data architecture is designed, created, deployed, and managed by data architects with a background in technical system and data design—whereas information architects navigate on the interface between business and IT and often have backgrounds in business analysis or semantic modeling.

Even though we consider data architecture to be a key component of a "stable core," its design and operation increasingly needs to support different speeds of innovation by embracing agile concepts (as we have outlined in Sect. 6.3). In this context, in 2014, Gartner introduced the notion of bimodal IT as the "the digital world demands greater enterprise dexterity in creating value from technology" (Gartner et al., Bimodal IT: How to Be Digitally Agile Without Making a Mess, 2014). The practice of bimodal aims to overcome one-size-fits-all constraints, but at the same time tries to avoid an ungoverned and unconstrained mode of operation. It essentially is the practice of managing two separate styles of work: one is focused on stability and predictability; the other on agility and exploration.

According to the Gartner IT Glossary "Mode 1 is optimized for areas that are predictable and well-understood" (Gartner, IT Glossary Bi-Modal IT, n.d.). In a business intelligence context, this means producing standardized, reliable, and automated data output supported by a well-governed and stable data architecture. It focuses on exploiting what is known, while iteratively and selectively renovating legacy environments to meet future requirements. It is worth mentioning that a data architecture following Mode 1 supports an information architecture with the same characteristics—i.e. standardized, reliable, and predictable information assets.

Mode 2, according to Gartner, "is exploratory, experimenting to solve new problems and optimized for areas of uncertainty" (Gartner, IT Glossary Bi-Modal IT, n.d.). It is often open-ended and tolerating failures. In a business intelligence context, these can be data-driven initiatives that begin with a hypothesis or model that is tested and adapted during a process involving short iterations, potentially adopting a rapid prototyping or Minimum Viable Product (MVP) approach.

Incorporating both modes in a business intelligence architecture is essential for BI value creation because data-driven decision-making requires both a predictable and standardized information supply as well as capabilities for exploration. It is worth noting that each mode requires a different governance style and organizational environment (see Chap. 5). The avoidance of an explicit bimodal approach and related requirements for information about a derived data architecture requirements results in a one-size-fits-all conflict. Either this results on overregulating governance for all information assets and data objects which most likely will harm flexibility and speed of decision support. Or the result risks limiting the reliability of decision-relevant information and underlying data.

How best to incorporate these modes into a BI strategy depends, among other things, on the organization's attitude and intended strategic use of information and data. This attitude may vary from industry to industry due to the regulatory landscape and reputational risk of data breaches. Hence, a good starting point for a BI strategy is to clearly describe the organization's strategic positioning with regard to the use of data.

Table 6.4 Characteristics of a data strategy

Characteristic	Compliance	Business opportunities
Focus	Regulatory compliance, data quality, and governance	Identify business opportunities
Data provisioning and usage	Stable core, corporate focus	Extension to stable core, agile delivery, citizen development
Data-governance ambition	Formal authority and adherence to given guidelines	Unconstrained data universe and access to data
Architectural driver	Single version of truth	Tolerance for multiple viewpoints and openness for new explorative results
Bimodal mode	Mode 1	Mode 2
Variety	Structured	Semi and unstructured
Volume	Little	Big
Velocity	Low	High
Retention policy	Retained in source and/or the EDW	Deleted soon after creation, if captured at all. Alternatively stored in data lakes.
Metadata	Documented	Undocumented
Security policy	Secured	Unsecured
Source	Human generated	Machine generated
Management maturity	High	Low, if any
Processing	Centralized	Decentralized
Origin	Internally generated	Internally and externally generated
Cost per record	High	Low
Value measured at	Value at the record level	Value at the aggregate level
Ease to extract value	Generally simple to exploit	Generally difficult to exploit
Value exposed in	Systems of record	Systems of innovation

In principle, we can distinguish between two main approaches:

- Compliance-oriented
- Business opportunity-oriented

The elements of each approach can be described by a set of key characteristics as shown below in Table 6.4.

The majority of organizations will lean toward one of the two strategies, and hence allocate budgets and resources to a data and governance architecture that reflects their positioning. However, a tailored data architecture allows to combine the demands of both strategies on each of the characteristics illustrated in Table 6.4.

To enable a tailored and modern data architecture, the following imperatives need to be taken into account:

- Trusted data
- Connected data
- Flexibility of architecture choice

Trusted Data

As data landscapes become increasingly complex, businesses are challenged with managing the inflow of structured and unstructured data from multiple sources such as applications, files, databases, data warehouses, and data lakes. For enabling organizations to extract value from the data and share it within the organization, a Mode 1 approach is required. This means that data architecture and data management solutions must provide ubiquitous data access while at the same time ensuring data security, privacy, and integrity under all circumstances. Only when these conditions are met can a company rely on their data.

Connected data

Connected data is essential in a time where data is being generated in vast quantities from various sources both inside and outside of the organization, making it challenging to gain real-time information on current corporate performance. When businesses aim to commercialize innovative data scenarios to attain a comprehensive view of their business, they must merge diverse data sets—whether big data, transactional data, or analytical data—to form a singular data universe. The strategy for managing data must offer the capacity to connect all data easily while avoiding unnecessary duplication and movement.

Flexibility of architecture choice

If a Mode 2 approach is a valid consideration, the chosen architecture must support this mode of operation. This has several implications. For example, an organization must have the flexibility to choose where to store and process its data. The data management solution must make certain that data can be stored and processed in any cloud and on hybrid environments (cloud/multi-cloud/on-premises). In selected cases, the architecture and related governance must allow the flexibility to experiment in situations of uncertainty. Only when these requirements are fulfilled, can an organization ensure that technology decisions are powered by business priorities instead of vice versa.

Reference Data Architecture

The foundation of a traditional BI data architecture is a unified (core) data warehouse. Data warehouses were designed to provide a harmonized data pool for overall evaluation purposes across organizational silos and technical system boundaries. A unified approach does not necessarily mean only one physical system, it rather means that at the semantic level of the underlying data model an integrated approach is pursued. Especially in large companies, there may be several data warehouses besides a leading Enterprise Data Warehouse, for example due to historical reasons, due to a need for separating specialized data domains, for security reasons, or simply for accelerating delivery speed.

In recent years, traditional data warehouse architectures (operating mostly under a Mode 1 approach) have come under pressure to modernize. New architecture patterns developed for big data and real-time processing (Mode 2 approach) have established themselves in corporate data architectures to address the growing influx of data and the need to make it accessible and actionable in a decision-making context.

Figure 6.11 below illustrates a data warehouse reference architecture combining both Mode 1 and Mode 2 characteristics:

The reference data architecture is structured into four layers (data sourcing and storage, data integration, data warehousing, and federated data warehousing) and shows how both modes (stable core and agile extension) can be incorporated. Please note that both modes can be combined on different layers. As this book is not primarily about architecture, we will only shortly introduce the key concepts.

Stable Data Core

The key characteristic of a classic BI data architecture remains relevant to this day—a stable and reliable core data warehouse, providing the enterprise-wide data foundation.

Data architecture tends to be relatively stable as data structures persist even when technologies evolve. When considering the main business objects managed by a given organization (such as, for example, customers, products, organizational units), they are relatively few compared to the number of applications, processes, or technologies using them. According to the TOGAF® documentation, "they provide architects with a stable and concentrated point of view on the architecture across the information systems." Whereas "applications and technologies evolve very quickly and are often owned by external partners providing infrastructure or application services, data is a unique, stable part of the architecture owned by the organization" (The Open Group®, 2020).

Therefore, processes to define and govern the stable core like data governance, master data management, and meta data management continue to be of high importance (see Chap. 5).

Data Warehousing

Data warehousing is the standard approach to achieve a stable and reliable data foundation on an enterprise level. It provides the data back-bone for corporate business intelligence. Enterprise Data Warehouses (EDWs) can serve up to 80% of a typical organization's data and information supply. They are architected around core data objects and data stores which are typically designed in star or snowflake schemas. These schemas are built to last for a long period of time and establish a "single source of truth" for corporate data from which ideally all standard reporting needs can be fulfilled. The goal of data warehousing is to build a long-term quality-assured data platform (sometimes known as corporate memory) able to support historical analyses across different systems and organizational units in a consistent and high-performance manner. This goal remains relevant to most enterprises today and cannot be achieved within transactional systems alone—especially in fragmented and non-standardized system environments. However, as data warehouses are built with this long-term perspective in mind, they require significant effort to design, create, maintain, fine-tune, and change. Consequently, traditional data warehouses can be very costly to operate and lack the agility to incorporate entirely new data requirements quickly.

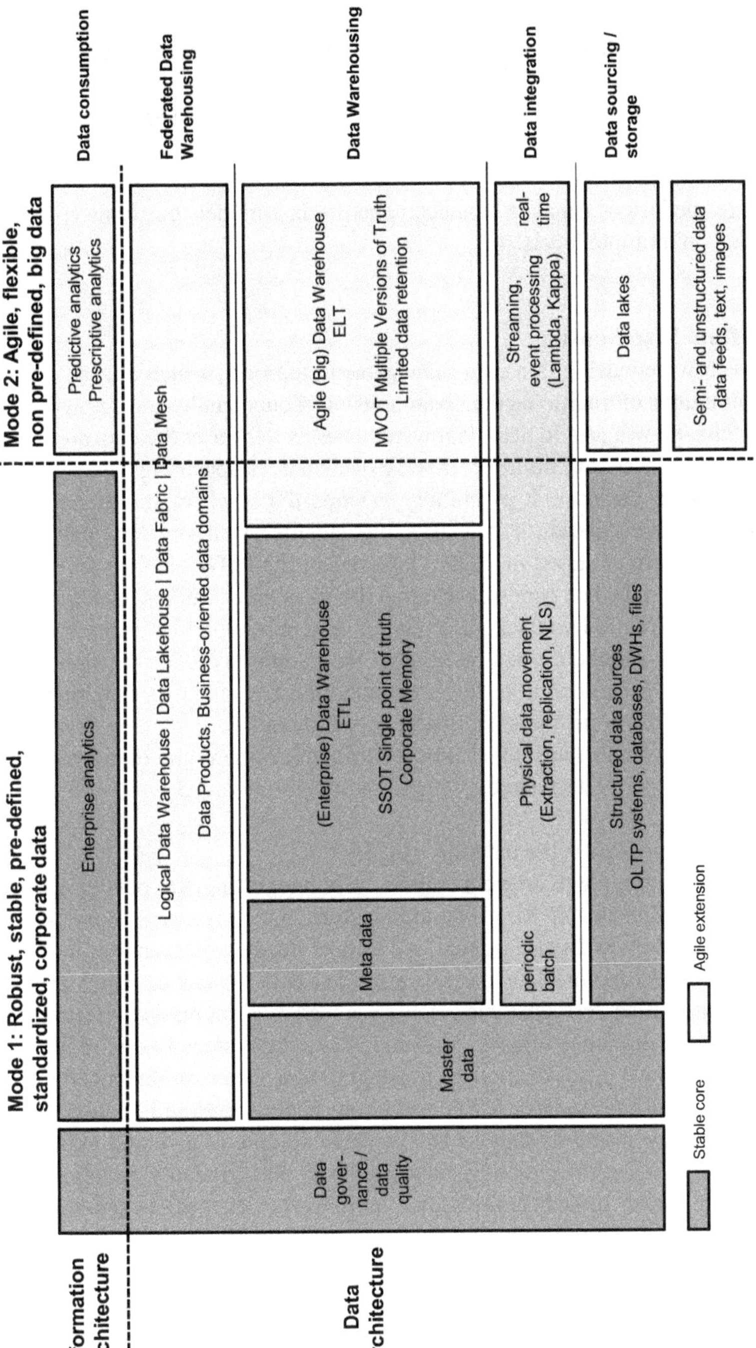

Fig. 6.11 Unified reference data architecture (© Exner/Zunic 2024. All Rights Reserved)

Additional down-sides of traditional data warehouses include:

- Data is typically updated via batch processes only and is hence not available in real time.
- Regular reconciliation efforts are required between source data and DWH data.
- High degree of data persistency and redundancy significantly increases the data footprint.
- Multi-layer persistency makes enhancements to data models costly as changes are needed on multiple levels.

Federated Data Warehousing

Federated data warehousing is a data management approach which aims to overcome the limitations of traditional data warehousing. Conceptually, a federated data warehouse (also known as a logical data warehouse) is a layer in the data architecture which enables access to multiple, diverse data sources appearing as one "logical" data source to the user. It essentially extends the reach of traditional data warehouses by enabling access to data lakes, big data files, web services, and Cloud applications. As Gartner stated in 2020, "inherent in the LDW architecture is the recognition that a single data persistence tier and type of processing is inadequate to meet the full scope of modern data and analytics demands" (Gartner et al., 2020).

The logical data warehouse can be seen as the natural evolution of traditional data warehouses, which allows a step-by-step modernization of the data architecture without having to re-invent the established data foundation. For many organizations, logical data warehousing can also be an attractive opportunity to more seamlessly connect isolated data sources which historically emerged and were never integrated.

A good example of this is the banking industry:

Banks typically struggle to create a unified, fully integrated data foundation that integrates both the Finance & Risk data architecture, which is a regulatory "must have" with the bank's own strategic and operational needs. For example, it is not uncommon that banks are unable to easily consolidate data from all customer touchpoints into an integrated 360° customer view or to feed relevant market information into operational performance reports. As banking is a data-intensive and regulated industry it continuously faces challenges to adapt to new data requirements on vast amounts of data and rarely dares to renovate core applications and architectures. These challenges are primarily caused by the sheer volume of data and organizational complexity but are magnified by the complexity and criticality of core banking applications which have become major inhibitors of change. In many cases therefore to meet new requirements, isolated custom-built applications, data warehouses, and third-party solutions were introduced around the core banking applications which exacerbate the problem of creating a common data foundation across the bank. Logical data warehousing can be an attractive option to consider mid-term in this case, as a renovation and consolidation of the core architecture is a multi-year and very costly transformation.

A BI strategy should therefore analyze the grown data architecture, identify the root causes resulting in the current pain-points, and describe a path to overcome these. Key questions from a data architecture perspective that should be addressed include: Has a stable core been established? Which additional alternative "cores" have been built and are they still relevant? Which parts should or must be integrated or consolidated? Which additional "new" data demands require an entirely different approach to data architecture and integration? How can a logical data warehouse be built taking an evolutionary approach?

In addition to opening the data architecture, logical data warehouses can also be considered as an opportunity to de-layer and de-clutter historically grown data warehouses. Enabled by innovations in database technology and increasingly lower memory and storage costs, logical data warehouses are today able to limit the amount of physically persisted data to a minimum and use Virtual Data Models (VDMs) to logically connect data objects and data layers. This can dramatically lower the costs of adjusting or enhancing existing data models, as less physical data is affected by the change.

Data Lakes

A data lake is, in essence, a very large store of data. Unlike traditional databases or data warehouses, it contains data in its original raw format. The data lake can be populated from a variety of sources—the data stored can be structured or unstructured and does not need to be validated or reformatted before being saved. In addition to text or number-based data, the data lake can also record images, videos, or other data formats. Structuring and, if necessary, reformatting of the data concerned is only carried out when the data is required.

The data lake offers several advantages. Thanks to the large amount of data stored, more in-depth analyses are possible. This can result in real competitive advantages for companies. Because the data is stored in its raw format without prior structuring or reformatting, storage processes are carried out very quickly. The requirements of the data lake in terms of computing power are low for storing even large amounts of data. In contrast to a data warehouse, the data lake offers many more "built-in" options for evaluating the raw data. Whereas the data warehouse is limited to pre-defined data views required for subsequent analyses, the data lake absorbs all data and does not limit the analysis options when storing the data.

One disadvantage is that a data lake has high requirements in terms of data protection and data security. The more data that is stored and the more relationships that can be established between the various data, the more complex they are to protect. The data lake needs a well-thought-out security and data protection concept as well as a mature, role-based user control with different access rights.

Some companies use a data lake as a cost-effective default storage for all kinds of raw data available in the organization. Once available in the data lake, they can pull and transform the data into a data warehouse for further analysis and/or integrate results of big data analyses via a logical data warehouse. Others use it only for archiving to offload outdated historical data from the transactional systems. Some enterprises separate their traditional data warehousing from the data lake entirely.

For example, they use the data lake as a data store for big data analytics only, using completely different tools, governance processes, and users. Others again take an even more offensive approach and use the data lake as their primary source of analytics, while keeping traditional warehousing to a bare minimum.

A BI strategy should provide guidance on the use, co-existence, and integration of data lakes with the data warehouse in the overall data architecture.

Data Science

The goal of data science is to discover relationships, trends, and patterns in large sets of data (big data). It applies statistical methods such as regression analysis, cluster analysis, conjoint analysis, data profiling, fuzzy logic, neural networks, and machine learning to make predictions or detect anomalies. The insights generated by data science are unique as they cannot be gained with traditional data warehousing approaches. In fact, data science is to some extent the inverse approach to traditional business intelligence. Business intelligence typically pre-defines the analytical dimensions (sphere of analysis) as an analytical foundation to answer standard pre-defined questions. Hence, it organizes data into schemas and aggregate views for a specific purpose. Data science overcomes this constraint of pre-defining the analytical dimensions. Consequently, it starts with a new, unconstrained question or hypothesis. Subsequently, it tries to find answers based on large sets of data and metadata. It tries to link different information sources and derive new insights via statistical methods. Data science is a growing discipline which is increasingly recognized as a competitive differentiator. Examples of use cases for data science include:

- Predict customer buying behavior
- Predictive maintenance of machinery
- Customer segmentation
- Fraud detection

A BI strategy needs to address the role of data science and how it will be integrated into the overall data architecture. It should also provide guidance around the business use cases and how they can be supported within the data architecture.

> In summary, we can conclude that traditional data warehouse approaches remain relevant for enterprise-wide analytics. However, to achieve a true bimodal architecture including the ability to integrate new data sources quickly as well as applying advanced statistical methods to data (e.g., for predictions, decision automation, or anomaly detection), additional approaches to analytics are needed.

A modern BI data architecture manages to integrate different analytics approaches and provide a seamless consumer experience across different analytical tools, data, and processes.

Key considerations for developing a BI Strategy

- Define your organizations' positioning on the "data offense"/"data defense" continuum and derive a corresponding target data architecture.
- Define the strategic relevance of a "Single Source of Truth" (in principle). If considered strategically relevant, specify for which enterprise-wide data assets.
- Describe on a high-level your enterprise data warehousing strategy and its intended target state.
- Describe your position and strategy regarding Big Data and how do you intend to use and integrate big data and data lakes in your data architecture.
- Describe the ownership for enterprise data architecture (per domain).

6.6.4 Application Architecture

Application architectures describe the behavior and purpose of business applications, how they interact with each other and with users. They focus mainly on the interaction between the applications rather than their internal structure. This involves, for example, defining the interaction between application packages, modules, databases, and middleware systems in terms of their functional coverage and integration points.

The key objective of application architectures is to ensure that the *suite of applications* being used by the organization is robust, integrated, scalable, reliable, and maintainable.

The application architecture should be business driven and shaped by functional requirements derived from the business architecture. Therefore, in large organizations, applications (or application portfolios) are often managed by a business or IT owner. To relate IT applications to the business architecture, it is good practice to assign the IT application landscape to business functions and or business capabilities.

This helps application architects and application owners to easily identify gaps ("white spots"), overlaps, and redundancies in terms of functional coverage and application integration. Application architectures typically evolve constantly, because every new IT project or initiative adds new features (functional coverage), new interfaces (additional applications), or both to the application architecture.

If the process of integrating new applications or sunsetting outdated applications in the application architecture is not managed from an overall portfolio perspective, an organization risks an uncontrolled growth of complexity also known as "analytical chaos." Application architects must not only understand and manage the dynamics of functionality and integration, but also help to shape the deployment strategy and keep an eye out for technology risks that could impact the growth and/or operation of the application.

> A holistic BI strategy should evaluate if and how the key enterprise-wide analytical business capabilities (outlined in the business architecture) are functionally supported by the as-is application architecture. It should also sketch a target state application architecture based on identified functional white spots or redundancies.

BI strategies also need to discuss and evaluate transformative architecture modernization strategies that can help elevate analytics maturity to an entirely new level. If these aspects are not discussed and decided as part of a BI strategy process, they are likely not going to be addressed at all. An application architecture should make at least the following aspects transparent:

- Consolidating application or application landscapes
- Outsourcing applications to external service providers
- Deploying parts of the application landscape in the Cloud
- Sunsetting applications

This target picture can then be used as a communication tool to align new planned initiatives and projects with a strategic plan or roadmap.

To communicate and visualize the application architecture including the evolution from an as-is to a target state in a BI strategy, it is useful to map applications to business dimensions, capabilities, or layers.

One variant is to map the structure of the information architecture (i.e., analytic domains) to the data transformation layers within the data architecture. This enables an easy identification of central integration points and white spots in the architecture (see Fig. 6.12 Variant 1). An alternative is to map the applications only to dimensions from the business architecture like company codes, lines of business, geographies, physical locations (see Fig. 6.12 Variant 2). By classifying each application via relevant metadata (i.e., owned by which line of business, belonging to which architecture layer, physically deployed in which location…etc.), different perspectives can be produced.

To summarize, the common overarching goals of creating a BI application architecture include:

- Reduction in the number of similar/redundant technologies and applications
- Reduction of complexity by introducing BI application standards
- Reduction of complexity by reusable solution components
- Standardization and consolidation of functions for DWH environments and mapping to BI applications (e.g., ETL framework, backend connectivity functions, etc.)
- Establish scalable, configurable modules for initializing complete DWH environments

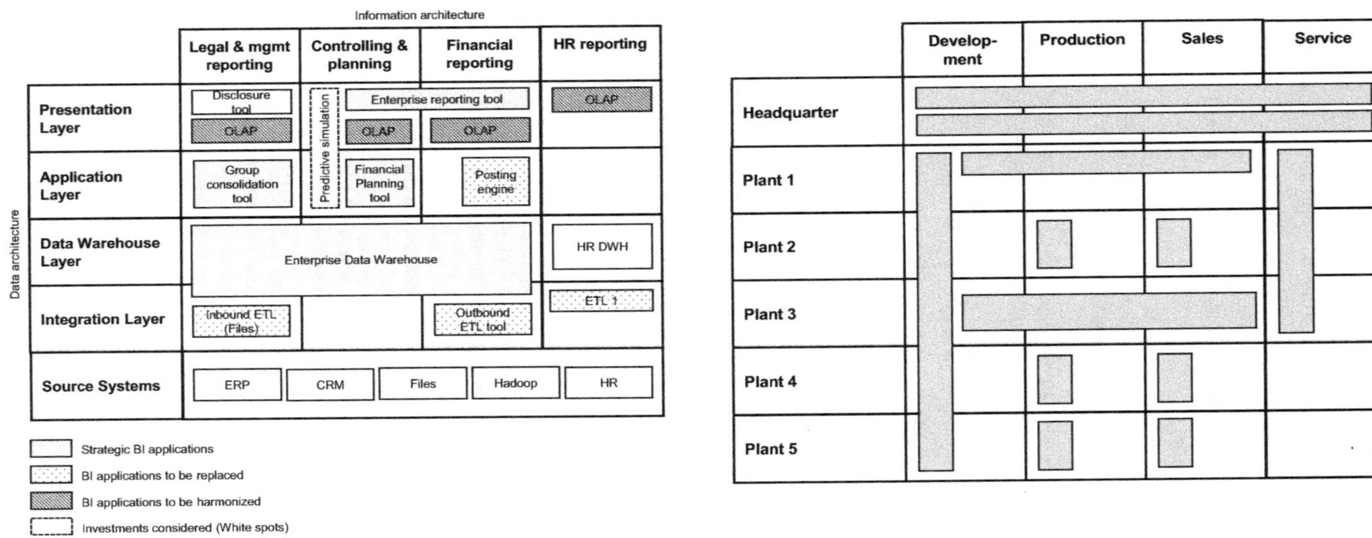

Fig. 6.12 Alternative views on BI application architectures (© Exner/Zunic 2024. All Rights Reserved)

A well-designed application architecture achieves this by:

- Establishing a governance and ownership structure to advance the BI landscape
- Creating transparency about the existing BI application landscape
- Supporting the planning of the future BI landscape
- Reducing interfaces within the BI landscape
- Increasing process and organizational coverage by identifying "white spots" in the application landscape

Key considerations for developing a BI Strategy

- Create an enterprise-wide inventory of the BI application landscape, underlying usage rates, status within application lifecycle, age, maintainability regarding required skills.
- Continuously evaluate to what extent the key business functions are supported by the current application architecture (for example, via surveys). Identify if the functional coverage is sufficient or in case of lacking functionality, which solutions are used to by-pass the enterprise applications ("shadow IT").
- Evaluate usage and adoption of enterprise BI applications vs. spreadsheets.
- Assess potentials for cost-cutting by standardizing and consolidating applications which serve similar or redundant purposes.
- Derive a target application architecture for enterprise-wide BI and ensure alignment with strategic business priorities and related analytics needs.

6.6.5 Technology Architecture

The technology architecture supports all other architecture layers by creating the physical and virtual infrastructure required for application services to run. It is a key component within the wider architecture and incorporates all requirements from the previously mentioned layers. Therefore, it manifests the art-of-the-possible in technology reality.

The key priority of technology architecture is to provide stable and continuous system operations according to defined service levels. At the same time technology architectures need to ensure that the technology platform is flexible and scalable enough to support changes introduced by new requirements and project implementations in other architecture layers.

It is therefore critical that technology architectures are tightly aligned to all other architecture layers.

Typical challenges facing technology architectures include:

- IT architectures become more and more complex and difficult to scale
- Growing heterogeneity of technologies and vendors

- Growing compliance requirements (for example, data security (GDPR), SOX, data center compliance standards)
- Increasing operational costs
- Majority of technology budget is spent on operations, little or no budget allocated to infrastructure renovation or innovation

Technology architectures are dealing with the virtual and physical infrastructure ("bare metal") components that are essentially underlying all other logical components of the architecture. They are traditionally built around more or less fixed, predefined service levels. This often presents a challenge in terms of elasticity and dynamic scaling to meet usage patterns or seasonal peaks.

One solution for this challenge is addressed by cloud computing.

BI architectures in the Cloud

According to the National Institute of Standards and Technology (NIST), cloud computing can be described as a model for enabling convenient, on-demand network access to a shared pool of configurable computing resources (for example, networks, servers, storage, applications, and services) that can be rapidly provisioned and released with minimal management effort or service provider interaction (NIST, 2011).

The essential characteristics of Cloud deployments are:

- On-demand self-service
- Resource pooling
- Rapid elasticity
- Metered consumption-based service
- Broad network access

There are three main Cloud service models:

- SaaS (software-as-a-service)
- PaaS (platform-as-a-service)
- IaaS (infrastructure-as-a-service)

All three service models lend themselves well to a BI context and should be evaluated carefully in a BI strategy development. Typically, a key aspect to be discussed is that a cloud based model essentially replaces high upfront IT investments (CapEx), with continuous operational running costs (OpEx).

We will outline some examples below.

Software-as-a-service:

BI application architectures are often characterized by a huge variety of front-end applications that essentially offer very similar solution capabilities and have large functional overlaps. This is exacerbated by the huge diversity of vendors and product portfolios in this domain. In addition, buying decisions are often entirely based on local business preferences disregarding the impacts they have on growing

IT complexity and efforts. One possible path out of this vicious circle is to provide users access to state-of-the-art BI tools in a public cloud environment. This takes away the entire effort of installing, patching, upgrading, and customizing the software on-premise, while enabling the users to consume latest product innovations and features. In addition, the application architecture becomes more elastic and scalable, as the provisioning of resources is based on pay-as-you-use basis.

Even if this approach suggests maximum flexibility, care must be taken to ensure that this does not result in uncontrolled growth that is difficult to manage. In addition, new governance models need to be considered and orchestrated on an enterprise-wide level. Especially in hybrid constellations of mixed cloud and on-premise deployments, certain guardrails or at least guidelines need to be established and governed. One key aspect to consider is the continuous delivery in a cloud model driven by the software vendor in contrast with the discrete, release-based delivery in an inhouse on-premise setup.

Platform-as-a-service:

The same principle introduced above for BI applications can also be applied for entire data platforms. Imagine for example, that an organization aims to modernize its data platform and rethink the way it integrates data from a wide variety of sources to become more flexible and cost-efficient in providing its BI services to users. An attractive alternative to a pure on-premise based data platform deployment is a platform-as-a-service approach (PaaS). This type of Cloud service model offers data management and data integration services (APIs) in the Cloud. This model can be used, for example, for efficiently integrating big data sources, training or using machine learning models and algorithms or building prototypes for testing/validating new software in a sandbox environment. Going even a step further, software vendors meanwhile offer data warehousing services in the Cloud which allow customers to build their logical or physical data warehouses including the connectivity and layered architecture in a PaaS model. Even though in many industries data security and compliance regulation might challenge or even limit this option, it might still be attractive complement to the existing data architecture for certain use cases.

Infrastructure-as-a-service:

Infrastructure-as-a-Service (IaaS) is a form of cloud service model that provides equipment and infrastructure components including storage, hardware, servers, and networking components to support operations. The IaaS provider owns the equipment and infrastructure and is responsible for housing, running, and maintaining them. An IaaS client typically pays on a per-use basis reflecting the amount of resources used over time. Additionally, the arrangement will involve an agreed service level in terms of availability and response to demand.

This service model is typically used as a foundational entry step into a cloud strategy to achieve higher and dynamic scalability in the technology architecture allowing for a usage-based allocation of resources and payment.

Like any other technology strategy however, a cloud service strategy has to be considered in relationship to the overall strategy of the IT organization, as well as the overall company strategy. It is advisable to ensure that a BI strategy continuously aligns with the IT corporate cloud service strategy and to derive a relevant roadmap for adoption of Cloud BI.

Key considerations for developing a BI Strategy

- Anchor business intelligence strategy with or within the corporate cloud service strategy.
- Provide traceability of business intelligence consumer requirements across all architecture layers, ultimately including the technology architecture.
- Translate BI consumer requirements into BI service level expectations.
- Evaluate if and to which extent BI Cloud service models should play a future role in the overall BI architecture.
- If applicable, define a concrete roadmap for a BI transition into the Cloud including the new and potentially obsolete technological capabilities that this transition requires.

7 Now Take Your Next Steps

As we have learned throughout the various chapters of this book, developing a BI strategy is not easy. It requires a good understanding of the fundamentals, a broad knowledge of the various factors contributing to business intelligence success, strong communication skills, and more.

This chapter aims to conclude the previous chapters with a more concise overview.

However, we strongly recommend our readers not to confuse this chapter with a checklist where you just tick the boxes, and you are done. Instead, we believe this chapter will help our readers summarize and recapitulate some selected essentials contributing to developing a BI strategy. We should not forget that the BI strategy is a means of enabling the Intelligent Enterprise. In this sense, we consider the practice of developing a Business Intelligence strategy to be somewhat of an art.

Business Intelligence is closely related to decision support. However, what are the essentials, what are we aiming for, and how do we achieve a setup that gives confidence that we are on the right track? These and many other questions arise when we ask ourselves what Business Intelligence is about.

First of all, Business Intelligence should not be confused with buying the latest technology. Instead, Business Intelligence encompasses a wide variety of disciplines, domains, and skills that serve the purpose of … what actually? Quite frequently, we finish this sentence with "decision support." However, decision support is a rather generic term, and indeed, all BI practitioners can agree on this as the primary purpose of business intelligence. However, that would just be replacing one broad term with another and would not add much value. Instead, we need to dig deeper.

R. Exner, A. Zunic, *The Path to an Intelligent Enterprise*, Future of Business and Finance, https://doi.org/10.1007/978-3-031-69914-6_7

In our book, we discussed that supporting a decision is not necessarily a decision made. Moreover, even a decision made does not necessarily change anything by itself. Only when the decision is translated into actions and consequently put into practice will it materialize into a concrete and intended impact. This intended impact will result in revised data, allowing a fact-based validation of whether the previous facts have been transformed into new facts due to the intended impact. Therefore, the main goal of Business Intelligence can be summarized as improving the SPEED TO IMPACT.

The given context of Business Intelligence is the business with its multiple strategies. What sounds evident in the headlines turns out to be a challenge in practice because business strategies are often not sufficiently aligned or even contradict each other. From this perspective, a key anchor of BI value should be the close alignment of corporate and functional strategies with business intelligence. As we learned in Chap. 2, this alignment can have multiple facets, ranging from envisioning new strategic opportunities based on data-driven business models to monetizing data.

Taking advantage of emerging opportunities is a significant challenge for many organizations and is often envisioned as part of a visionary future state scenario. One of the reasons for this is that to take advantage of these opportunities, the entire organization must be rebuilt on continuous and increasing agility and innovation. Considering that the existing mindset of a typical workforce is often still constrained by current ways of working and limited by organizational boundaries, it becomes understandable that the goal of an Intelligent Enterprise often remains visionary.

Returning to our core topic of BI strategy. What should a BI Strategy describe? As we previously discussed, it is highly recommended to use concise yet comprehensive language to provide easy-to-understand answers to the fundamental questions along the BI strategy development journey. These answers range from the organization-specific definition and scope of Business Intelligence to a comprehensive assessment of the current capability portfolio and the development of an ambitious but still feasible new performance level of business intelligence.

Strategy in general, and in our context BI strategy in particular, should be seen as a promise to the organization to realize the most viable set of business intelligence activities. This aims to achieve the published goals, thus providing a transparent value add of business intelligence to the entire organization.

This promise requires among others a renewed portfolio of products and services, which typically must challenge existing, historically grown structures and data design. If these structures are supposed to remain unchanged, it is no wonder that companies are challenged to adapt their business structures in an agile way and, for example, to manage their margins on the latest products, service offerings, and bundles. In addition, if companies want to become data-driven, it should be evident that data structures should serve this purpose. Therefore, data structures must not just be treated as a means, but as a prerequisite to achieve the desired results.

In this context, the BI strategy should provide guidance on removing structural inconsistencies and redundancies to strengthen corporate efficiencies. This should be done in a holistic way, which is a prerequisite of seamless data-driven decision-making. A corporate steering model must not be solely based on financial KPIs but also include nonfinancial KPIs. Overarching ownership for data-driven decision-making and obtaining infrastructure (processes, solutions, governance, etc.) in place needs to be defined.

If BI is accepted as a critical element to support steering on all organizational levels by accelerating "SPEED TO IMPACT," then BI strategy must include strategic alignment with the businesses. Decision-making, execution, and ultimately intended impact will still be the key differentiator between theory and practice. BI strategy development should aim for a clear and recognizable uniqueness and value contribution. Otherwise, BI will increasingly struggle to prove its relevance and value compared to the typically transparent costs. As a result, BI runs the risk of being sidelined.

As we have learned, the speed of the innovation curve is becoming increasingly steeper. Speed is king, and every organization should strive to remove barriers to acceleration. What is true for organizations in general should be valid for BI in particular. Consequently, a BI strategy should self-critically evaluate opportunities to learn faster, innovate faster, and develop and deploy faster. These opportunities must be translated into meaningful guardrails by the BI strategy.

Creating a BI strategy requires processes and activities that, when executed, lead to the desired outcome of the existence or revision of a BI strategy document. A transparent, understandable, and meaningful structure of these processes and activities provides guidance on the sequence and describes what the first steps are, what comes next, and so on. However, this is still just describing theories of how it should work. To walk the talk, it is essential that a designated "someone" takes ownership and ensures that all activities needed to produce the intended BI strategy are carried out ("BI strategy owner"). As long as there is no real name of a person assigned to be the "someone," it can be taken as an indicator that this essential prerequisite is not yet met.

But, of course, this is not enough. In any organization, where typically different people with individual ways of thinking, communicating, and collaborating want to join forces in a meaningful way, it is obvious that some common rules of the game need to be established. These rules of the game can be called governance. As we discussed in Chap. 4, governance in general, as well as BI governance, encompasses a variety of dimensions.

In addition to a well-managed and balanced BI product portfolio as an effective governance and communication tool for aligning management and strategic priorities with BI capabilities and resulting BI products, we learned about the high relevance of data governance. Only if data governance is perceived as a key priority throughout the entire enterprise will the BI products implemented be able to generate value.

In Chap. 5, we learned that the trustworthiness of data is a hygiene factor that needs to be fulfilled even without explicit requests. However, the challenge is to design BI governance structures and architectures for stability while at the same time allowing sufficient flexibility to introduce change and innovation to achieve continuous adoption and value.

Therefore, our advice is to link enterprise-wide initiatives as closely as possible to KPIs of corporate strategy and demonstrate how they influence business outcomes strategically. This includes but must not be constraint to measuring adoption rates and user satisfaction.

The absence of a holistic BI architecture framework is one of the reasons why companies fail at BI projects and, as a result, fail at making their BI strategies successful. To support our readers in managing this challenge, we explored in Chap. 6 some fundamental BI architectural guidelines, including a stable core and a business-oriented and broad "anticipatory" mindset. Not to forget the recommendation to aim for maximizing reuse of high-value reporting and data assets by promoting agile project delivery based on top of the stable core as default.

Our book concludes by detailing existing architectural layers, starting with business architecture, information architecture, data architecture and closing with the typical, frequently with the term architecture associated, application architecture and technology architecture. A BI strategy must support the current operating model described by business architecture. However, in case the current operating model and underlying business architecture are intended to be changed, business intelligence needs to be involved right from the start.

Creating an inventory of information assets across the enterprise is a prerequisite for gaining efficiency and eliminating redundancies. At the same time, it is a crucial artifact of a well-established information architecture, the absence of which points to a lower level of business intelligence maturity. Additionally, it concretizes the connection (or disconnection) and integration with business architecture. Understanding user groups and users with their needs and usage behaviors is critical for achieving the intended BI value contribution efficiently. An organization that calls for "customer centricity" externally but neglects the need for it internally is inconsistent and confusing to the workforce.

We outlined some arguments why it is advisable not to confuse information architecture with data architecture and why BI practitioners should continuously evaluate the extent to which the current application architecture supports key business functions. With such a systematic approach in mind, BI practitioners will be able to identify whether functional coverage is sufficient, or, in the case of missing functionality, which solutions are being used to bypass enterprise applications, leading to a well-known phenomenon called "shadow IT." The requirements of business intelligence consumers should be traceable across all architectural layers, including the technology architecture. Of course, the emerging BI cloud service models, with their strategically intended future role in the overall BI architecture, should be evaluated frequently to draw the correct conclusions in time.

We called our book "The Path to an Intelligent Enterprise." This is because we strongly believe it is a path to the "Intelligent Enterprise" rather than a well-developed highway. Along the way, just like on a highway, there are many crossroads or junctions where decisions must be made. It is like driving a car. The first time you drive by yourself, you may feel hesitant or unsure, what will come next, what are the others doing? However, step by step, each of us has become more advanced and experienced, so with a lot of practice, it becomes more and more an art. Similarly, we can think of the art and practice of developing a Business Intelligence strategy as an essential lever to approach the Intelligent Enterprise.

We have learned that developing a Business Intelligence Strategy is a journey, not a fixed future state scenario, not something to be ticked off like a checklist. Accepting all the uncertainties, it is essential that we do not need an unfilled role called "somebody," but a real Mr. or Ms. Business Intelligence who owns the issue is driven by passion for getting it done and walks the talk.

We need courage and confidence: Courage to face the challenges and bring the questions up for discussion at all levels with the confidence that they will be answered. In other words, a strong "can do" mentality.

Your next step will put you on the path to the Intelligent Enterprise.

The art and practice of Business Intelligence strategy begins NOW.

Good luck!

References

Alexopoulos, P. (2020). *Semantic modeling for data - Avoiding pitfalls and breaking dilemmas*. O'Reilly Media.

Bloomberg, J. (2018, 29 April). Digitization, digitalization, and digital transformation: Confuse them at your peril. Retrieved 14 October, 2023, from https://www.forbes.com/sites/jasonbloomberg/2018/04/29/digitization-digitalization-and-digital-transformation-confuse-them-at-your-peril/#3d4077c32f2c

Cebotarean, E. (2011, 15 Febraury). *Journal of Knowledge Management, Economics and Information Technology*. (E. a. Journal of Knowledge Management, Ed.). Retrieved 21 March, 2023, from http://www.scientificpapers.org/wp-content/files/1102_Business_intelligence.pdf

Chamoni, P., & Gluchowski, P. (2016). In P. Gluchowski & P. Chamoni (Eds.), *Analytische Informationssysteme – Einordnung und Überblick* (5th ed.). Springer Gabler. https://doi.org/10.1007/978-3-662-47763-2_1

Eckerson, W. (2004, 18 November). *In search of a single version of truth: Strategies for consolidating analytic silos*. TDWI. Retrieved 05 December, 2023, from https://web.archive.org/web/20050314185644/http://www.tdwi.org/Publications/WhatWorks/display.aspx?id=7300

European Commission. (2023). *Corporate sustainability reporting*. (E. Commission, Editor, & F. S. Contact Directorate-General for Financial Stability, Producer). Retrieved 14 March, 2023, from https://finance.ec.europa.eu/capital-markets-union-and-financial-markets/company-reporting-and-auditing/company-reporting/corporate-sustainability-reporting_en

European Union, 1.-2. (Ed.). (2023). *European Union - Shaping Europe's digital future*. DESI 2023 dashboard for the Digital Decade. Retrieved 14 October, 2023, from https://digital-decade-desi.digital-strategy.ec.europa.eu/datasets/desi

Friedag, H. R., & Schmidt, W. (2016). *Pocket guide - Balanced scorecard - The European approach*. Retrieved 15 May, 2023, from http://www.scorecard.de/wp-content/uploads/2021/11/Balanced-Scorecard_A5_final_2016-04-12.pdf

Gartner. (n.d.). *Gartner Glossary: Analytics*. Retrieved July 30, 2023, from https://www.gartner.com/en/information-technology/glossary/analytics

Gartner, The Practical Logical Data Warehouse, Henry Cook, Rick Greenwald, Adam Ronthal, 9 December 2020. This Gartner report is archived and is included for historical context only.

Gartner, Dawson, P., Lowendahl, J.-M., & Gaehtge, F. (2023, July 24). *Gartner, Understanding Gartner's hype cycles*. Retrieved from https://www.gartner.com/en/research/methodologies/gartner-hype-cycle

Gartner, Feinberg, D., & Russom, P. (2022). *Hype cycle for data management*. This Gartner report is archived and is included for historical context only. Retrieved 20 November, 2023

Gartner, Hostmann, B., Rayner, N., & Herschel, G. (2009, October 19). *Gartner business intelligence, analytics and performance management framework*. This Gartner report is archived and is included for historical context only. Retrieved 30 July, 2022, from https://www.gartner.com/

R. Exner, A. Zunic, *The Path to an Intelligent Enterprise*, Future of Business and Finance, https://doi.org/10.1007/978-3-031-69914-6

imagesrv/summits/docs/apac/business-intelligence/BI-Analytics-PM-Framework-166512.pdf. This Gartner report is archived and is included for historical context only. GARTNER is a registered trademark of Gartner, Inc. and/or its affiliates and is used herein with permission. All rights reserved.

Gartner, IT Glossary Bi-Modal IT. (n.d.). *Gartner IT Glossary for Bi-Modal IT*. Retrieved from https://www.gartner.com/en/information-technology/glossary/bimodal

Gartner, Hype Cycle for Artificial Intelligence, Afraz Jaffri, Farhan Choudhary, 8 July 2022. This Gartner report is archived and is included for historical context only.

Gartner, Hype Cycle for Analytics and Business Intelligence, Peter Krensky, 14 July 2022. This Gartner report is archived and is included for historical context only. HYPE CYCLE is a registered trademark of Gartner, Inc. and/or its affiliates and is used herein with permission. All rights reserved.

Gartner, Bimodal IT: How to Be Digitally Agile Without Making a Mess, Mary Mesaglio, Simon Mingay, 15 July 2014. https://www.gartner.com/document/2798217. Retrieved 11.04.2023. This Gartner report is archived and is included for historical context only

Hackathorn, R. (2003, 01 July). *TDAN.com*. (I. Bolder Technology, Ed.) Retrieved 19 November, 2023, from https://bolder.com/wp-content/uploads/2019/10/Minimizing_action_distance.pdf

Luhn, H. (1958). A business intelligence system. *IBM Journal of Research and Development. IBM Journal*. https://doi.org/10.1147/rd.24.0314

Müller-Stewens, G., & Lechner, C. (2005). In S. Poeschel (Ed.), *Strategisches Management - Wie strategische Initiativen zum Wandel führen* (3rd ed.). Schäffer Poeschel Verlag. Retrieved 27 October, 2023. ISBN-13: 978-3-7910-2467-7.

NIST. (2011, 09). *National Institute of Standards and Technology*. The NIST Definition of Cloud Computing. Retrieved from https://csrc.nist.gov/publications/detail/sp/800-145/final

Osterwalder, A., & Pigneur, Y. (2010). *Business model generation*. Wiley.

Roland Berger Strategy Consultants. (2016, 21 May). *Digitization of industry in full force*. (Roland Berger Strategy Consultants, & BDI Bundesverband der Deutschen Industrie e.V., Eds.) Retrieved 03 October, 2023, from https://www.rolandberger.com/en/Insights/Publications/Digitization-of-industry-in-full-force.html

Rosenfeld, L., & Morville, P. (2002). *Information architecture for the Web and beyond* (2nd ed.). O'Reilly Media.

The Open Group®. (2001). *TOGAF® - Frequently asked questions*. The Open Group Architecture Framework®. Retrieved 07 October, 2023, from http://www.opengroup.org/public/arch/p1/togaf_faq.htm

The Open Group®. (2018). *Content metamodel*. The Open Group Architecture Framework®. Retrieved from https://pubs.opengroup.org/architecture/togaf9-doc/arch/chap30.html

The Open Group®. (2020). *Information architecture: Business intelligence & analytics and metadata management reference models*. The Open Group®.

United Nations (UN). (1987). *Report of the World Commission on Environment and Development: Our common future*. (United Nations, Ed.) Retrieved 05 July, 2023, from http://www.un-documents.net/ocf-02.htm#I

Westenberger. (2018). *Data analytics 2018: Studie BI-Strategie & Industrialisierung*. TH Köln. Retrieved 07 December, 2023.

Wright, T. (2022, 27 July). *How to write a vision statement (With examples, tips, and formulas)*. (Cascade, Editor). Cascade. Retrieved 21 April, 2021, from https://www.cascade.app/blog/write-good-vision-statement

Yadav, S. (2015, 18 December). *The Kano Model – A tool to prioritize the users' wants and desires*. (I. D. IxDF, Editor). Retrieved 09 January, 2023, from https://www.interaction-design.org/literature/article/the-kano-model-a-tool-to-prioritize-the-users-wants-and-desires

Zachman, J. A. (2008). *Zachman international enterprise architecture*. John Zachman's concise definition of The Zachman Framework™. https://zachman-feac.com/

Index

A

Agile BI delivery, 192, 198
Analytical chaos, 167, 231
Analytical dimensions, 4, 61, 103, 141, 144, 230
Analytics, 5, 6, 19–21, 23, 24, 62, 71, 76, 84, 103, 104, 158, 166, 170, 171, 174, 175, 180, 190, 191, 199, 200, 202, 206, 208–211, 228, 230–232, 234
Application architectures, 191, 205, 211, 231–236, 242
Approach for evaluation, 178
Architectural silos, 192
Artificial intelligence (AI), v, 6, 9, 10, 19, 21, 24, 25, 75, 79, 80, 82, 83, 184, 186, 191, 207, 215

B

Backlog, 88, 135, 199, 218
Best practice, 108, 153, 179, 200, 206
BI applications, 13, 17
BI architecture goals, 196–202
BI architecture ownership, 190
BI architectures in the Cloud, 235
BI business model, 37
BI Center of Excellence (BI CoE), 179
BI Competence Center (BI-CC), 157
BI Development Center (BI-DC), 179, 183–184
BI governance, 11, 13, 16, 20, 112, 134, 152–179, 182–188, 201, 241
BI maturity model (BI-MM), 116
BI organization, 13
BI processes, 13, 17, 103, 141
BI product portfolio, 159, 161, 162, 241
BI strategy development, 2, 17, 25, 27, 34, 35, 39, 44, 66, 74, 81, 132, 147–149, 181, 207, 235, 240, 241
BI strategy development lifecycle, 135
BI strategy journey, 10
BI strategy lifecycle, 137
BI strategy process at a glance, 137
BI technology trends, 17, 22–25
BI usage trends, 20–21
BI value contribution, 17, 22, 25, 27, 40, 50, 61, 136, 141, 181, 185, 188, 222, 242
BI vision, vi, 26, 125–134, 138, 139, 147
Big data, v, 20, 21, 158, 166, 167, 184, 207, 225, 228–231, 236
Bimodal IT, 223
Business architecture, 190, 192, 205, 206, 208, 210–216, 219, 222, 231, 232, 242
Business model, 22, 37, 44–50, 63, 64, 188, 212, 214
Business process performance (BPP), 103
Business Process Reference Models (APQC), 204, 206, 208, 214

C

Canvas, 12, 13, 212
Capabilities, 5, 8, 15, 16, 19–21, 23, 24, 26, 31, 36, 44, 46, 56, 57, 78, 80, 82, 83, 96, 108, 111, 121, 133, 134, 159, 161, 183, 187, 190, 205, 208, 211, 212, 214, 216, 223, 231, 232, 235, 237, 241
Capital Expenditure (CapEx), 82, 235
Center of Expertise (CoE), 63
Cloud Business Intelligence (Cloud BI), 20, 200, 237
Collection of information, 100
Commodity, 78, 81
Communication barriers, 11, 177
Communication design, 221

R. Exner, A. Zunic, *The Path to an Intelligent Enterprise*, Future of Business and Finance, https://doi.org/10.1007/978-3-031-69914-6

Connected data, 224, 225
Consideration of dynamics, 134
Continuous improvement, 155, 167
Continuous innovation, 75, 78
Conversational, dialog-oriented AI, 19
Core, 3, 8, 13, 16, 25, 27, 31, 32, 55, 60, 61, 64, 65, 72, 75, 91, 130, 141, 142, 146, 147, 155, 157, 160, 177, 180, 182, 183, 188, 191, 198, 200–202, 211, 212, 223–226, 228, 229, 240, 242
Corporate strategy, 40, 44, 97, 98, 135
Customer centricity, 46, 242
Customer journey, 32–34, 44, 46, 47

D
Data architects, 223
Data architecture, 21, 208, 222, 226
Data-as-a-service, 22
Data-driven, 6, 9, 10, 20, 36, 44–46, 58, 61, 62, 65, 70, 74, 118, 157, 166, 170, 172, 174, 175, 186, 188, 190, 191, 193, 202, 223, 240
Data-driven decision making, 7, 62, 65, 66, 70, 174, 175, 191, 193, 223
Data governance, 160, 173, 191, 197, 198, 201, 226, 241
Data lake, 200, 229
Data management, 13, 17, 24, 25
Data monetization, 22
Data science, 6, 19, 24, 158, 191, 202, 218, 230
Data warehouse, 3, 4, 166, 200, 202, 209, 225, 226, 228–230
Data warehousing, 167, 200, 207, 226, 228–231, 236
Decision made, 7, 240
Decision-making, v, vi, 7–10, 19, 24, 31, 41, 44–46, 48, 50, 54, 58, 60, 80, 82, 84, 85, 118, 152, 154, 157, 170–172, 176, 181, 184–186, 188, 190, 195, 201, 202, 207, 208, 214, 215, 225, 240
Decision support, 3, 11, 25, 26, 46, 50, 56, 61, 63, 66, 68, 170, 201, 223, 239
Decompose, 96
Decomposition methodology, 99
Dependencies, 6, 34, 112, 145, 146, 153, 169, 195
Design thinking, 161, 219, 221
Digital, vi, 9, 10, 18, 44, 50–58, 78–81, 98, 174, 175, 177, 193, 214, 223
Digital content, 57
Digital Economy and Society Index (DESI), 51
Digitalization, 50–56, 58
Digitalization strategy, 56
Digital maturity, 51, 58, 174, 175
Digital processes/interactions, 55, 57
Digital tools and solutions/assets, 57
Digital transformation, 52, 53
Digital twin, 9
Digital workforce, 56, 57
Digitization, 52
Do more with less, 67, 68
Drill-down, 5, 15, 77
Driver trees, 15

E
Efficiencies, 67
Efficiency gains, 180
Embedded analytics, 19
End-to-end, v, 31–33, 36, 46, 53–55, 57, 59, 60, 70, 84, 118, 157, 180–182, 184, 206, 214, 215, 222
End-user adoption, 155, 164
Energy economics, 72
Enterprise architecture (EA), 195, 203
Enterprise architecture framework, 209, 210
Enterprise Architecture Management (EAM), 207
Environment, Social, Governance (ESG), 69
ESG ratings, 71
Everything as a Service (XaaS), 81
Exponential growth, 52, 75, 78, 79
Extract Transform Load (ETL), 82

F
Feature gravitation, 77, 78
Federal Enterprise Architecture Framework (FEA), 204
Finance, vi, 4, 17, 32, 36, 40, 41, 56, 59–67, 69, 70, 73, 82, 94, 98, 99, 144, 155
Flexibility of architecture choice, 224, 225
Forecasting, 6, 20, 76, 82, 83
Forward-looking, 35
Fuzzy, 17, 70, 219, 230

G
Gaps, 38, 74, 116, 117, 136, 222, 231
Gartner Hype Cycle, 23, 24
Governance, 11, 20, 55, 57, 152–156, 161, 169, 171, 200, 224
Governance views, 112, 113

Grow (in output) without growing (input), 67
Guardian of the stable core, 177
Guidance, 2, 12, 25, 30, 59, 61, 66, 72–74, 81, 88, 91, 96, 97, 99, 115, 116, 121, 123, 125, 133, 140, 153, 155, 161, 172, 174, 208, 209, 230, 240, 241

H
Hidden rules, 6, 34
House of Strategy, 89, 90, 92
How to decompose, 94–103
How to improve captured input, 105–115
Hygiene factor, 160, 186, 241

I
Information assets, 85, 216, 218, 219, 222, 223, 242
Information ecology, 217
Infrastructure-as-a-service (IaaS), 236
Innovation think tank, 58
Intelligence space, 6, 9
Intelligent Enterprise, v, vii, 6, 9–10, 18, 25–27, 52, 56, 118, 119, 127, 214, 240, 242, 243
Internet of Things (IoT), 215
Inter-system competition, 79
Inventory of information assets, 220

K
Kano, 75–78
Key anchor of BI value, 240
Key benefits at a glance, 116
Key elements to be governed, 168
Key Performance Indicators (KPIs), 57, 61, 84, 90–92, 141, 208

L
Legacy BI solutions, 132
Lifecycle, vi, 23, 78, 156, 158–161, 168–170, 172, 173, 179, 194, 198, 218, 234
Localized governance, 173
Logical data warehouses, 229

M
Machine learning, 6, 9, 10, 60, 80, 230, 236
Machine-human competition, 80
Master data, 13, 17, 65, 98
Maturity assessment, 115, 117, 118, 121, 122
Maturity framework, 116, 117
Maturity judgment, 121
Maturity model, 115–118, 121, 123
Minimum Viable Product (MVP), 223
Mission, 91
Multi-business-model configurations, 49
Multi-dimensional analysis, 5, 8
Must-have requirements, 76

N
Natural Language Processing (NLP), 19
Network economy, 53
New generation of users, 18
New technologies, 18–20
New user experiences, 18
Non-Financial Reporting Directive (NFRD), 70

O
Operational efficiency, 72
Operational excellence, 59, 91
Operational expenses (OpEx), 82, 235
Organization, 13, 16, 143, 154, 177–188
Organizational design, vi, 35, 36, 48, 50, 152, 154, 177, 178, 211

P
Pain-points, 11–13, 25, 99, 229
Performance gap, 38
Personal biases, 7
Platform-as-a-service (PaaS), 20, 235, 236
Prediction, 6, 21
Prescription, 6
Profitable growth, 45, 46, 48–50, 54, 79, 80
Project Portfolio Management, 13, 17

R
Reduction of complexity, 134
Reference data architecture, 225
Repository of all initiatives, 175
Root-cause analysis, 9, 68, 118, 136

S
Semantic modeling, 217, 221
Shadow IT, 15, 166, 234, 242
Silos, 16, 21, 26, 32, 62, 74, 174, 192, 198, 201, 225
Single source of truth, 167, 226
Single version of truth, 174
Software-as-a-service (SaaS), 235

Speed to impact, 7, 8, 84, 240, 241
Spreadsheets, 3, 15, 22, 132, 234
Stable core, 134, 177, 191, 202, 242
Steering model, 13, 16, 21, 51, 62, 63, 66, 240
Strategic cornerstone, 94, 96
Strategic impulse, 37, 140, 142–147
Strategic objectives, 15, 88, 96–98, 105, 172
Strategy House, 88–92
Sustainability, vi, 15, 40, 43, 45, 62, 65, 69–74, 193, 194
Sustainability management, 69, 73
Sustainability performance, 70, 72–74
Sustainable, 31, 32, 45, 47, 60, 62, 63, 72, 79, 118, 132

T

Target ambition level, 38
Target Operating Model (TOM), 62, 63, 134, 211
Taxonomy, 144, 205, 206, 219
Total cost of ownership (TCO), 164, 196–200
Technical debt, 198
Technology architecture, 195, 205, 211, 234, 236, 237, 242
The Open Group Architecture Framework (TOGAF), 204, 205, 208–210
Tool kit for strategy aligned BI, 87–123
Tornado of exponential growth, 79
Trace back, 96, 102
Trend categories, 17
Trusted data, 224, 225

U

Unified reference data architecture, 227
Unique selling proposition (USP), 90

V

Value contribution, vi, 10, 11, 17, 22, 25, 26, 35, 50, 54, 65, 74–76, 78, 79, 81, 87, 90, 96, 99, 102, 111, 135, 145, 146, 152, 155, 156, 164, 185, 196, 203, 241
Virtual Data Models (VDMs), 229
Vision, 91, 125–133
Vision statement, 125, 126, 129–132, 139
Volatility, uncertainty,complexity, and ambiguity (VUCA), 199

W

Walk the talk, 34, 175, 241
What a BI Strategy is NOT, 10
What is a BI Strategy, 10

Z

Zachman framework, 204

GPSR Compliance
The European Union's (EU) General Product Safety Regulation (GPSR) is a set of rules that requires consumer products to be safe and our obligations to ensure this.

If you have any concerns about our products, you can contact us on

ProductSafety@springernature.com

In case Publisher is established outside the EU, the EU authorized representative is:

Springer Nature Customer Service Center GmbH
Europaplatz 3
69115 Heidelberg, Germany

www.ingramcontent.com/pod-product-compliance
Lightning Source LLC
Chambersburg PA
CBHW071700220925
32987CB00003B/207
* 9 7 8 3 0 3 1 6 9 9 1 3 9 *